DATE			

The City, The Immigrant and American Fiction, 1880-1920

by

DAVID M. FINE, 1934-
"

The Scarecrow Press, Inc.
Metuchen, N.J. & London
1977

Library of Congress Cataloging in Publication Data

Fine, David M   1934-
        The city, the immigrant, and American fiction, 1880-
1920.

        Bibliography: p.
        Includes index.
        1. American fiction--History and criticism. 2. Im-
migrants in literature. 3. City and town life in literature.
I. Title.
PS374.I48F55   813'.4'093   77-6297
ISBN 0-8108-1038-7

CONTENTS

FOREWORD

Early in 1932 proletarian novelist Albert Halper complained in a magazine article ["Notes on Jewish-American Fiction," Menorah Journal, 20 (Spring 1932), 61-69] about what he regarded as the scarcity of quality Jewish-American fiction. Echoing Mike Gold's famous quarrel with the irrelevancy of Thornton Wilder ["Wilder: Prophet of the Genteel Christ," New Republic, 69 (22 Oct. 1930), 266-267], Halper lashed out at the failure of Jewish authors to deal with the contemporary and the immediate. There have been a good number of talented Jewish-American writers, he noted, but too few of them have been willing to venture outside the commercially-safe literary territory of the ghetto. Fresh at first, ghetto material to Halper had deteriorated into cliché and anachronism in the decade of the twenties--a decade marked by the emergence of the East European Jew from the urban ghettos. Jewish fiction had become almost identical with ghetto fiction, with romantic and sentimental tales of "bearded men and mothers, of sacrifices so that little Hyman could continue his violin lessons or Deborah with her writing." Halper could, of course, find plenty of examples to prove his point, yet not all the ghetto fiction of Halper's time could be so easily dismissed. Only two years before his article appeared, Jews Without Money, Mike Gold's harrowing portrait of Lower East Side life in the early years of the century, was published; and what Halper could not then know was that two years after his complaint--in 1934--Henry Roth's marvelous evocation of a ghetto boyhood, Call It Sleep, would appear. In that same year, moreover, the first volume of Daniel Fuchs's Williamsburg trilogy would be released.

What all of this suggests--placing Halper in later perspective--is that the immigrant ghetto had become by the thirties on the one hand a literary cliché, a persistent source of romantic and sentimental outpourings, but on the other, a rich vein still capable of yielding to the right talent fresh insights into the immigrant experience and important truths about a modern urban America torn by economic, industrial, and ethnic conflict. The ghetto "tradition" or "genre" which Halper assailed--and which is the subject of this study--stretches back before him almost a half-century to the 1880's, when the massive presence of immigrants from the most distant and unfamiliar regions of Europe was first felt in the city. This is the beginning of the period historians have traditionally, and somewhat misleadingly, labeled "new" immigration, distinct from "old" immigration in terms both of the different national and ethnic origins of the newcomers and their tendency--for social as well as economic reasons--to settle overwhelmingly in densely-packed urban enclaves. In terms of sheer numbers, the migration was predominantly Italian (most from Sicily and the poorer southern regions of the peninsula), with East European Jews, Poles, Bohemians, and a good number of other groups adding to the stream.

The stream widened steadily until the World War I years, when the rampant nativism brought on by the war and the Bolshevik revolution led to a series of restrictive laws which effectively shut off South and East European immigration and marked the end of America's long era of unrestricted immigration. With few newcomers arriving to replace the immigrants who were resettling uptown and in the new suburbs, the ghettos in the twenties began to lose their distinctive colors and blend gradually into the larger city. Of course one can still discern the outlines of some of the old immigrant neighborhoods in the larger eastern cities, but the lines have become fainter with time, the landmarks less recognizable.

My aim in this book is to examine a rather sizable body of fiction dealing specifically with urban immigrant life, written both by native-born and immigrant authors, and produced during the peak ghetto years, 1880-1920--the era bounded on one side by the beginning of massive South and East European immigration and on the other by the beginning of the decline of the old ghetto neighborhoods. The focus, in other words, is on fiction which is contemporaneous with the events it describes, which looks to the immediate present for its material rather than the past. The novels of Gold, Roth, and Fuchs are not only better-known to today's readers (and thus need no rediscovering) but look back in time for their material, however relevant their themes and attitudes are to the literary aesthetic of the 1930's. When the urban immigrants abandoned the traditional foreign quarters of the city--to be replaced in time by the so-called non-white ethnics, primarily Blacks, Puerto Ricans, and Chicanos--the fiction of the immigrant ghetto became increasingly a fiction of nostalgia. In Anzia Yezierska, John Cournos, Samuel

Ornitz, and later Gold, Roth, and Fuchs, we begin to get a different angle of vision--portraits of a life remembered, experiences recalled from some distance in time. A second generation perspective begins to take hold. Past tense replaces present.

The shift, of course, is gradual, like the generational shift itself, and can not be located in any single book or year. Abraham Cahan's The Rise of David Levinsky, published in 1917, however, might conveniently be cited to suggest the changing perspective of ghetto fiction. It was Cahan's last piece of fiction and among the first of many in the next decade and a half which would cast a backward glance at a disappearing immigrant milieu. Levinsky, successful American business entrepreneur, looks back in this first-person narrative over a half century of life (his own, and by extension, that of a whole generation)--the Russian boyhood, the flight to the promised land, the ghetto impoverishment, and finally the achievement of the American dream and the recognition that it was purchased at too high a cost.

Distance, obviously, provides perspective. The strength of Cahan's novel is its ironic point of view, and irony comes only through detachment and distance. Too few of the writers of the ghetto before Cahan were able to separate themselves far enough from their material to achieve any kind of perspective. Only by going beyond the ghetto--in time or space or both--could it be seen clearly. And yet this is not to say that the ghetto novelists of the twenties and thirties all saw it clearly. As Halper noted, the stereotypes and stock plot contrivances which typified the earliest ghetto fiction persisted for half a century into the thirties. Literature "obeys" not only life but its own conventions. By the late nineteenth century certain habitual ways of depicting the urban poor in fiction were well-established. When the European immigrant became the subject of much of this "bottom dog" fiction, he absorbed the familiar sentimental portraiture devoted to slum dwellers since the eighteenth-century urban novels of Defoe, Smollett, and Fielding. Whether the ghetto story-tellers were immigrants or native-born Americans, whether they wrote as "insiders" or "outsiders," they assimilated a literary tradition and with few exceptions clung stubbornly to it.

In this sense immigrant fiction in the period 1880-1920 marks not so much a new "tradition" as the extension of an old one in a new direction. The literature drew heavily on familiar, long-held, and therefore comfortable, assumptions, and yet by exploring a new subject, the non-Anglo urbanite, this literature helped shape the course of contemporary American fiction, just as the new urbanites helped shape the course of contemporary American society. Proletarian fiction of the thirties and "minority voice" fiction are rooted solidly in urban immigrant literature. Hence the importance of examining its attitudes, assumptions, and themes. Surprisingly, very little has been written about this body of fiction despite the vast amount of work done by historians (and still being done too, particularly "quantitative" studies) on this major phase of European immigration. Books and articles have appeared on the literature of particular national or ethnic groups (e.g., Jewish-American, Italian-American), on immigrant autobiographies as cultural documents, on special topics which touch immigrant literature (e.g., radical fiction, the city in fiction, the poor in fiction), and on a few of the more prominent immigrant authors (e.g., Abraham Cahan), but a comprehensive study of the fiction of the urban immigrant has not before been attempted.

For reasons which will become clear in the narrative the majority of this fiction concerns the East European Jewish immigrant, but my intent has been to explore the fiction of the whole range of immigrant groups--including the earlier-settling Irish and Germans--which made up the cosmopolitan American city in the last two decades of the nineteenth century and the first two of the twentieth. One fascinating body of fiction I have not dealt with is the Yiddish-language fiction written by ghetto Jews. As such tales were hardly read outside the walls of the ghetto, they can not be thought of as comprising a significant part of the American literary heritage. Nor do I discuss works about immigrant life written in other languages and subsequently translated into English, such as Henri Sienkewicz's After Bread.

The structure of the book reflects my desire throughout to emphasize both the continuity of urban immigrant fiction with earlier modes of city fiction and the simultaneous groping for new perspectives, for new ways of seeing, which connects ghetto fiction with later literature concerned with the "disenfranchised." Immigrant fiction responded both to the times and to literary convention, and I have tried to keep both allegiances in view. Chapters I and II place the literature in the turn-of-the-century cultural milieu--the period's fierce nativism and xenophobia, the various urban reform movements, and the cosmopolitanism of a few of its visionaries. Chapter III, while centering on Stephen Crane's Maggie and Abraham Cahan's Yekl--both first novels which reached the public in 1895--tries to set off these ground-breaking works against a long tradition of slum fiction going back to the early eighteenth century. I have gone farthest afield in this chapter, but only to illustrate how solidly entrenched stereotyped slum portraiture is in British and American fiction. The following two chapters describe some of the native-drawn portraits of the immigrant which began appearing in the nineties. The first of these, Chapter IV, looks at the profusion of sentimental tales stressing the bizarre, exotic, and colorful features of ghetto life. Local color, it would seem, went urban in such tales. Chapter V examines the immigrant labor novel, tracing its factual grounding in the cataclysmic labor warfare of the period--Haymarket, Homestead, "Packingtown," and the "Great Revolt" of New York's sweatshop workers. The evolution of such fiction from sentimental and middle-class muckraking to a more complex proletarian and socialistic literature is an important part of the story. The final two chapters, VI and VII, examine novels written by immigrants themselves about their experiences in the urban ghettos and sweatshops. Most of these works are, unfortunately, hardly more revealing than the fictional portraits done by native-born writers, but in a few, notably Abraham Cahan's later fiction, the immigrant is at last seen from the "inside" instead of the "outside."

Perhaps more important than uncovering--or recovering--a body of urban fiction which, having inherited traditions from the nineteenth century, helped pave the way for the twentieth, is the fact that this fiction so clearly illustrates the reciprocal relationships between imaginative literature and the culture of which it is a part, a relationship which remains constant in any age or culture. Immigrant fiction in these years responded specifically and concretely to an unsettling contemporary reality and in turn helped shape that reality in the minds of Americans. Fiction here, and always, is both mirror and lamp, structuring reality as it reflects it, creating it as it refracts it. In confronting these novels and tales we come face to face not only with some of the facts of our recent history, but with the source of some of our most persistent urban myths, beliefs, and attitudes. More than a record of national events, these works are a record of our national consciousness.

ACKNOWLEDGMENTS

I wish to thank American Studies (University of Kansas) and American Jewish Historical Quarterly (Brandeis University) for allowing me to reprint here material from articles I have written which appeared in these journals. Full citations of these articles are contained in the Bibliography. Of the many people who have aided and encouraged me, I would like to single out two: Professor Blake Nevius of the University of California, Los Angeles, for his great help in the early stages of the preparation of the manuscript, and Professor David Peck, my colleague and good friend at California State University, Long Beach, for his careful reading of the text and his incisive commentary on every part of it. I owe thanks also to the Foundation of California State University, Long Beach, for awarding me a grant which enabled me to carry on much of the research. On a more personal note --to my grandfather, Benjamin Fine (1880-1975), whose real-life story is told again and again in the novels described in this study, I owe a debt which can never be repaid. The memories he shared with me, years back, of his daring escape from Czarist Russia and his life on New York's Lower East Side have taught me what no book or professor could about the immigrant generation and the making of Americans. Finally, I want to thank my wife Nancy, both for her invaluable editorial help in preparing the manuscript and for her constant support, encouragement, and enthusiasm. This book is dedicated to Nancy with love and gratitude.

THE BEATEN MEN FROM BEATEN RACES:
SOME NATIVIST VIEWS

The Literacy Test Act of 1917, passed over the veto
of President Wilson, marked the beginning of the end of
America's open-door immigration policy. Enacted in the
midst of the xenophobia engendered by the World War, the
measure, mild as it seems today, was the first major legislative victory for nativists and restrictionists and prepared
the way for further, more stringent immigration laws. In
1921, the first quota law was adopted and in 1924 the John-
son-Reed "National Origins" Act was approved, though not
fully implemented until the end of the decade. These meas-
ures climaxed a debate over the desirability of continuing unlimited immigration which had been raging for about forty
years and established a national immigration policy which
would last for approximately forty more years.

The bases for restriction in the immigrant laws of
1917, 1921, and 1924 made it clear that the real purpose of
these acts was not so much to reduce the total number of
Europeans entering the country as to reduce to a trickle the
number arriving from South and East Europe. Behind these
acts lay the assumption that an immigrant's country of origin was the best index of his capacity for assimilation.
Since the early eighties when a southerly and easterly shift
in the geographic origins of the European immigrant flow began to be recognized, the cry for curtailment of immigration
became increasingly more insistent. The most recent arrivals,
the forces for restriction argued, came from inferior racial
stock, represented the most backward elements of backward
nations, and had come almost exclusively for mercenary reasons and had no desire to become good citizens.

The 42-volume report of the Dillingham Commission,
established by Congress in 1907 to study the immigration is-

sue, corroborated the views of a growing body of Americans.[1]*
The "old" immigrants, it was argued, came from countries
in northern and western Europe--from the same nations, that
is, which supplied America's first citizens. They spread
widely into the interior of the country, blended easily with
their earlier-arrived countrymen, and after a period of adjustment became good Americans. The "new" immigrants,
by contrast, were from far different cultures, were clannish,
and resisted Americanization. Their numbers included higher
percentages of males, of "birds of passage" who returned
home after a stay, of unskilled workers, and of illiterates.
Moreover, the report insisted, they were not motivated by
the same high ideals of democracy as were earlier-arriving
immigrants, but were frequently mercenaries and failures
lured here by the steamship companies and unscrupulous employment agents who scoured Europe for her cast-offs.

Most of these charges have been laid to rest by recent
historians of immigration, who, rejecting the existence of
such clear-cut distinctions between "old" and "new" immigrants, have demonstrated that nineteenth- and early twentieth-century immigration is best viewed as a single continuous
process. With the exception of certain groups--the East European Jews fleeing Czarist oppression, for instance--similar
economic changes uprooted "old" and "new" immigrants from
their native lands. That these changes in the peasant economy were felt first in northern and western Europe and then
spread south and east accounts for the gradual shift in the
geographic origins of America's immigrants which began in
the last decades of the nineteenth century. Historians have
also rejected the notion that the two groups were homogeneous
entities. There was considerable variety--cultural, religious,
linguistic, intellectual--within each group. Both, moreover,
had their share of unskilled workers, "birds of passage," and
illiterates. Further, the distinction between the two large
bodies is blurred by the fact that in 1882, the year frequently
cited as marking the dividing line, the entrance of Germans,
who along with the Irish had been the chief constituents of the
"old" immigration, reached its highest annual level (250,000).
Not until 1896 did the yearly influx of southern and eastern
Europeans surpass that of northern and western Europeans,
and not until several years into the new century did the difference between the volume of the flow from southeastern
Europe become significantly greater. [2] As late as 1910 Ger-

---

*See Chapter Notes, beginning on page 149.

mans were still the largest foreign-born group in the country, ahead of the Russian Jews, Austro-Hungarians, Irish, and Italians. 3

The observer of the American city in that year would have been more impressed--or depressed--by the variety of national and ethnic groups crowded together in the foreign quarters of the city than by the replacement of one group by another. Irish and German colonies were well-established in the large cities long before the coming of the southern and eastern Europeans. The Irish were overwhelmingly urban settlers; almost 87 per cent of the Irish-born, it has been estimated, lived in cities, while 67. 5 per cent of German-born were city dwellers. The southeastern Europeans, though, showed an even higher proclivity to settle in cities. 88. 6 per cent of the Russians, 84. 4 per cent of the Italians, and 80 per cent of the Poles lived in cities. 4 Ethnic diversity was a clearly marked feature of the urban landscape in the early years of the twentieth century--as it is today.

If the newest arrivals settled in the cities in greater proportions than earlier-arriving immigrants, the reasons were more complex than an inherent clannishness. Most of the newcomers were without the capital required to move to the interior and establish farms. They came, moreover, at a time of urban consolidation. Many were unskilled and opportunities for unskilled labor were concentrating in the cities. Even those who were skilled in old-world trades were finding their handicraft skills of little use in a society being transformed by urban-industrial manufacturing. New inventions in production technique were making it possible for unskilled laborers to do jobs that previously required skilled workers. The immigrants in these years were feeling the same urban pull as were rural natives who by the thousands were abandoning their farms and moving to the cities. Complaints, thus, about the immigrant flooding of the cities were in essence complaints about urban and industrial concentration. For the immigrant there were social and psychological advantages to urban settlement as well. The city offered the newcomer, who in language and social customs resembled native Americans less than did earlier immigrants, important social benefits--the opportunity to live and work among those who spoke his language, ate similar foods, enjoyed the same recreation, and heeded the same religious demands. Economic necessity combined with social convenience and the need for security to make the history of late nineteenth- and early twentieth-century European immigration a large part of the history of America's urban development.

The immigrant provided the American city not only
with the bulk of its population but with its characteristic
mosaic-like ethnic configuration. The newcomers flocked to
the neighborhoods settled by earlier-arriving co-nationalists,
most often situated on the edge of the downtown business district. Here low-cost housing, unskilled labor opportunities
within walking distance, and the chance to settle among Old
World neighbors were available to the immigrant. In prein-
dustrial times the downtown area had provided housing for
many of the city's wealthy, who for reasons of prestige and
convenience preferred to be near the city's center. In the
face of the industrial and commercial growth of the downtown
area and with the development of urban transportation systems,
however, the wealthy retreated to suburban locations and the
center of the city became almost exclusively an immigrant
residential area. [5] As the newly-arrived immigrants joined
their countrymen in the central city, the area reached greater
density levels and divided itself into more and more separate,
distinct ethnic units or ghettos, based on Old World regional
affiliations. The population pressure exerted by the newcomers on the downtown area, moreover, often forced earlier-
arriving immigrant settlers of the region to move out and re-
locate in other parts of the city. The coming of the Italians,
East European Jews, and Poles to New York's downtown
ghettos, for instance, drove the Irish and Germans further
uptown--almost as group migrations--just as wealthy natives
had withdrawn from the city's center in earlier decades under
the pressure of urban change. The phenomenon of one group
forcing another "uptown" was repeated in all the large cities. [6]

The density of the immigrant communities and their
geographic spread across the face of the city alarmed urban
reformers and nativists. Much of the blame for the mounting problems of the city was placed on the conspicuous newest arrivals. With their "bizarre" and "exotic" appearance,
their strange customs and habits, and their "clannishness,"
they became highly visible targets. They had, moreover, the
bad luck of arriving just when Protestant nativism was in one
of its periodic upswings. The Haymarket riots of 1886 did
more than anything else to link the immigrant with radicalism
and anarchism, and the event was followed by a resurgence
of popular xenophobia. In the eighties, hostility toward the
immigrant was not directed specifically at the southeastern
European, but early in the following decade as the differences
between the older, more assimilated groups and the newest
arrivals became apparent, the latter were singled out by the
nativists. [7] In the xenophobic literature of the day the new-

comer absorbed much of the traditional hostility to foreigners
which had surfaced periodically throughout the nineteenth century. He was seen as being in the hands of foreign powers,
as depressing native wage standards by his willingness to
work for almost any pay, and as importing subversive political ideologies and alien religious beliefs.

The assault against the recent immigrant, though, was
fueled by more than traditional native xenophobia. A new nativist attack, led by a group of New England intellectuals
(with imported ideologies of their own), was clearly underway
in the nineties. Following the lead of European race scientists and waving the banner of Anglo-Saxonism, these patrician exclusionists warned that the continued entry of southeastern Europeans would dilute and eventually wash away any
traces of the people who built the nation. Instead of producing a superior man compounded of the hardiest of the world's
people, immigration, they argued, was causing the submer-
gence of the best native stock. Characteristically, they expressed the process in terms of Anglo-Saxon "race suicide"
or biological "reversion," through intermixing, to a more
primitive type. The foundation for the acceptance of racial
theories was laid in the successful campaigns waged against
the Chinese in the West, in the post-Reconstruction South's
attempts to restrict the Negro's power by stressing his in-
feriority, and in the widespread conception of the racial de-
ficiencies of the "heathen" Filipino following the Spanish war.
All three cases contributed to the belief that certain races
were unfit for the tasks of self-government.[8]

According to the Anglo-Saxon point of view, the American was the descendant of a long line of English-speaking
people, a line which had passed through the Reformation in
England, had settled the New England colonies, and had always supplied a model for order, stability, and self-government. America was not an emerging society, its values to
be shaped by the myriad of immigrants who chose to come
here, but a fixed and stable society, its cultural and political
values formed from its first European settlement. The "new"
immigrant, either through hereditary constitution (as the more
race-conscious maintained) or through environmental conditioning over the centuries, was seen as incapable of ever at-
taining the high level of civilization which characterized the
Anglo-American. The more remote--geographically and cul-
turally--his origins were from England, the greater was the
threat. Massachusetts Senator Henry Cabot Lodge, an advocate of the literacy test requirement as early as 1890 and

one of the founders of the Boston-based Immigration Restriction League, typified the New England Anglo-American point
of view. Our open-door policy, he maintained, allowed the
admission of "races most alien to the body of the American
people and from the lowest and most illiterate classes among
those races. "[9]

Even more outspoken than Lodge was his fellow New
Englander, Francis A. Walker, professor of political economy
at Yale and later president of the Massachusetts Institute of
Technology and Superintendent of the Census. Walker's great
fear was Anglo-Saxon "race suicide. " He argued that the
heavy influx of immigrants was producing a reaction among
the native population. Unwilling to live and work under the
depressed conditions produced by immigration, Americans
were no longer reproducing at the same rate as they had in
the early years of the nation, and as a result the immigrants
were replacing the native population. The first drop in the
native birthrate occurred, according to Walker, around 1830,
when widespread European immigration began. During the
1880's the arrival of the "new" immigrant caused an even
greater drop in the native birthrate. [10] Americans, he argued, were simply refusing to compete with the foreign-born.
Again and again he sounded the alarm:

> The entrance into our political, social, and industrial
> life of such vast masses of peasantry, degraded below
> our utmost conceptions, is a matter which no intelli-
> gent patriot can look upon without the gravest appre-
> hension and alarm. These people have no history be-
> hind them which is of a nature to give encouragement.
> They have none of the inherited instincts and tenden-
> cies which made it comparatively easy to deal with the
> immigration of the olden times. They are beaten men
> from beaten races; representing the worst failures in
> the struggle for existence. [11]

In the following decades the intellectuals intensified
their assault. Edward A. Ross, professor of sociology at the
University of Wisconsin, denounced the social effects of "new"
immigration in his book The Old World and the New (1914).
Ross agreed with Walker that native Americans would choose
"race suicide" to existence under the foul living conditions the
immigrants were creating. [12] Robert DeCourcy Ward, a Harvard professor of climatology and one of the founders of the
Immigration Restriction League, argued that the principles of
eugenics established by Sir Francis Galton in England must be

applied to the human population in America to reverse the de-
generative trend brought on by immigration. Here, he maintained, "the eugenically less desirable portion of the community is furnishing a disproportionally large share of the next
generation.... But clearly if the race is to progress, the
fitter part should be the most fertile. "[13]

In The Passing of the Great Race (1916), Madison
Grant, a lawyer, anthropologist at the American Museum of
Natural History, and founder of the New York Zoological Society, summarized the pseudo-scientific racial polemic which
reached its zenith as America prepared for war. Beginning
with the familiar three-part European race classification--
Nordic, Mediterranean, and Alpine--he insisted, as his European teachers had, that races differ not only physically but
intellectually. The Nordics are the natural "rulers, organizers, aristocrats" of society. Until the Civil War these were
the people who settled America and gave it its distinctive ra-
cial--and thus intellectual--qualities. With postwar prosperity
and the need to build railroads and operate large factories
the "hordes of newcomers" were lured here. Earlier immigrants had been Nordics who "came of their own impulse to
improve their social condition," but the recent immigrants
were the most depressed members of the most backward nations. America was advertised to them as a land of easy
wealth and

> ... European governments took the opportunity to un-
> load upon careless, wealthy, and hospitable Americans
> the sweepings of their jails and asylums. The result
> was that the new immigration ... contained a large
> and increasing number of the weak, the broken, and
> the mentally crippled of all races drawn from the low-
> est stratum of the Mediterranean basin and the Balkans
> together with hordes of the wretched, submerged popu-
> lations of the Polish ghettos. Our jails, insane asy-
> lums, and alms houses are filled with this human
> flotsam and the whole tone of American life, social,
> moral, and political, has been lowered and vulgarized
> by them. [14]

Grant went on to predict that "in large sections of the country
the native American will entirely disappear. " Not wanting to
intermarry, he will commit racial suicide, and our large
cities will be filled with "ethnic horrors. "

The Passing of the Great Race, appearing on the eve

of the Literacy Text Act's adoption, climaxed the racial ar-
guments which helped to turn the tide for passage of the law
but by no means defined the wide range of native opposition
to immigrants which had been gathering strength since the
nineties. Opposition came from a variety of sources, many
of which were non-racial or only peripherally racial. Conservative businessmen, who traditionally had encouraged immigration, reversed their position during the hard times of
the nineties with their fear of unemployment, labor unrest,
and radicalism. Organized labor opposed the new immigrant
because he was difficult to organize, lowered wage standards,
and was often used as a strike-breaker. [15] Many clerical
leaders, following the lead of Congregationalist minister
Josiah Strong, opposed unrestricted immigration on the grounds
that cities with large foreign populations were infested with
crime and immorality. In general, the increasing polarization of the city, the growth and spread of slums and ghettos,
the steadily rising crime rates, and the escalating labor warfare were significant factors in the growing popular opposition
to unlimited immigration. Race ideology by itself was not
responsible for the legislative victories of the restrictionists
but was significant to the degree that it provided an apparent-
ly scientific rationale to the popular xenophobia that had been
on the rise in America since the eighties.

Early in that decade, in 1883, while the first large
boatloads of Italians and East European Jews were arriving
at Castle Garden, Henry James, then 40, left his native New
York and set sail in the opposite direction, for London. He
remained abroad for the next 20 years, returning to America
in 1904 for the visit which would occasion his remarkable volume of observations, The American Scene (1907). James left
New York before the full impact of industrialism and immigration
was felt on the city. The mass exodus from southern and
eastern Europe was just beginning. When he returned to his
birthplace, several million immigrants had arrived and the
entire face of the city had changed. Symbolically, on the
site of his former home in the Washington Square neighborhood stood a shirtwaist factory. Skyscrapers, tenement
houses, uptown mansions, and expansive hotels dominated the
city's landscape, blotting out the vista of the rivers. Everywhere he saw strangely-dressed foreigners speaking hybrid
languages like none he had heard in Europe.

The confusion of polyglot Manhattan both fascinated and
appalled him, and he spent time exploring the Italian and Jewish sections of the city. He found the Italians strangely silent

in the New World. They were not at all like the Italians of
the Old World but produced a "neutral and colourless image."
These New World Italians "meet us, at every turn, only to
make us ask what has become of that element of the agree-
able address in them which has, from far back, so enhanced
for the stranger the interest and pleasure of a visit to their
beautiful country. "[16] What is it about the "ambient air" in
America, he asked, that has robbed the Italians of their true
nature and turned them into a brooding, taciturn, and "colourless" people.

    Of the Lower East Side Jews he was more apprehen-
sive. He recalled the anguish he felt after spending an evening with friends in the ghetto. The teeming, frenzied, polyglot life of the ghetto reminded him of a zoo: the crisscross
of metal fire escapes on the tenement buildings he likened to
cages, the inhabitants scurrying about their business, to
squirrels or monkeys. He was intrigued by the vitality of
the Jews, by what he called their "intensity of aspect," but
puzzled as to how they could be assimilated. On what terms
would assimilation take place, and would it be good for the
country?

        ... in these haunts of comparative civility we saw the
        mob sifted and strained, and the exasperation was the
        sharper, no doubt, because what the process had left
        most visible was just the various possibilities of the
        waiting spring of intelligence. Such elements consti-
        tuted the germ of a 'public' and it was impossible ...
        to be exposed to them without feeling how a new thing
        under the sun the resulting public would be. That was
        where one's 'lettered' anguish came in--in the turn of
        one's eye from face to face for some betrayal of a
        prehensile hook for the linguistic tradition as one had
        known it [pp. 138-39].

The "Accent of the Future," to James, might conceivably "be
destined to be the most beautiful on the globe and the very
music of humanity ... but whatever we shall know it for, certainly, we shall not know it for English--in any sense for
which there is an existing literary measure" (p. 138).

    To dismiss James as simply another Anglo-Saxon rac-
ist is too simple. His apprehension over the newcomers was
not merely a matter of race or ethnicity but sprang from a
larger source--the absence of community or real society in
America. Everywhere James looked, on his return to New

York, he saw people uprooted, alienated, divided. The immigrants exacerbated the fragmentation of the metropolis. They were, as foreigners and urbanites, doubly alienated. Race consciousness was not missing in James--it could not have been, given his background--but it fails to explain the full range of his fears.

Xenophobia was not restricted to the intellectuals of New York or New England, even though the vast majority of the newest arrivals from Europe were settling in the eastern cities. In the West and Midwest, as well as on the East Coast, Anglo-Saxon race-consciousness played a significant part in the period's imaginative literature. In the imagination of the American West of the eighties and nineties, the urban Jew stood for the power and greed of the East Coast. He was identified with the exploitative capitalism which was forcing the West into subjugation. Ignatius Donnelly, an active Minnesota reform legislator and later Populist candidate for President, presented in his anti-utopian novel, Caesar's Column (1890), the Populist view of a society controlled by an oligarchy consisting largely of Jews, who, risen from peddlers in a laissez-faire economy, work their cruel revenge on Christians for their ancient persecution. Underlying the book's vision is the hysterical fear of the growing power of Jewish millionaires the world over and their economic strangulation of the Anglo-Saxon. The novel attempts to project into the future what Donnelly sees as the inevitable result if East Coast capitalism were to go on unchecked for the next hundred years. A small group of wealthy, arrogant, selfish "Semitic" rulers would reduce the vast hordes of the world's people to abject slavery. On the familiar "two nations" theme is superimposed the racial ideology of the American West. It is the Jewish bankers who control the world:

> The task which Hannibal attempted so disastrously, to subject the Latin and mixed Gothic races of Europe to the domination of the Semitic blood as represented in the merchant city of Carthage, has been successfully accomplished in these latter days by the cousins of the Phoenicians, the Israelites.... The world is today Semitized. The children of Japhet lie prostrate slaves at the feet of the children of Shem; the sons of Ham bow humbly before their august dominion. [17]

In Caesar's Column, Christina Jansen, a Swedish girl engaged to Maximillian, one of the leaders in the revolutionary "Brotherhood" which seeks to overthrow the oligarchy,

represents one of the last vestiges of Nordic purity and nobility in America. She is described as blonde and blue-eyed.
The daughter of a poor blacksmith, whose family devotion,
honesty, and pride are seen as Nordic and thus as Anglo-
Saxon characteristics, Christina is forced to waste a gifted
voice singing in a cheap music hall. Of the Jansen family
Maximillian tells the narrator Gabriel Weltstein:

> This is the stuff of which was formed the masterful
> race that overran the world under the names of a doz-
> en different people. Ice and snow made the tough
> fiber, mental and physical, which the hot sun of south-
> ern climes melted into the viciousness of more luxuri-
> ous nations. Man is scourged by adversity, and
> leveled into mediocrity by prosperity. This little fel-
> low [Christina's younger brother], whose groans are
> between his set teeth, has in him the blood of Vikings
> [pp. 209-210].

In a scene which rather crudely symbolizes the rape
of Nordic purity by the dark "southern races," Christina is
attacked and stabbed in the throat by the Jew, Nathan Brederhagen, when she resists his advances. Brederhagen is cast
as the parvenu-son, "a reckless, drunken, useless spend-
thrift, with no higher aim in life than wine and women." He
is identified in the novel with the sensuousness of the Mediterranean race, a characteristic Gabriel had noticed in the
leader of the oligarchy, the Prince, who "showed signs of
sensuality and dissipation, in the baggy, haggard features."

The leader of the Brotherhood, Caesar Lomellini, of
Italian extraction but South Carolina birth, represents the
victimized farmer. Crushed under the lion's paw of mortgage,
railroad favoritism, and usury, he has been reduced to an
animal, his physical appearance reinforcing the savagery of
his nature. The description given of him, in fact, suggests
the primitive "reversion" the race scientists were warning
would result from unchecked immigration. [18] Second in command under Caesar in the revolutionary brotherhood is a Jew,
portraying another, quite different populist Jewish stereotype,
the sinister, alien radical. The physical description, like
that of Caesar, is highly suggestive. He is old and withered,
his head is crooked to one side, and his face is dominated by
a hooked nose and two large fangs which protrude from his
mouth.

The erection of the enormous column out of bodies of

oligarchs and workers alike, a task ordered by the drunken
Caesar after a destructive revolution, signals the total failure of the Brotherhood, so long submerged in poverty that
all idealism has been bred out of it.

An agrarian reformer, Donnelly in this novel attacks
both the forces of East Coast financial power and violent,
anarchic revolution, both identified in the populist mind with
the Jew. The fact that the column is erected by the surviving professional men and intellectuals, while the men of
brawn give the orders, underscores for Donnelly the perversity of revolution. His own voice is that of Gabriel Weltstein, whose speeches often derive from the Populist platform
and who at the novel's end sets off for Africa to establish an
agrarian colony.

The Nordic racism and the intense xenophobia which
Donnelly reveals in this novel and which formed a significant
part of the populist mind, can be traced in a number of other
writers of the American West. Owen Wister, a Westerner if
not by birth then by inclination, identified his western heroes
with Anglo-Saxon ideals. In "The Evolution of the Cow-
Puncher," the "cow-puncher" is portrayed as the purest Anglo-Saxon type remaining in America, the noble, courageous,
self-reliant man of action in direct contrast to the effete "de-
based and mongrel" people who have infected the eastern
cities, "encroaching alien vermin, that turn our cities into
Babels and our citizenry into a hybrid farce, who degrade
our commonwealth from a nation into something half pawnshop, half broker's office."[19] Because the West required
Anglo-Saxon fortitude, he added, "You will not find many
Poles or Huns or Russian Jews in that district." Frank Norris, another Westerner in spirit who identified some of his
heroes with Anglo-Saxon characteristics, did not generalize
as Wister did about the newcomers, but included among his
nastiest characters the urban immigrant. The portrait of
Zerkow, the Polish Jew in McTeague, shows the persistence
in the West of the old Shylock stereotype, as that of S. Behr-
man in The Octopus suggests the fear of the Eastern Jewish
oligarchy.

The coupling of progressivism and nativism is inherent
in many of the Western writers of the period. It can be seen
in Norris, in Theodore Roosevelt, in Edward A. Ross (who
attended Stanford University and identified with the anti-Orien-
tal movement in California before his teaching career at Wisconsin), and, most obviously, in Jack London. With London

the tension between the two positions reaches an extreme
form: socialism and Anglo-Saxon racism, the attraction toward Marx on the one hand and Nietzsche on the other, the
quest for social justice and the glorification of the Teutonic
superman. The fiction he wrote during the second decade of
the twentieth century--when nativism and xenophobia were at
a peak--includes a number of heroes with pronounced Nordic
racial features and proud consciousness of their Anglo-Saxon
heritage. Billy Roberts, for instance, in The Valley of the
Moon (1913), has the typically Anglo-Saxon "short, square-
set nose," "rosy cheeks," "firm, short upper lip," and "well-
molded, large, clear mouth." He resembles, we are told,
the blond, Nordic warrior who leaps from a boat during the
invasion of England in a picture cherished by the heroine,
Saxon Brown, whose name clearly identifies her heritage. [20]
In Mutiny on the Elsinore (1914) the unnamed narrator, a pas-
senger on the ship, notices that the men in command are
blond, while the crew are dark-haired: "Every one of us
sits aft in the high place is a blond Aryan.... Ninety per
cent of the slaves that toil for us are brunettes."[21] Early
in the novel he sums up much of his Anglo-Saxon race superiority: "... ours is a lordly history, and though we may
be doomed to pass, in our time we shall have trod on the
faces of all peoples, disciplined them to obedience, taught
them government, and dwelt in the palaces we have compelled
them by the weight of our right arms to build for us" (p.
149).

      Other writers lacked the confidence of Jack London
that the Anglo-Saxon race would continue to prevail in the
New World. A brief story published in Collier's in 1912 en-
titled "What Is an American?" lays bare the whole range of
nativist fears. A simplistic parable, it contrasts the lives
of two workmen--the alien and the American--in a New England quarry. Masso, an Italian immigrant, lives in a filthy
shack with his wife and five children, while native-born Ezra
(who we are told is really the dispossessed heir to the land
on which the quarry is situated) shares an immaculate cottage
with his wife and one son. Masso is a "bird of passage,"
trying to earn enough money to buy a farm in the old country.
He has come here for the high wages, and when his salary is
cut, he takes his sons out of school and puts them to work.
Ezra, by contrast, simply tightens his belt, refusing to de-
prive his son of an education. And while Masso and his wife
continue to have more children, Ezra chooses "race suicide"
rather than compete. He believes in "the ideal of progress,
of breeding better than he had bred, the idea that demanded

a certain standard of living. And rather than forgo that ideal
Ezra committed race suicide. "[22] When both men are killed
under a falling boulder, the author tells us that Masso, with
his huge progeny will continue his line, while Ezra with only
a single son may not.

As patently absurd as the tale is, it was not alone in
the period's popular fiction, particularly as the European
crisis flared and as the race scientists prolonged their attacks through the middle of the century's second decade. In
Catherine Metcalf Roof's The Stranger at the Hearth (1916),
a novel which appeared the same year as Madison Grant's
The Passing of the Great Race, one of the characters, a native New Yorker, sums up much of the period's popular xenophobia:

> You can't deluge a country with strange people whose
> racial psychology, habits, and standards are totally at
> variance with its original inhabitants and evolve a good,
> clean, consistent type. On the contrary, you get ex-
> actly what we have in America to-day,--an oil and
> water democracy with a money standard in which to a
> great extent, the personal and material standards of
> the least progressive classes in continental Europe are
> replacing the altruistic Anglo-Saxon ideals of our orig-
> inal democracy. We aren't Americanizing them.
> They are de-Americanizing the country.... [23]

Anna Varesca, the novel's heroine, is the wife of an
Italian count. Returning to New York for a visit after ten
years in Italy, she finds the city overrun with immigrants
from South and East Europe. On a shopping trip she is jos-
tled and brushed against by "peasant types," which seem to
her "the farthest possible remove from that which through
many generations has inherited the right to the title American. " The result of her contacts with the new Americans is
to kindle a virulent Anglo-Saxon racism. Married to an Italian nobleman, she had considered herself "Continental," but
she comes to recognize a similarity between her husband,
"the finely civilized and subtilized Latin aristocrat," and the
"rude products of Eastern Europe" she finds on the city
streets. She perceives a marked contrast between the "ex-
pressive races" of the South and the "controlled Anglo-Saxon
who sets justice above impulsive sympathy. " The effect of
the visit is to alienate her from her husband and to draw her
toward the native patrician, Daniel Griscomb. The contrast
between the two men--the temperamental, emotional Mario

and the restrained, polished Daniel--defines the novel's conflict.   Mario's suicide in an insane fit of jealousy confirms
the portrait of the hot-blooded Mediterranean Miss Roof would
have us accept.   Early in the novel Anna confides her distaste for New York to Daniel, and he responds in one of the
nativistic set-piece speeches which recur throughout the novel:
"Of course, New York isn't America; it isn't even a sane
place.   It is full of people that don't know what an American
is.... It isn't a place to live in.   I hope--every sane person must hope--to get out of it some day" (p. 86).

There was, of course, another side to the question.
If the large Eastern city was becoming uninhabitable, the
fault might lie less with the depressed standards the immigrant brought than with the degrading living and working conditions he found here.   And while native-born patricians,
race-conscious social theorists, labor leaders, and agrarian
reformers were denouncing the most recent immigrants and
urging restrictive legislation, other Americans, taking their
cue from the progressive sociologists and social workers,
were demonstrating that environment and not heredity or race
was the primary determinant of immigrant acculturation.
The urban reformers and novelists who will be considered in
the following chapter interpreted the process of acculturation
variously but shared the belief that American institutions
were at least in part responsible for the squalid conditions
under which the immigrants lived and worked.

II

REFORMERS, AMERICANIZERS, AND COSMOPOLITANS:
THE CASE FOR THE IMMIGRANT

To the urban reformers of the eighties and nineties
the tenement house, the slum environment, and the sweatshop
were the factors most directly responsible for the failure of
the recent immigrant to assimilate with the native population.
To those who saw the need to "elevate" the immigrant by ex-
posing him to the best in American life, the overcrowded and
squalid living conditions of the newcomer stood as the chief
obstacle. Behind the concern for tenement reform was the
belief that slums were to blame for crime, disease, sexual
immorality, and alcoholism among the immigrant youth.
Charles Loring Brace, founder of the Children's Aid Society,
expressed this attitude in The Dangerous Classes of New York
and Twenty Years Work Among Them (1872). The immigrant
children, he maintained, uprooted from parental guidance in
overcrowded slum neighborhoods and growing up among thieves
and toughs, were the "dangerous classes." Josiah Strong,
evangelist, civic reformer, and opponent of unrestricted immigration, expressed grave concern in a book called Our
Country because "the hoodlums and roughs of our cities are,
most of them, American-born of foreign parentage. "[1]

In focusing on the potency of housing and neighborhood
improvement, the reformers all but ignored the strength of
the immigrant's cultural conditioning. In believing that by up-
grading the physical environment of the immigrant they could
hasten his assimilation, they overlooked his ethnic or national
background, his religious beliefs and demands, his community
needs, his educational level and his employment opportunities.
Jacob Riis, the best-known of the period's advocates of tene-
ment-house reform, epitomized this limited environmental determinism in his widely read How the Other Half Lives (1890),
a compilation of sketches of life in New York's immigrant
colonies drawn from his twelve years as police reporter for
the Tribune and the Sun. Theodore Roosevelt, who was then

New York's Police Commissioner and who often accompanied
Riis on his rambles through the city's foreign quarters, was
greatly influenced by the work, citing it in his autobiography
as "an enlightenment and an inspiration for which ... I could
never be too grateful."[2]

Riis, an immigrant from Denmark, was neither a
trained social scientist nor a careful scholar, but a reporter
who cared, as Lincoln Steffens characterized him, about what
he reported, and who saw the human drama behind each piece
of news.[3] How the Other Half Lives, based on photographi-
cally illustrated articles he prepared for Scribner's magazine,
was the first of ten books in which he was to concern himself with the slums. The book is not only a plea for tene-
ment-house reform but for the rehabilitation of the entire
slum environment. Sweatshops, child labor, saloons, stale
beer dives, opium dens, and prostitution all came under his
observation. Behind the work lay the assumptions that (1)
improving the physical environment of the immigrant quarters
would improve the safety of the whole city through better san-
itation and that (2) better housing would provide a moral boost
to the immigrant and ease his Americanization. The tenement house and the slum environment were the children of
"public neglect and private greed." Influenced by his association with Alfred T. White, who built New York's first model
tenement house in Brooklyn, demonstrating that decent housing
was not incompatible with profit, Riis never lost his confidence that private enterprise would right its wrongs once it
was shown the need and the way.

How the Other Half Lives is largely a guided tour of
the city's immigrant colonies, a local color portrait of the
ghettos, comprised of personal reminiscences and impression-
istic sketches. Riis's characteristic method of winning sympathy for reform was to pile one pathetic case study upon another, punctuating them with indignant outcries often couched
in Scriptural rhetoric: "The tenements today are New York,
harboring three-fourths of its population. When another generation shall have doubled the census of our city, and to that
vast army of workers, held captive by poverty, the very name
of home shall become as a bitter mockery, what will the harvest be?"[4] Riis does not absolve the immigrant from all
blame for his destitution. Some groups have risen from the
ghettos faster than others; some in their "clannishness" have
stubbornly resisted Americanization. Riis, as the immigrant
who succeeded in America and who titled his autobiography
The Making of an American, had little patience with

immigrants who were slow to adopt American attitudes and values. In his unshakeable faith in private enterprise, his stress upon Americanization--a one-way process in which the immigrant did all the adjusting--and his commitment to environmental determinism, he typifies the middle-class, liberal reform spirit of his age.

His importance lies in his calling attention vigorously and dramatically to the need for tenement reform and thus paving the way for subsequent reform legislation, which would be climaxed by the work of the Tenement House Commission of 1900. Lawrence Veiller, the Commission's secretary and principal author of its scrupulously documented Report, was an outspoken critic of tenements who, unlike Riis, had little faith that private enterprise would improve tenement houses on its own initiative even if it were shown that profits and decent housing were not necessarily incompatible. The minimum standards for air, light, and space which the Report recommended were incorporated in the stringent 1901 Tenement House Act. [5]

Attempts to restrict the number of tenants who could live in a tenement flat frequently met with resistance from the immigrant himself, who depended upon boarders to help pay his rent. The reformers, who recognized the dangers to health and safety posed by overcrowding, often found themselves at odds with the tenement dwellers to whom overcrowding was a necessity. The same opposition of reformer and immigrant grew out of sweatshop reform legislation. However intolerable the tenement sweatshop was, it provided employment for thousands of Jewish, Italian, and Bohemian families. The immigrant community depended on this piecework which enabled whole families to work together, often in their own tenements, multiplying their earning capacity and offering little interference with religious and dietary observances. The system with all its horrors enabled thousands to survive.[6]

During the nineties reform journalists frequently called attention to the evils of the sweatshop system. [7] Their concern focused primarily on unregulated female and child labor and the public health menace created by producing clothing in crowded, unsanitary tenements. A recurrent image in the reform journalism of the day was the "consumption" or cholera victim lying on a pile of cut goods which would soon be turned into clothing and sold in expensive stores. To Jacob Riis, one of the greatest evils of the system was the unregulated labor of children, which retarded the process of Americaniza-

tion. The sweatshop perpetuated the separation of the immigrant community, isolating the immigrant child and preventing his being exposed to broad American ideals. Working
alongside his parents in a tenement workshop all day, he had
no time for education or even to learn English. And the
"sweater," to Riis, "no worse than the conditions which
created him," had, lamentably, a vested interest in perpetuat-
ing the isolation and ignorance of his workers.

The concern for urban reform as a precondition to the
Americanization of the immigrant is central to Lucia True
Ames's 1889 novel, Memoirs of a Millionaire, a work al-
legedly based on the career of philanthropist-reformer Mildred
Brewster. Miss Ames, herself an active philanthropist
throughout her life, argues through her heroine that the decline in American--and to her this meant New England--ideals
is the chief cause of the failure to assimilate the recent immigrant. America's urban problems, the book asserts, are
not simply the results of the "new" immigrant invasion but of
the abnegation of responsible citizenship by the "better classes." Greed, vulgar materialism, and political irresponsibility and apathy on the part of the native population have sown
the seeds of anarchism and crime among the immigrant population. Addressing a group of clergymen in Chicago, Miss
Brewster said, "The danger to this great city to-day is not
so much from the dynamite of the anarchist as from the in-
difference and inactivity of the men and women who have your
brains, your wealth, your culture, and many of them your
nominal Christianity. "8

The solution to the immigrant problem is not to be
found in exclusion or restriction but in the Americanization
both of the immigrant and the privileged native population
along the lines of the New England tradition:

> No, not America for Americans, but America for
> American ideals and institutions! And welcome be he,
> whether of our own land or any other, who, seeing
> what God has destined this fair land to be as leader of
> the nations, seeing it as its early founders saw it,
> shall give heart and brain and hand to purifying and
> redeeming it lest indeed it be the land of the 'Broken
> Promise' [p. 224].

Americanizing America is the task Mildred Brewster
saw as the primary one. The nation would first have to be
made over before the immigrant could be made into an

American. Like Riis, she maintained that crowded, unsanitary immigrant housing, the product of unregulated capitalistic expansion, is a block to the Americanization process, and
one of her first projects was to build a row of model tenements (to which she quaintly affixed names of Puritan significance: Scrooby, Leyden, Plymouth, Mayflower, Bradford,
Brewster, Carver, and Winslow). The close connection she
makes between decent housing and morality is one frequently
made by the reformers of the eighties and nineties. Her
housing scheme, which included cooperative cooking service,
roof-top playgrounds, kindergarten and nursery services, bunk
beds, and game rooms, is seen as the first step in the Americanization of the immigrant.

Her position is clearly within the optimistic reform
tradition of the late nineteenth and early twentieth century.
Like the New England patrician exclusionists, she stressed
the need to preserve America's Anglo-Saxon heritage, but
countering them, she argued that it is the America the immigrant finds, not the Europe he brings, which is the key to
assimilation. Environment and present opportunity, not
heredity and past conditioning, are the vital ingredients.

Other writers as well were concerned with the failure
of American institutions to provide acceptable models for
the newcomers. Finley Peter Dunne was fond of having his
shrewd Irish bartender, Mr. Dooley, ridicule the clichés of
the restriction movement, particularly when those clichés
were uttered, as they often were, by earlier-arriving immigrants. In one installment of the popular newspaper feature,
Dooley recalls to Hennessy a conversation he had with
Shaughnessy:

> 'He was in yisterdah an' says he: "Tis time we done
> something to make th' immigration laws stronger,"
> says he. "Thrue fr'e ye, Miles Standish," says I;
> "but what wud ye du?" "I'd keep out th' offscourin's
> iv Europe," says he. "Tis not so seeryus as it was
> befure ye come," says I. "But what ar-re th' immy-
> grants doin' that's roonous to us?" says I. "Well,"
> says he, "they're arnychists," he says; "they don't as-
> symilate with th' counthry," he says. "Maybe th'
> counthry's digestion has gone wrong fr'm too much rich
> food," says I; "perhaps now if we'd lave off thryin' to
> digest Rockyfellar an' thry a simple diet like Schwartz-
> meister, we wudden't feel th' effects iv our vittels," I
> says. "Maybe if we'd season th' immygrants a little
> or cook thim thurly, they'd go down better," I says. '9

The problem, Dooley knows, is not what the immigrant brings but what he finds here.   The unparaphraseable bartender goes on a little later to attack Hennessy's nativism:

'Well,' said Mr. Dooley, 'as a pilgrim father on me gran' nephew's side, I don't know but ye're right. An' they'se wan sure way to keep thim out.'

'What's that?' asked Mr. Hennessy.

'Teach them all about our instichoochins before they come,' said Mr. Dooley [pp. 53-54].

The "old" immigrant's hostility to the "new," which Dunne ridicules in this sketch, was noticed by many native observers.   In much of the fiction concerned with the politics and labor of the ghetto, exploiters of the recent immigrant are earlier-arriving or second-generation immigrants.   The Irish are the oppressors of the recently-arrived Lithuanians in Upton Sinclair's The Jungle (1905).   In Sidney Nyburg's The Chosen People (1917), the German-Jewish industrialists exploit the labor of the Russian Jews.   Throughout the fiction of the Jewish ghetto, the German-Jewish "sweater" or landlord is a stock villain figure, more contemptible than the native-born oppressor, because he has betrayed his own people.

Economic motives aside, the mutual antipathy between "old" and "new" immigrant, particularly between German and Russian Jew, forms a significant aspect of immigrant psychology.   The relationship between the worlds of "uptown" and "downtown," German and Russian, English- and Yiddish-speaking Jew, was fraught with distrust, shame, and jealousy, stemming in large part from the differing conditions under which each group entered.   Unlike the earlier-arriving German Jews, the Russian Jews were fleeing from political conditions which placed their very lives in jeopardy.   The older immigrant often brought some capital with him and shared in the pioneering of the commercial growth of the city, notably the department store boom.   The Russian Jew, by contrast, arrived most often without capital and at a time marked by industrial consolidation.   Opportunity was concentrated in a few urban domestic industries, particularly the garment trades, although some newcomers entered commerce as peddlers or small shopkeepers, catering to the immigrant trade. Such conditions, together with the factors of insecurity in a new land and the language barrier, fostered the separatism, the cohesiveness, and the solidarity of the Russian-Jewish community which the German Jews found degrading.   A product of conditions more conducive to assimilation, the German Jew, also an urban dweller, prided himself on his rapid Americanization and was embarrassed by the persistence of Old World habits, language, dress, and orthodoxy in his East European coreligionists. He feared that the progress he had made in gaining recognition for himself among his Christian neighbors would be lost with the influx of poor Russian Jews, with their long black coats (dubbed "Prince Isaacs" in distinction to Prince Alberts), sidelocks, pushcarts, and ghetto clannishness. To the uptown Jew, beginning to feel comfortable in America, the downtown Jew was a subversive influence that could only serve to endanger American ideals and undermine his own hard-won position. The uptown community resented the attention given to the downtown immigrant in the press--notably in Lincoln Steffens' Commercial Advertiser-- and in fiction. Abraham Cahan's 1896 novel of the Lower East Side, Yekl, and the popular stage adaptation of Israel Zangwill's Children of the Ghetto were widely denounced by uptown Jews. Lincoln Steffens remarked in his Autobiography that as a police reporter on Lawrence Godkin's New York Evening Post he received complaints about the attention he gave to the ghetto:

> The Post observed all the holidays of the Ghetto. There were advance notices of their coming, with descriptions of the preparation and explanations of their sacred, ancient, biblical meaning, and then an account of them as I saw these days and nights observed in the homes and churches of the poor. A queer mixture of tragedy, orthodoxy, and revelation, they interested our Christian readers. The uptown Jews complained now and then. Mr. Godkin required me once to call personally upon a socially prominent Jewish lady who had written to the editor asking why so much space was given to the ridiculous performances of the ignorant, foreign East Side Jews and none to the uptown Hebrews. I told her. I had the satisfaction of telling her about the comparative beauty, significance, and character of the uptown and downtown Jews. I must have talked well for she threatened to have me fired, as she put it. [10]

Although much of what the German Jew gave to the Russian Jew in charity was motivated by the wish to rid the latter of the stigmas of the Old World, there was, nevertheless, a deep-felt concern for the newcomer's plight. Psychologically, many an uptowner recognized in the strange,

Old World figure something of his own past, the traditions
from which he had drifted in the New World. One of the
pervasive themes in Jewish-American fiction of this century
is the emancipated second- or third-generation Jew's traumatic recognition of his past, usually objectified in the form
of an Old World father-figure who appears suddenly to haunt
the American Jew. [11] There was also among many German
Jews the recognition of the traditional obligation of Jew to
Jew, rich to poor, and they gave large sums in aid. In the
debate over immigration restriction, it should be added, the
German Jew was among the most insistent of the voices de-
manding that the gates remain open.

        The attitude of the Russian Jew toward the German
was no less ambivalent. On the one hand, the newcomer had
little use for those who had repudiated tradition. The German Jew was labeled "goy" (gentile) and "meshamud" (apostate) by the ghetto dwellers. Louis Wirth in his pioneering
sociological study of the ghetto quotes from an anonymous immigrant autobiographical manuscript which reveals this attitude:

> When I first put my feet on the soil of Chicago, I was
> so disgusted that I wished I had stayed at home in Rus-
> sia. I left the old country because you couldn't be a
> Jew over there and still live, but I would rather be
> dead than be the kind of German Jew that brings the
> Jewish name into disgrace by being a Goy. That's
> what hurts: They parade around as Jews, and down
> deep in their hearts they are worse than Goyim, they
> are meshamuds. [12]

On the other hand, the Russian Jew felt pride in the achievements of some of his coreligionists from Germany. Men like
Jacob Schiff, Meyer Guggenheim, and Julius Rosenwald were
held in high esteem in the ghetto. Success and social climb-
ing were not absent as ideals among the Russian Jews, and
such names reminded the ghetto dwellers of the possibility of
an immigrant's and a Jew's succeeding in America.

        During the middle and late eighties, before the East
European Jews attracted the notice of native-born writers,
Henry Harland wrote several novels about New York's German
Jews in which he criticized their unwillingness to assimilate
with the native population, anticipating, ironically, the criticism German Jews were to level at their downtown brethren
a decade or so later. Raised in Connecticut, Harland attended

Harvard Divinity School for a year and then settled in New
York, where he came under the influence of Felix Adler and
the Ethical Culture movement.   Under the name "Sidney Luska" he wrote these early novels of New York Jewish life before emigrating to England to help edit The Yellow Book.
The German Jews, whom he had come to know through Ethical Culture and as a student at the City College of New York,
appear in the novels as fabulous, mysterious, exotic, almost
mythical creatures tied to the yoke of a long "racial" past
which they are unable to throw off.   Harland had a message
to preach: salvation through assimilation and assimilation
through intermarriage.   Yet his characters are usually unsuc-
cessful in their attempts to escape the past.   An occult tie
binds them to the Old World and prevents them from fully
participating in the New.   As a result the Jew in America is
lost, destined to wander hopelessly around the periphery of
society.   This seems a strange attitude for a writer whose
Jewish acquaintances included thoroughly assimilated, successful men like Felix Adler, but Harland was working with a
tried-and-true formula for the presentation of the Jew in
literature.

     Ernest Newman, the musician in As It Was Written:
A Jewish Musician's Story (1885), is a schizophrenic Jekyll-
Hyde character, a sensitive violinist and affectionate lover as
well as a psychopathic murderer, bound by the curse of his
dead father.   He is accused of murdering his fiancée after
she is found dead in her apartment a few hours after he had
left her but is acquitted by the court for lack of motive.
Later he comes into possession for the first time of a letter
his father had written from his deathbed years earlier forbidding him to marry since all the women in the family for several generations had been unfaithful.   The letter named the
father of Ernest's fiancée as the man who had betrayed him
and ended by imploring the son to take revenge.   The knowledge initiates in Newman an automatic writing state in which
he reveals how he murdered his fiancée while in a trance.
He has been controlled unaware by the past.   Harland has
employed the bizarre circumstances symbolically to portray
the Jew's inability to extricate himself from his past.   Newman is the "new man" in name only.

     The protagonist of The Yoke of the Thorah (1887) is
another sensitive, "spiritual" Jew, a painter, Elias Bacharach,
who is in love with a gentile girl.   Despite the warnings of
his uncle--an old orthodox rabbi with whom he lives--that he
must never marry the girl, he arranges for their wedding,

but while the ceremony is underway, he collapses and becomes seriously ill. Whether his collapse is the result of
the uncle's chicanery, the power of suggestion on a highly
sensitive artist, or his own sense of "racial" guilt, he re-
covers to renounce the girl and his own intended apostasy.
He marries instead a rather coarse, crude Jewess, the daughter of a parvenu merchant family, and lives to regret his
choice. Haunted by the memory of his lost love and chained
to a dull, bourgeois wife, he ends by committing suicide in
Central Park. Intermarriage was the chance Harland offered
his protagonist to escape "the yoke of the Thorah," but Bacharach was unable--or perhaps unwilling--to take it.

In Mrs. Peixada, which came out the previous year,
the Jewish heroine Judith--cast in the familiar mold of the
suffering, dark-haired exotic beauty--is more fortunate. With
the sudden death of her old Jewish husband, who had imprisoned her, she is released to wed the successful gentile
lawyer Arthur Ripley. Peixada, the villainous husband, is
another version of the well-known opposite stereotype from
the lovely Judith--the rich, greedy pawnbroker, complete here
with a hawk's beak for a nose, yellow fangs for teeth, claws
for hands, and talons for fingers.

Despite the existence of such unsavory stereotypes, Harland in these early works retained a sympathy for the German Jew, but saw his hope for future happiness only in complete assimilation. Because of certain scenes in these novels
in which he depicted the coarse, materialistic uptown Jews
with their talk of the marketplace and their saleable daughters,
and because he deplored the separateness of the Jews, Harland was attacked widely by uptown Jewish readers. Ironically these same readers were in the next decade to deplore the
clannishness and separateness of the recently-arrived downtown Russian Jews and to boast of their own assimilation. [13]

Like other writers considered in this chapter, Harland
maintained a vision of an America whose values and attributes
had been fixed along English and Protestant lines since the
earliest European settlement. Americanization in this vision
presumes movement in only one direction: the immigrant
sheds his past--rids himself of cultural traits which are at
variance with Anglo-American ideals--and adjusts to the beliefs and behavior patterns of his adopted land. "Anglo-conformity," a term which has been used in recent times to describe this view of the national ideal, was the dominant but
not the only attitude toward assimilation. [14]

The "melting pot," another traditional concept, based on entirely different assumptions about America, reemerged conspicuously in the writings and social experiments of some liberal Americans in the late nineteenth century. The melting pot, as the metaphor suggests, involves the blending and fusing of diverse elements. The New World, according to this rival interpretation of assimilation, is a place of new men. The national character is not fixed and determined from the past but is continually being shaped and given direction by all those who choose to come to America. In the crucible of America each immigrant adds his own heritage to the mixture he finds here. Since Hector St. John de Crevecoeur described for Europeans in his Letters from an American Farmer in 1787 a country where "individuals of all nations would be melted into a new race of men," the melting pot concept has had its adherents here. Emerson expressed his faith that "the energy of the Irish, Germans, Swedes, Poles, and Cossacks, and all the European tribes ... will construct a new race, a new religion, a new state, a new literature, which will be as vigorous as the new Europe which came out of the smelting-pot of the dark ages."[15] Oliver Wendell Holmes had his Autocrat affirm, "We are the Romans of the modern world--the great assimilating people."[16] And later in the decade Herbert Spencer described a new American who, through non-Anglo admixture, would be "more plastic, more adaptable, more capable of undergoing the modifications needful for complete social life."[17]

As America's faith that it could continue to harbor Europe's dispossessed began to collapse under the pressure of the hordes of "new" immigrants, the settlement house movement with its melting-pot credo emerged to help reaffirm that faith. From its inception in Dr. Stanton Coit's Neighborhood Guild in 1886 (later the University Settlement under Columbia's Seth Lowe), the settlement movement was dedicated to bridging the gap between the two worlds through mutual understanding and respect. The Americanization of the immigrant was no longer to be simply a one-way street. Instead of being urged to shed his Old World past as rapidly as possible, the immigrant was encouraged to retain what was best in his background and adopt what was best in the native tradition. Natives and immigrants, "haves" and "have-nots," were to live and work together, each learning from the other. In the nineties, settlement houses scattered throughout the East Side of New York and in Chicago, Boston, and Philadelphia were providing a wide variety of community services--education, manual training, playgrounds and kindergartens, clubs, amusement and recreation, nursing and public health. In addition the settlement workers were active in agitation for tenement and labor reform.

Among the more vigorous of the settlement agitators was Jane Addams, who in 1889 founded Chicago's Hull House, the most successful and best-known of the settlement experiments. Miss Addams, who was born in comfortable surroundings in Cedarville, Illinois, in 1860, conceived her plan while on an educational trip to Europe, after having seen some of the effects of industrial labor on East London working girls. When she returned, she bought an old mansion on Halstead Street which became the nucleus of Hull House. In addition to its role as an agency for the improvement of living and working conditions in the largely foreign West Side of Chicago, Hull House, as Jane Addams conceived it, was to serve as a liaison between the cultural traditions of the native and the immigrant. [18]

Her first book, Democracy and Social Ethics (1902), reveals what the first thirteen years at Hull House had taught her: that the immigrant poor are not simply a "class" but a different culture with values often at odds with those of middle-class America; that poverty is not necessarily the result of idleness or indolence (there are overtones of this traditional Anglo-Saxon view persisting in Riis); and that the social worker must be chary of applying her own middle-class standards to the immigrant, whose differing standards are rooted in far different realms of experience:

> Because of this diversity of experience the visitor is
> continually surprised to find that the safest platitude
> may be challenged. She refers quite naturally to the
> 'horrors' of the saloon, and discovers that the head
> of her visited family does not connect them with 'hor-
> rors' at all. He remembers all the kindnesses he has
> received there, the free lunch and treating which goes
> on, even when a man is out of work and not able to
> pay up; the loan of five dollars he got there when the
> charity visitor was away and he was threatened with
> eviction. He may listen politely to her reference to
> 'horrors,' but considers it only 'temperance talk.'[19]

Hull House grew from a single structure to a complex of thirteen buildings with a large staff ministering to a variety of immigrant needs. Projects like the Labor Museum reflected the House's basic concern for preserving the

contributions of the immigrant's past. The museum was set
up to demonstrate the evolutionary nature of industry, the
continuation of the past in the present, and the contribution
of Old World culture to the New. It was an attempt to remind the immigrant, particularly the child, of his link with
the past and his contribution to the present, and to bridge the
generation gap in the face of alienating New World experiences. From its beginning as a place where Old World tools
and machines were exhibited, the museum evolved into a shop
where immigrants came to manufacture goods in the Old
World manner. Some few supported themselves by selling
these goods. In Twenty Years at Hull House (1910), Miss
Addams explained its value: "These women and a few men
who came to the museum to utilize their European skill in
pottery, metal, and wood demonstrate that immigrant colonies
might yield to our American life something very valuable, if
their resources were intelligently studied and developed."[20]
A two-way process of adjustment rather than the one-way
Americanization formula advocated by Jacob Riis and some of
the period's other reformers was the way of the settlements,
and with such pioneers as Dr. Stanton Coit, Seth Lowe, Lillian Wald, and Jane Addams, organized and effective social
work had its birth in America.

Journalist Hutchins Hapgood had none of the reform
zeal of the settlement founders but shared with them the belief that the new immigrant offered something of positive value
to American life. In the preface to the first edition of The
Spirit of the Ghetto (1902), a compilation of his newspaper
and magazine sketches of life in New York's Jewish Lower
East Side, he revealed the attraction he felt toward the ghetto:

> I was led to spend much time in certain poor resorts
> of Yiddish New York not through motives either philan-
> thropic or sociological, but simply by virtue of the
> charm I felt in men and things there. East Canal
> Street and the Bowery interested me more than Broad-
> way and Fifth Avenue.[21]

Like Jane Addams, Hapgood spent his childhood in
small-town Illinois. He was born in 1869 in the Mississippi
River town of Alton, but his ancestors dated back to Massachusetts Bay's earliest settlement. He returned to the Massachusetts his father had left and, with his brother, Norman,
studied at Harvard. He graduated with honors in 1892, went
on to get a master's degree, and taught English composition
for a while at Harvard. At his brother's urging he left

Cambridge for a job with the New York Commercial Advertiser, one of several young Harvard men city editor Lincoln
Steffens had attracted to the Advertiser's staff. Norman Hapgood, whose interest in drama led him to the discovery of
the Yiddish theatre, was as impressed as Hutchins was with
the cultural life of the ghetto. In 1916 he wrote:

> In New York City it is from the Russian Jews, who
> are the mass of poor Jews in America, that the real
> contribution to American life is likely to come, be-
> cause their aspirations are spiritual, their imagination
> alive. The Jews on the East Side are extraordinary
> and interesting. Often when I have been rather tired
> of the New York that everyone sees, I have gone
> down on the East Side to the theatres, clubs, cafes,
> and felt that I was in a universe that was young and
> full of hope. 22

Hutchins Hapgood discovered the same "spirit of the
ghetto," which he sought to convey to native readers in his
sketches. America's spiritual life would be enriched by the
orthodox and tradition-oriented Russian Jews. The scholarly
and intellectual Old World Jews of the ghetto--his "Prophets
without Honor" and "Submerged Scholars"--were his most revered figures, happy contrasts to those who sold their birth-
rights for the material distractions of the New World. Quaintly anachronistic, "submerged in old traditions and outworn
forms," the old ghetto Jew retains for Hapgood an essential
dignity and nobility in resisting the ways of the New World.

Hapgood was introduced to the theatres and coffee-
houses of the East Side by his friend and co-worker on the
Advertiser, Abraham Cahan, and the charm of the ghetto was
never lost on him. Like Lincoln Steffens, Hapgood saw the
literary value of the ghetto as stemming largely from the conflicts and contrasts its life presented. Steffens, looking back
over these years in his autobiography, recalled the literary
appeal the ghetto had both for him and for his staff.

> The tales of the ghetto [he observed] were heart-break-
> ing comedies of the tragic conflict between the old and
> the new, the very old and the very new.... We all
> know the difference between youth and age, but our ex-
> perience is between two generations. Among the Rus-
> sian and other eastern Jewish families in New York it
> was an abyss of many generations; it was between
> parents out of the middle ages ... and the children of

the streets today.... Two, three thousand years of
continuous devotion, courage, and suffering for a
cause lost in a generation. [23]

Hapgood, throughout The Spirit of the Ghetto, explores
this conflict in its many manifestations: the old orthodox Jew,
the young "allrightnik," the utopian socialist; the values of the
synagogue and those of the theatre; the Jewish home and the
American street; the Cheder (Hebrew School) and the public
school. Perhaps even more than for its contrasts and conflicts, the ghetto attracted him as a source of intense intellectual fervor and passionate concern for literature and the
theatre. The line between fiction and non-fiction in Hapgood's
sketches is not always clearly drawn. Although based on
firsthand observation of real people, his impressions are
highly colored by his enchantment with the life he saw. His
heroes of the ghetto--the scholar Moses Richerson, the poets
Eliakim Zunser and Morris Rosenfeld, the storytellers Solomon Libin and Abraham Cahan, the playwright Jacob Gordin,
and the artist Jacob Epstein--are eulogized and idealized.
Epstein, who illustrated the first edition of the book, is described in terms which Hapgood might have applied to himself:

He tells the truth about the ghetto as he sees it, but
into the dark reality of the external life he puts frequently a melancholy beauty of spirit.... [W]hile really remaining faithful to the external type, his love for
the race leads him to emphasize the spiritual and human expressiveness of the faces about him [pp. 259-
261].

Hapgood's individual portraits are filled with this "melancholy beauty of spirit," particularly his portraits of the
pious Old World Jews. Among the younger intellectuals and
writers of the ghetto, he discovered a far different spirit,
one of tough-minded, critical realism: "Mellowness, com-
placency, geniality, and calmness are qualities practically unknown to the intellectual Russian Jews, who, driven from the
old country, now possess the first opportunity to express
themselves" (p. 40). He sees realism as an inborn quality
of the Jewish mind. Of his literature, the Jew asks himself
two questions: Is it natural? and, Is it true? His tastes
have been shaped by his own bitter experience and by the fiction of Tolstoy and Chekhov. Many of the ghetto's intellectuals are more Russian than Jewish. Sensuousness, he points
out, is a characteristic absent from Jewish literature: "A

Keats is a Jewish impossibility" (p. 98). There is the love
of beauty but little enjoyment of pure form. This, he suggests, accounts for the sparsity of Jewish achievement in the
plastic arts. In the best ghetto art, the traditional melan-
cholic spirit comes together with a critical realism, as in
the bitter, impassioned sweatshop poetry of Morris Rosenfeld,
the ghetto's "singer of labor. "

Hapgood's only strong antipathy in the ghetto was to
the political "isms" preached by the younger Jews in the
cafes. He saw them as repudiations of both traditional faith
and American ideals. The Spirit of the Ghetto closes with a
short parable about a young, intellectual anarchist woman,
which illustrates his disgust with the direction some of the
younger ghetto dwellers were taking. Sabina has so thoroughly dedicated herself to her political cause that when she discovers that she is in love with a man, she commits suicide,
feeling betrayed and vulgarized by the intrusion of her emo-
tions.

The collection was followed eight years later by another group of sketches, Types from City Streets (1910),
which again reveal Hapgood's romantic preoccupation with the
charm and intensity of life in the ghetto. The scope of this
collection is broader. The tales deal with the Irish Bowery,
Little Hungary, and segments of native low life as well as
the Jewish ghetto. His announced aim was to demonstrate
that in the "common" and "low" life of the city lies a still
unexplored region of literary interest. To enter this region
with sympathy and curiosity is to discover "life which is open,
direct, honest, accessible, and charming. " The poor have
been exposed more directly to raw experiences. They have
lived more deeply and assimilated their experiences more
fully. What they have to say, therefore, has real value for
the writer. They are, to Hapgood, "cultivated" in a real way,
through real experience.

> People who have reached 'de limit' are full of rich
> material for literature. They have nothing to con-
> ceal.... You can take not only your plots from the
> lives of these people, but you can also derive the
> vigor and vitality, the figurative quality of your style,
> from the slang and racy expressions of your lowly
> friends. [24]

This kind of romantic rationale for the literary treatment of the urban poor was anything but novel in 1910. As

we shall see in the following chapter, Hapgood is following in
a long line of "literary slummers" who well before the end
of the nineteenth century were issuing such defenses for their
preoccupation with slum material. Of greater interest in
Hapgood's sketches are the benefits to native life he attributed
to the immigrants.

Hapgood saw the foreign influence on American life as
a wholly benevolent one. He portrayed the native urban type
as a nervous, frenetic, palpitant man who has no time for
books, art, leisure, philosophy, or contemplation. He likened
him to "the nervous system of a frog in the psychological laboratory which the operator, by the application of acid, galva-
nizes into unmeaning activity" (p. 114). The foreigner is
changing all this; he has come with his art, his love for the
contemplative life, his Gemütlichkeit, which Hapgood trans-
lates as the Bohemian spirit of urbanity and "intelligent loaf-
ing." The Italians and the Germans are the best representa-
tives of this Gemütlichkeit. The Jews, on the other hand,
are "intellectual debauchees," "full of passion, storm, and
stress." Refugees from Russian persecution, they are bel-
ligerent and stormy and "lack the repose and balance which
is an essential of the true Bohemian" (p. 120).

Most of the book consists of sketches, short stories,
anecdotes, snatches of conversation, and interviews Hapgood
collected on his rambles through the immigrant quarters of
New York. Grouped under such headings as "The Pathos of
Low Life," "Life's Little Misfits," "The Bowery Sentiment,"
and "The Town's Philosophers," they present a highly colorful if exaggerated and distorted account of the city's foreign
life. One of his interests here, as in The Spirit of the Ghetto, was the misfit, the immigrant who dangles between Old
World and New, feeling at home in neither. He tells the
familiar story of one such misfit, the son of a ghetto Jew,
who moved from the Lower East Side, changed his name, and
became a writer. Returning to the ghetto in search of local
color story material and his own roots, he finds himself pa-
tronized by the cafe intellectuals. He becomes a misfit
among his own people. He wants to return but cannot, and
he senses his double alienation.

The sketch titled "A Domestic Bohemian" serves as a
kind of metaphoric statement of the point of view Hapgood es-
pouses throughout the collection. An allegory or parable of
the local colorist who must go beyond surface impressions to
get an inside view of his subject, the story tells of a physi-

cian who frequents an immigrant cafe where almost daily he
observes with some annoyance and distaste the Bohemian,
Yahi, one of the cafe's regular patrons.   Yahi is "an un-
pleasant person to look at ... sallow, long face, tawdry
clothes....   Yellow was the color of his skin as well as of
his face. "   One day the physician, called to Yahi's sick
wife, finds the man poor but kindly, fatherly, and affectionate:

> There was nothing serious the trouble and we re-
> turned to the dining room, where Yahi made me drink
> a bottle of beer and talked of the last French novel,
> stopping now and then to pat his son on the head, and
> run into his wife's bedroom to see whether anything
> was the matter.
>
> I left the flat with the reflection that the civilized
> point of view was a trivial one after all; and that Yahi
> at heart was not 'yellow' a bit [p. 176].

Yahi is Hapgood's "intelligent loafer" type, the tolerant,
pleasant, philosophical immigrant whom Europe was supplying
New York in increasing numbers, and whom the native writer
recognized only when his curiosity and sympathy had enabled
him to go beyond rough surfaces.   From the low life of the
city, particularly from its immigrants, came the "stuff of literature. "   Here, Hapgood believed, was life without prejudice
or pretension.

Despite his assertions to the contrary, Hapgood was
still the outsider with his nose pressed to the windows of the
ghetto, and his appreciative local color portraits of the immigrant are in their way as superficial and naive as those of
the less sympathetic "genteel" writers he castigated.   Romantic and sentimental treatment of the urban immigrant characterizes much of the popular fiction of the ghetto (which will
be examined in subsequent chapters).   What gives Hapgood's
writing its chief interest today--and its value in the early
years of the new century--is its confident and optimistic assertion of the melting-pot ideal at a time when many native
Americans were losing that confidence.   To this son of one
of America's oldest families, America was in need of the
values of the immigrant to redeem it from the frenetic, un-
reflective life ushered in by the urban-industrial age.   To
Hapgood, it was not a question of what America could offer
the immigrant, but what the immigrant could offer America.

The term "melting pot" gained currency in 1908 when

English-born novelist-playwright Israel Zangwill used it as
the title of his successful play about immigrant life in New
York.   Since then the term has undergone considerable shift
in meaning and has become, in the words of a recent observer, Philip Gleason, more a symbol of "confusion" than
"fusion."25 The term, Gleason demonstrates, was employed
in the second decade of the century to denote almost any view
toward assimilation favored by those using it.   During the
war years, with the fear of divided loyalties and the suspicion of all but "100 per cent Americans," the traditional optimistic view that the melting pot was working to produce a
stronger America by blending the best elements of Old and
New World cultures lost ground to the view that the function
of the pot was to purge the "foreign dross" and "impurities"
from the immigrant.   In the popular mind the melting pot was
identified more and more closely with indoctrination.   As a
result of this shift those liberal critics who rejected narrow
Americanization as a cultural ideal tended also to reject the
melting pot, with its connotations of conformity and standardi-
zation.

One of those critics was philosopher Horace Kallen, a
student of John Dewey, son of German-Jewish immigrants,
and a supporter of Zionist causes.   In "Democracy versus
the Melting Pot," an influential two-part essay he wrote for
the Nation in 1915, he outlined the attitude toward acculturation which he would develop in his subsequent writings.   "Cultural Pluralism," the term he later gave to his position, rejected both the melting-pot assumption of the gradual fusion
of native and immigrant stock and the narrower doctrine of
assimilating the immigrant into the dominant existing culture.
He maintained that America is and should continue to be a
confederation of European nations and cultures.   He argued
for an America which would be

> a democracy of nationalities, cooperating voluntarily
> and autonomously in the enterprise of self-realization
> through the perfection of men according to their kind.
> The common language of the commonwealth, the lan-
> guage of its great political tradition, is English, but
> each nationality expresses its emotional and voluntary
> life in its own language, in its own inevitable artistic
> and intellectual forms.   The common life of the com-
> monwealth is politico-economic and serves as the foun-
> dation and background for the realization of the distinc-
> tive individuality of each natio that composes it.   Thus
> 'American civilization' may come to mean the perfec-

tion of the cooperative harmonies of 'European civilization' ... a multiplicity in a unity, an orchestration
of mankind. [26]

This extreme cosmopolitanism had another vigorous
defender in Randolph Bourne. America has the unique opportunity, Bourne argued, to become a "trans-national," cosmopolitan culture--a little Europe, with national distinctions pre-
served yet all groups cooperating for the good of society. [27]
Instead of imposing Anglo-Saxon traditions--the superiority of
which he doubted--upon immigrants and calling it Americanization, we should, he claimed, recognize that America is a
land of immigrants and that each immigrant culture has in-
fused vitality, power, and variety into the nation. Narrow
Americanization and forced chauvinism stifle what is most
vital in America; our greatest asset is our multiplicity.

Recent events in such bi-cultural or poly-cultural
cities as Belfast, Jerusalem, Montreal, Nicosia (and all large
American cities as well) raise, of course, doubts as to the
efficacy of Kallen's and Bourne's cosmopolitan ideals in the
modern world, however eloquently they stated them. But
whether "an orchestration of mankind" or a "Trans-National
America" either accurately described what was taking place
in the nation or would be a successful model to follow in the
years ahead is not the issue here. The important point is
that their call for cosmopolitanism, for a poly-cultural society, was heard widely in the early twentieth century, attracted
a number of adherents, and stood as a liberal alternative to
Anglo-conformity and melting-pot fusion, particularly as these
two concepts blurred into each other.

In Vida Scudder's 1903 novel, A Listener in Babel, all
three positions are given expression. Hilda Lathrop, the
novel's upper-class heroine who goes to live and work in a
settlement house, listens early in the novel to her fellow
workers debate the question of immigrant adjustment. Philip
Mervyn, a lawyer, expresses the cosmopolitan ideal:

It seems to me very doubtful whether the future is to
see one American race. As I watch these hordes
sweeping down upon us, another image rises before
me--why not an Italian city here--a Hungarian colony
there--a Swedish, a German--all preserving their racial autonomy, as they certainly seem inclined to do
so far, but held together by political union? [28]

Another of the settlement workers, Miss Saltonstall,
counters with the opposite ideal of Anglo-conformity: "We
shall get it through the schools. We shall indoctrinate all
these foreigners in time--all the worthy ones at least--with
the great American tradition" (p. 75).

Janet Frothingham, a third worker, expresses the
melting-pot concept, which was basic to the settlement movement and which Miss Scudder ultimately affirms in the novel
by having her heroine embark upon a rather vague Jane Ad-
dams-like scheme of bringing together peasant handicraft and
modern industry:

> ... and if we ignore the wealth of traditions which our
> emigrants bring us, we ignore still more their crea-
> tive powers.... The English stock needs enrichment.
> It has developed on our soil a civilization with strong,
> fine traits, but arid, hardened, materialized, nervous.
> Wouldn't that civilization profit by the gifts of other
> races, less competent in action, it may be, but with
> more aptitude for emotion and dream [pp. 80-81].

Whether, in fact, the "gifts of other races" were contributing anything valuable to American life was a question
Americans debated throughout this stormy period. In the half
century between 1870 and 1920 nearly twenty million immigrants came to America, and, for better or worse, American
life was deeply affected by their presence. Jane Addams and
Hutchins Hapgood, who were drawn to the ghetto for entirely
different reasons, shared the belief that the recent immigrant
was supplying stable values desperately needed in a rapidly
changing industrial society. Born in the rural Midwest of old
American families and raised in comfortable surroundings,
Addams and Hapgood both saw in the immigrant a hope for
redeeming some of the order which had gone out of American
life. They carried forward into the urban age America's traditional melting pot ideology. By contrast, Jacob Riis, the
"old" immigrant who arrived penniless and achieved success
in America, conditioned his approval of the "new" immigrant
on his willingness to cast aside his past and assimilate with
the native population. The urban landscape would first have
to be improved before the immigrant could be expected to become a good American, but Riis was quick to criticize the
immigrant who seemed reluctant to adopt the ways of his new
land. He sought to reform the slum environment in order to
smooth the way for the Americanization of the immigrant. He
sketched the ghetto's derelicts, paupers, and street arabs.

Hapgood, on the other hand, sketched its artists, poets, and scholars.   Riis examined its crowded tenements and saloons; Hapgood its theatres, schools, and coffee houses.   Beginning with different assumptions about the nature of American life, the journalists, sociologists, and social workers who explored the ghetto reached different conclusions about the immigrant's contributions to that life.   What they had to say established the main lines of the immigration debate and furnished much of the ideological content for the fiction of the ghetto.

Fiction, however, has its literary as well as its sociological roots, and the fiction of the urban immigrant has one of its major sources in the conventions of the tenement tale, which became a vogue in the century's last two decades.

III

PLUMBING THE CITY'S DEPTHS:
ABRAHAM CAHAN, STEPHEN CRANE
AND THE TENEMENT TALE TRADITION

In 1896 Appleton published Abraham Cahan's first novel,
Yekl, A Tale of the New York Ghetto, and reissued Stephen
Crane's Maggie, A Girl of the Streets, brought out privately
and pseudonymously three years earlier.   Neither the Bowery
nor the immigrant Lower East Side of New York were new
subjects for fiction at that time.   For more than a decade
magazines had been featuring stories and sketches of slum
life.   The city's "other half" had become, by the mid-nineties,
a product of proven marketability, one which the writer who
wanted to demonstrate his contemporary social relevance could
hardly resist.   What made the almost simultaneous printing of
Maggie and Yekl significant was that in these two slim first
books, Crane and Cahan--then unknown to each other and from
entirely different backgrounds--launched a dual assault upon
the romantic conventions which had come to be identified with
the tenement tale.   While neither author was able to avoid entirely the condescending tone which had always characterized
the fictional treatment of the poor, the protagonists in these
two novels were far different from the self-sacrificing, noble,
and heroic tenement dwellers readers of the nineties had come
to expect in their fiction.   The slum denizens of Crane and
Cahan were vain, assertive and self-seeking, and in portraying them as such, the authors undermined the sentimental assumptions of the popular tenement tale.

No two contemporaries could seem less alike.   In background, training, and temperament they belonged to different
worlds.   Cahan, the son of an impoverished Talmudic scholar
from a small shtetl near Vilna, emigrated penniless to America in 1882 among the advanced guard of the large Russian-
Jewish migration which was to last through the second decade
of the twentieth century.   At the age of thirty-six he had established himself as a cultural leader of New York's Lower

East Side ghetto. He had worked in sweatshops, served as a
"walking delegate" to the new unions springing up in the ghetto, taught English to immigrants in East Side night schools,
helped edit the Yiddish Arbeiter Zeitung and published articles and sketches in both the Yiddish and English press. [1]
His active life would continue for more than a half-century,
dominated by his successful editorship of the Forward, which
he turned into America's largest circulation Yiddish daily.
With the possible exception of The Rise of David Levinsky,
his fiction would be forgotten.

Crane, by direct contrast, was the son of an upper-
middle-class New Jersey Methodist minister. He spent his
adolescent years not in a Russian shtetl but in Asbury Park,
an affluent New Jersey resort. And his knowledge of the
slums was not, like Cahan's, the product of enforced daily
contact, but of his fascination with the submerged population
of the Bowery and Tenderloin districts, where he spent a
good deal of his time between 1891 and 1895. Maggie was
written early in 1893 when he was living with some students
in an East Side rooming house. [2] When the book was reissued in 1896, he was only twenty-five, yet he would live but
four more years, his fame as a writer assured with the publication of The Red Badge of Courage in 1895.

If, then, Cahan drew his materials directly from the
life he knew first-hand and Crane from life observed from
the perspective of an outsider, the two stories don't reveal
this difference. A similar ironic and detached point-of-view
pervades both books. William Dean Howells noted the similarity between the two novels and paired them in a review for
the New York World. Of Cahan he said:

> I cannot help thinking that we have in him a writer of
> foreign birth who will do honor to American letters....
> There is much that is painful in his story, as there is
> much that is dreadful in Mr. Crane's work, but both
> of these writers persuade us that they have told the
> truth and that as conditions have made the people they
> deal with, we see their people. [3]

Howells was no stranger either to Cahan or Crane in
1896. He had read the 1893 version of Maggie--Crane had
sent him a copy--and was impressed by the young writer's
uncompromising urban realism. In January of 1896, after
Red Badge was published but before the reissue of Maggie,
he wrote Crane, "For me, I remain true to my first love,

'Maggie. ' That is better than all the 'Black Riders' and 'Red Badges'. "[4] He went on to contribute the Preface to the 1896 English edition of Maggie. Howells was also interested in Cahan's early work. Attracted to an early ghetto sketch, "A Providential Match,"[5] he sought out Cahan in 1892. They met in Howells' home, and encouraged by the famous man to write a novel about ghetto life, Cahan set out to work on Yekl, which he completed in 1895.[6] Howells was pleased with the manuscript and saw to its publication with Appleton after both Harper and McClure had rejected it.

Despite Howells' praise, both books were uniformly denounced for their sordid treatment of the lower class. Reviewers did not question the propriety of treating slum or ghetto material in fiction; the tenement tale was well-established both in England and America and stories of slum life were enjoying a vogue. What they attacked was the relentless depiction of rapacity and avidity they found in these books. The reviewer for the The Nation, for instance, labeled Crane "a promising writer of the animalistic school," which he defined as "a species of realism which deals with man considered as an animal ... but which neglects, so far as possible, any higher qualities which distinguish him from his four-footed relatives, such as humor, thought, reason, aspiration, affection, morality, and religion." Similarly, the reviewer of Yekl in The Bookman asked,

> Does Mr. Cahan wish us to believe that the types of life of the ghetto thus represented are truly representative of his race? That it is as sordid, as mean, as cruel, as degraded as he has shown it to be? For ... throughout the work there is not a gleam of spirituality, unselfishness, or nobility. [7]

To the reviewers both books exuded the odors of "Zola's stinkpot." Maggie and Yekl had become part of the larger battle fought over the limits of realism in the eighties and nineties. Cahan and Crane, like Zola before them, were guilty of turning men into beasts. How far they had come from the romantic conception of the poor in the tenement tale tradition can be seen by looking briefly at that tradition.

The genesis of tenement fiction both in England and America can be traced first of all to the spread of slums throughout such cities as London, New York and Chicago in the late nineteenth century and to the warnings of the social consequences of slums presented in such books as Charles

Loring Brace's The Dangerous Classes in New York (1872),
Charles Booth's multi-volume Life and Labour of the People
of London (1889 and 1897) and Jacob Riis's How the Other
Half Lives (1890).   Articles on slum life were appearing in
all the journals advocating a concern with contemporary problems.   In 1890 Arena introduced a series on poverty in American cities and under Benjamin Orange Flower's editorship
continued throughout the decade to feature exposes of the
slums. [8]   In 1891 Scribner's began a symposium on "The
Poor in the Great Cities" (published in book form in 1896),
which featured such contributors as Jacob Riis, Walter Besant and Joseph Kirkland.   The growth of the urban immigrant population, the proliferation of labor warfare, the physical spread and increasing density levels of the city's traditional slum areas and the public outcries over rising rates of
urban crime, vice and disease all combined to make the
slums increasingly visible and topical as the century drew to
a close.   The American City had taken on a foreign and tattered appearance which suggested endless literary opportunities.

        The roots of late nineteenth-century slum fiction, how-
ever, strike deeper soil than the contemporary reform concern.   The tenement tale vogue of the eighties and nineties
was the culmination of a long literary involvement with the
urban poor.   Charles Dickens was perhaps the writer most
directly influential to the slum novelists of the late nineteenth
century.   His treatment of the urban netherworld in several
novels combined the two features which were to dominate the
literary treatment of the city's poor in the following decades--
a humanitarian concern with the plight of the other half and a
fascination with the romance and adventure of slum life.
Dickens was, of course, not the first English novelist to feel
the literary attraction of London's slums.   The entire history
of the English novel from the early eighteenth century is, in
fact, linked closely with urban material.   London in the age
of Defoe, Fielding, and Smollett had a population in excess of
one million and was more than ten times the size of any other
English city. [9]   It had, by then, taken on many of the characteristics of the modern city which were to prove irresistible
to writers.   The geographic partitioning of the city by class
and occupation was already a marked feature.   To Joseph Ad-
dison, the essayist, London had become "an aggregate of several nations," which he looked upon with fascination. [10]

        To judge by the profusion of eighteenth-century pam-
phlets and sermons on the subject, what to do with the urban

poor was an issue of great concern.   Most of the accounts
viewed poverty more as a crime than a misfortune, an attitude which crossed the ocean and persisted stubbornly throughout the next century and--in some quarters--to the present
time.   Against this prevalent view, however, should be
placed the forward-looking pamphlets and novels of Daniel
Defoe.   In Moll Flanders and Colonel Jack, two novels he
published in 1722, Defoe voiced his concern with the failure
of the state to provide any positive steps toward the allevia-
tion of the causes of poverty. [11]   Environment, in Defoe's
world, is more important than heredity in shaping character.
Moll is born in Newgate Prison, and Colonel Jack, an ille-
gitimate child, is thrown on the streets as a young boy.   He
sleeps on the warm ashes of the glass house, earns a few
pennies by running errands, and learns to pick pockets.   Just
as Moll is a precursor of the fallen woman who will appear
in many guises in later urban novels, Jack anticipates the
plucky, resourceful street arab who is to become a stock
character in nineteenth-century slum fiction.   Like so many
of his later incarnations, Jack is rescued from his poverty
by a combination of effort and good fortune.

    Henry Fielding and Tobias Smollett also wrote sympa-
thetically of the urban poor.   Billy Booth, the protagonist of
Fielding's last novel, Amelia (1751), is to some extent a victim of his own imprudence and torpor but to a larger degree
of the callousness and voraciousness of the upper classes
which prevent him until the last pages of the novel from re-
gaining the commission he has been unjustly deprived of.   In
Fielding's many asides to his readers he insists that the
"good heart" can be found anywhere, but in the novel those
that have it are all poor.   The hero of Smollett's Roderick
Random is another disinherited youth, a "friendless orphan"
forced to make his way through the city of corruption and
greed, "jeered, reproached, buffeted, pissed on, and at last
stripped of all money. "

    It is significant that Fielding's Booth and Amelia, De-
foe's Colonel Jack, and Smollett's Roderick Random are not
of low parentage.   All of them are from upper- or middle-
class backgrounds.   Reduced to poverty through some form of
deceit, they recoup their fortunes after a number of sordid
adventures.   This is part of the romantic formula of the slum
novel inherited by Dickens and passed on to his late nineteenth-
century literary heirs in England and America.   For the de-
serving poor--whether born into poverty or robbed of a birth-
right--there was always the hopeful prospect of rescue.   Even

George Gissing, the most important of Dickens' followers in
the slum tradition and a far more relentless and cynical de-
picter of slum life than his predecessor, was not averse to offering an escape to his worthy slum dwellers. Walter Besant,
even more than Gissing, though, typifies the sentimental and
optimistic treatment of the urban poor in late nineteenth-century fiction, with its reliance on such panaceas for the poor
as private philanthropy, the assertion of Christian ethics, and
a change of heart among the wealthy.

In America the novels of Elizabeth Stuart Phelps and
Helen Campbell reveal similar moral outlooks. Miss Phelps's
The Silent Partner (1871) deals with the brutal working conditions in a Massachusetts textile mill. Like Dickens and Besant the remedy she offers the laborer is a change of heart
on the part of the employing class--the emergence of buried
good will, piety, and Christian ethics. Miss Campbell, a
student of New York's slums and author of books and articles
about the sweatshop system, wrote two novels in the mid-
eighties which argue the responsibility of the upper classes
to the lower. Miss Herndon's Income (1885) is a long, talky
novel about a group of wealthy New Yorkers who discover
their obligations to the exploited workers of the city. Led by
the title character and a regenerate capitalist named Long-
street, they undertake such schemes as the building of model
tenements and model factories outside the city limits so that
workers who are honest, loyal, and hard-working can lead
decent lives. Miss Melinda's Opportunity (1886), similar in
message, focuses on the scheme of founding a housing and
recreation center for New York working girls.

Other novels of the period offered similar panaceas.
Lucia True Ames's Memoirs of a Millionaire (1889) and Alice
Rollins' Uncle Tom's Tenement (1886) urge the remedy of
model tenements in place of the overcrowded, unsanitary, and
unsafe "dumb bell" tenements which dominated the slum landscape. Whatever the specific solution proposed in these reform novels, it was to be achieved through the assertion of
individual conscience and Christian morality--charity and good
will on the part of the rich and self-help and perseverance on
the part of the poor. The economic system itself was seldom
called into question. Capitalism works to the benefit of capitalist and worker so long as each class recognizes its duty
and obligation to the other. If workers are in chains, it is
not the system which is at fault, but a few misguided or selfish capitalists, who are unaware of or unconcerned with the
conditions they are creating and who must be won over to

Christian ethics. Sometimes it is not even the capitalists
who are at fault for the enslavement of the working class but
malevolent forces which control both employer and worker.
In Roy McCardell's Wage Slaves of New York (1899), an absurd melodrama which according to its preface enjoyed a
vogue in earlier serialized form, the factory workers are enslaved only because their benevolent, paternalistic employer
has been deprived of control of his plant by a pair of grotesque, nefarious schemers. More typically, though, it is
the apathy and social irresponsibility of the wealthy which
must be, and is, overcome in these slum novels.

        Implicit--and sometimes explicit--in such novels is
the belief that slums are dangerous breeding grounds for
crime, disease and anarchy, and that should the privileged
classes ignore their obligations to the poor the entire city
would soon be uninhabitable. Charity was also self-interest.
Lucia True Ames has her millionaire-reformer pontificate before an audience of leading New York citizens: "The tene-
ment-house question is not merely a question of brick and
stone, ventilation, bath-rooms, and four per cent; it is a
question largely of providing the best means for uplifting
spiritually, mentally, and physically these swarming masses."[12] In the audience are Felix Adler (founder of New
York's Ethical Culture movement), reformer-novelist Alice
Rollins, and Charles Loring Brace, director of the Children's
Aid Society. One can imagine Jacob Riis there also, nodding
his approval.

        At the same time that reform novelists and journalists
were warning about the social dangers of slum life, other
novelists were discovering in the slums a fascinating new region for urban local color. Hamlin Garland, who wrote that
authentic local color fiction must come from writers raised
in the area they wrote about, also insisted that the slum novel, if it is to have the ring of authority, must come from
one who has grown up in the slums.[13] But those who were
products of the slums seldom had the education or the leisure
time to write fiction, and most of the stories about slum
life, like those about the immigrant ghettos, came from the
pens of middle-class observers attracted to the slums if not
by a reform zeal, then by the picturesque, exotic, "Arabian
Nights" quality they discovered there. In most of the tales
we see the poor through the eyes of a sympathetic, benevolent
narrator drawn to the tenement districts as a journalist, a
settlement worker, or a young writer in search of urban color.
Henry Cuyle Bunner, editor of Puck, with headquarters on

Mulberry Bend--an Irish and later Italian quarter in lower
Manhattan--was a confirmed "literary slummer" who never
tired of the parade outside his window. He thought of Mulberry Bend as the "most picturesque and interesting" area in
the city. [14] Bunner's friend and collaborator, Brander Matthews, the playwright, scholar, and later Columbia University
professor of literature, also found New York's slums irresistible. He invented for his short story collection, Vignettes of
Manhattan (1894), the narrator Rupert de Ruyter, a Knickerbocker writer whose search for local color leads him to Mulberry Street's "Little Italy," where he finds the life "unfailingly interesting. "[15]

     Sometimes the narrator in the tenement tale is a
young writer, who, like Crane in his early Bowery sketches,
has undergone an "experiment in misery," disguising himself
as a Bowery bum in order to discover the hidden truth about
the poor. The point of view of this persona, then, is like
that of his readers, whom he conducts on a kind of guided
tour of the slums. Alvan Francis Sanborn, whose Moody's
Lodging House and Other Tenement Sketches (1895) and Meg
McIntyre's Raffle and Other Stories (1896) provide a wealth
of Boston Irish local color, is such a narrator. He claims
to have disguised himself as an unemployed laborer to live
among the poor in a cheap rooming house. What he discovers among Boston's tough Irish, though, is what Bret
Harte discovered among the rough-and-tumble gamblers and
prostitutes of the Sierra mining towns: honor among thieves
and a deep sense of loyalty and sacrifice for which, he says,
one looks in vain among the "better" classes. This is the
point of view which Hutchins Hapgood adopted in Types from
City Streets, and it is one which persists in the period's tenement fiction. Occasionally, when the subject is the immigrant community, derisive stereotypes appear--hard-drinking
and brawling Irish, beer-guzzling and anarchistic Germans,
stiletto-bearing Italians, and vulgar and penurious Jews--but
generally the portraits are idealized and sentimentalized,
avoiding the harsher outlines reformers and nativists were
painting. Whether the poor were native-born or foreign-born,
the qualities of courage, dignity, and stoical endurance are
those which stand out most consistently. Middle class readers were given in this fiction the kind of poor they wanted to
believe in and expected in their fiction.

     So while the desire to mirror the truths social scien-
tists, settlement workers, and reform journalists were revealing about the new urban America was a powerful force in

attracting writers to the slums, the novels which were produced owed more to the long tradition of sentimental portraiture of the poor in fiction than to contemporary urban reality.
In story after story the poor are depicted as ignorant and innocent victims of forces beyond their control, but free from
the moral debilities journalists and social scientists were linking with destitution.   Environment crushes bodies in these
tales, but leaves souls untouched.   Poverty is rarely degrading: more often it is ennobling.   Men are hard-working,
honest and uncomplaining; women self-sacrificing, courageous
and either inviolable or cruelly betrayed.   If the heroine
yields to the seducer it is only after a long, hard struggle,
as in the case of Cora Stang, the beautiful slum flower in
Edgar Fawcett's The Evil That Men Do (1889).   One of the
characters in Paul Leicester Ford's The Honorable Peter
Stirling (1900) spoke for most of the slum novelists of these
years when he said, "There is more romance in a New York
tenement than there ever was in a baron's tower--braver battles, truer loves, nobler sacrifices.   Romance is all about
us, but we must have eyes for it. "[16]   Chicagoan Isaac Kahn
Friedman made the same point in the "Proem" to his novel,
Poor People (1900).   Comparing the tenement house where
the novel's action takes place to a dark, gloomy mine, he
tells us that in the mine's "forbidding depths ... are hid glit-
tering nuggets of pure gold, and to him who diggeth deep and
diligently shall be given. "[17]   The prize nugget in Friedman's
novel is the young German Adolph Vogel, who valiantly overcomes an inherited alcoholism, writes the successful play
"Poor People," and thus wins the right to marry the narrator's daughter, having demonstrated the kind of inner strength
and determination that mark so many of the period's slum
heroes.

        The daily horrors of slum life, the wretched sweatshop
and tenement house conditions which the urban reformers were
describing in the press, were often enough dramatized in fiction, but the moral implications of these conditions--the effect
on inner character--formed little part in the literature.   Sensational journalistic exposés of the brutal crimes, bestiality
and rapacity bred by slum life may have been an important
factor in drawing story tellers to the slums; however, the portrayal of the poor in slum fiction derives more from the conventions of romantic, sentimental nineteenth-century fiction
than from the contemporary journalistic reports. [18]   Howells,
whatever his own squeamishness and ambivalence when it came
to the slums, [19] took note of this pervasive sentimentality in
slum fiction.   In an 1895 editorial on the popularity of Edward

Townsend's Bowery gamin, "Chimmie Fadden," he wrote that
middle-class readers "must have toughness idealized, and they
must have the slums cleaned up a little ... if they are to
have them in literature."[20]

    Jacob Riis's work reveals this characteristic shift
which occurred when the reform journalism became fiction.
In How the Other Half Lives, a collection of articles, accompanied by photographs, on New York's slum neighborhoods,
he insisted repeatedly that the slum environment is degrading
as well as destructive, but in his fictional sketches collected
in Out of Mulberry Street (1897) the poor retain a kind of
moral innocence, faith and idealism in the face of their poverty.   In one sketch a young waif's belief in Santa Claus so
touches the older gamins in a dormitory for street youths
that they gather their meager savings to fill his Christmas
stocking.   In another tale, a young tough, arrested when the
police break up a gang war, escapes his arresting officers to
rescue an infant he sees wander in front of an oncoming
streetcar.   In still another, an old ghetto slippermaker works
day and night at his trade in a tenement flat, depriving himself of food and sleep in order to have Yom Kippur day free
to worship and fast.   Riis claimed in the Preface to Out of
Mulberry Street that the material for these stories came from
"the daily grist of the police hopper in Mulberry Street"
(where he was assigned as a police reporter), but his treatment of the material, his nagging insistence on the heroism
of his slum dwellers, suggests a stronger fidelity to the conventions of fiction than to the facts the reform journalists--
himself included--were digging up.

    It is to Riis's credit as a story-teller that he doesn't
rescue his characters from their poverty.   There are none
of the sudden and melodramatic reversals of fortune for the
worthy poor which one finds in the slum novels of Dickens,
Besant, and Gissing in England and Edward Townsend, Helen
Campbell, and Elizabeth Stuart Phelps in America.   Death is
prevalent in these sketches--usually in the form of a bizarre
accident resulting from unsafe living and working conditions.
Taken collectively, these mawkish stories of Riis all seem to
say that the slum environment destroys life but not the in-
domitable spirit of the poor.   Physical impoverishment is not
to be equated with spiritual impoverishment.

    This blend of cynicism and sentimentality, the stance
which resulted perhaps out of necessity from the police reporter's experience, characterizes the greater number of the

period's tenement tales. Many of the writers, like Riis, were
reporters who found the brief story focusing on the single in-
cident--only a step removed from the journalistic sketch--the
most congenial medium for depicting slum life. They were
more interested in representing the elemental struggle between
man and his environment, acted out every day in the slums,
than in extended plot or character development. Often a collection of stories set in a single locale (a neighborhood, a
block or even a single tenement building) with some of the
same characters reappearing gives the semblance of a novel,
but in such collections there is rarely any continuity of plot
from episode to episode. The practice of grouping tenement
sketches in this way may have originated with Arthur Morri-
son's London collection, Tales of Mean Street (1894). It appears in America in James Sullivan's Tenement Tales of New
York (1895--largely West Side New York Irish), Julian Ralph's
People We Pass (1896--German and Irish youths in a single
New York tenement house), Alvan Francis Sanborn's Moody's
Lodging House and Other Sketches (1895--Boston's poor Irish
settlement around Turley Street) and Isaac Kahn Friedman's
The Lucky Number (1896--a mixed immigrant community in
Chicago).

Another way of grouping tenement tales was around a
central character whose adventures could be followed in serialized publication. By far the favorite of such heroes was
the plucky, resourceful street arab--the kind Riis liked to
write about and Edward Townsend so successfully exploited in
his "Chimmie Fadden" sketches for the New York Sun. "Chimmie" is a Bowery tough who rescues the upper-class heroine
when she is assailed on a "slumming trip" and is rescued in
turn by being given a job as footman to the girl's father, af-
fectionately referred to by Chimmie as "'is whiskers." In a
long series of monologues Chimmie tells of his experiences
among polite society, allowing Townsend to reveal through his
young innocent the fundamental moral honesty of the slum boy
in contrast to the deviousness and connivances of the rich. [21]
Other popular versions of the idealized tough presented in
serialized form were George Ade's "Artie" and Richard Outcault's comic-strip creation, "The Yellow Kid" (born in the
Sunday edition of the New York World in 1895). Outcault also
created the slum comic strip "Hogan's Alley," which with
"The Yellow Kid" was continued in the World by George Luks
when Outcault moved to Hearst's Journal. [22]

The fictional focus on the street tough is not suprising
in light of the concern for the plight of the slum child voiced

by all the reformers. "The reform of poverty and ignorance must begin with the children," Riis maintained. [23] The slum child was both the most pathetic victim and, if he could be reached through schools, settlements and the church, the best hope for an end to the recurring cycle of urban crime, immorality and disease. What emerges in the fiction, though, is the street youth as hero more than as victim. Unlike Jimmie, the brother of Crane's heroine, the gamins in the popular slum fiction are more valorous than discrete, and they are kept occupied in tale after tale in rescuing women from would-be assailants or burning tenement buildings, and children from the paths of oncoming trains. A slight variation on this theme is James Sullivan's "Slob Murphey" (in Tenement Tales of New York). "Slob," despised by the neighbors in his West Side Irish tenement house because of his often cruel practical jokes, is crushed beneath the hooves of a milk-wagon horse. As he lies dying, he experiences beatific visions and in his last words implores his father to give up the drinking which has caused the family so much misery.

There are a number of other such young diamonds-in-the-rough in the popular tenement fiction of the nineties, good-bad boys who bear names like "Leather," "Skinny," and "Chalkey" (also from Sullivan's collection), "Skippy," "Nisby," and "The Kid" (from Riis's stories), "Yank" and "Petey" (from Julian Ralph's People We Pass), "Gallegher," "Snipes," and "Rags" (from Richard Harding Davis's Gallegher and Other Stories), "Chimmie" Fadden (Townsend), and "Patsy" Tulligan (from Stephen Crane's "The Duel That Was Not Fought"). These are some of the heirs to Peck's Bad Boys and to Horatio Alger's good boys like Phil the Fiddler, Mark the Match Boy and Ragged Dick. The street gamin's inherent cheerfulness, resourcefulness, philosophic turn of mind and stern sense of justice, as well as his picturesque raggedness, colorful dialect and metaphoric speech, combined to make him one of the most popular features of the tenement tale. The stories which dealt with such boys usually focused on incidents which revealed rather than shaped character, and what was revealed was a mettle and a capacity for heroism which normally lay hidden from the outsider's view. There was something reassuring to a middle-class audience to read about such gritty lads who like true Yankees could rise above their grim surroundings.

In the same way that the idealized gamin in most slum fiction differs from Crane's Jimmie, the slum girl who appears in these stories offers a striking contrast to Maggie.

As James Colvert has pointed out in his introduction to the
recent Virginia edition of Crane's Bowery Tales, Crane adopted many of the attitudes and assumptions about the slum girl
from popular reform tracts.   Whether or not he had actually
read the works of Thomas DeWitt Talmadge (author of The
Mask Torn Off), J. W. Buel (Metropolitan Life Unveiled) or
Jacob Riis, he was well aware of the prevalent point of view
which regarded the slum girl in terms of virtue overwhelmed
by a corrupting environment. [24]   Relating Maggie to attitudes
found in reform tracts of the eighties and nineties is a familiar strain in recent Crane scholarship, one which has all but
replaced the earlier emphasis on Crane's debt to Zola and
French naturalistic sources. [25]   Marcus Cunliffe in a short
piece in 1955 outlined some of the "American Background" of
Maggie, and since then this has been a common element in
discussions of the work. [26]

        The treatment of Crane's heroine certainly follows the
broader lines of the "virtue overwhelmed" theme found both
in the reform tracts and the popular fiction, but Crane's
story differs from other versions in his having resisted casting Maggie in the role of the long-suffering heroine struggling
to maintain her purity against the wiles of a ruthless seducer
--often from the upper classes. In Fawcett's The Evil That
Men Do, for instance, the heroine succumbs to her seducer
only after a long, hard struggle--with him and with herself.
She ends, typically, as a prostitute and finally is murdered--
or at least enters into a kind of unspoken suicide pact with an
old lover who has sunk as low as she.

        In some important ways Fawcett's novel anticipates
Crane's.   Despite its lapses into melodrama, its loose, episodic construction, and its discursiveness, the novel is more
relentless than most of its contemporaries in depicting the
brutalizing effects of slum life.   There is little possibility of
escape for any of the characters.   Cora, "a delicate blush-
rose in the midst of all this murk and soilure," lives in a
Bowery tenement surrounded, like Maggie, by vulgarity,
drunkenness, and violence.   She successfully resists the advances of the coarse son of her landlady only to be deceived
by the unctuous son of a wealthy alderman.   "She had tried
very hard to be good," Fawcett tells us in language strikingly
similar to Crane's, "but she had failed hopelessly. "[27]   For
Cora, as for the nineteenth-century heroine, the wages of sin
are death.   The author, though, makes a strong case in defense of Cora.   The lower-class virgin has been sacrificed to
the passions of the upper class.   He rails at the double

standard which allows men to avoid the consequences of their lust while their victims face a life of shame. At the same time, he attacks the rich who use their wealth to evade responsibility for their acts. Cora "pictured him [the alderman's son] as standing before the world at the side of an honored wife, himself unsuspected of the crime for which she [Cora] ... must reap the single harvest of degradation" (p. 298).

A far different version of the slum flower theme is contained in Edward Townsend's A Daughter of the Tenements (1895), which deals with a girl who rises from the world of sweatshops and fruitstands to a successful career as a dancer. Carminella in this novel is the female counterpart of Townsend's dauntless hero Chimmie Fadden. Luck and pluck for both provide the ticket out of the slums. In a letter to Katherine Harris, to whom, presumably, he had sent a copy of the 1896 Maggie, Crane wrote with what seems like some bitterness: "My good friend Edward Townsend--have you read his Daughter of the Tenements?--has another opinion of the Bowery and it is certain to be better than mine."[28]

In Crane's version of the Bowery and in Cahan's of the nearby Lower East Side, the poor are neither mettlesome heroes who rise--morally or actually--above their surroundings nor innocent and passive victims of an implacable environment. The characters in Maggie and Yekl are aggressive, self-seeking, and self-justifying. They ignore obligations to others if such obligations stand in the way of their desires. As Pete uses and discards Maggie when Nell comes along, Yekl abandons his "greenhorn" wife and child for the more Americanized Mamie Fein. Uncomfortable moral insights or sensations are dismissed as not being applicable to them. Pete insists to the end that he is a "good feller." Jimmie dismisses the similarity between his own seductions and Pete's violation of his sister. He "wondered vaguely, if some of the women of his acquaintance had brothers. Nevertheless, his mind did not for an instant confuse himself with those brothers nor his sister with theirs."[29] He will not admit to himself for long the thought that Maggie "would have been more firmly good had she better known why" (p. 115). Maggie, after her "fall," instinctively shrinks from the "painted" women in the music hall (p. 108). And disconsolate Mary Johnson cries "I'll fergive her" after the girl's suicide. Similarly, Yekl ("Jake") justifies his abandonment of his wife by blaming her for holding him back. Like Pete, he sees himself as a gallant, and wallows in self-pity at his fate after

Gitl and their child arrive in America. "All his achievements seemed wiped out by a sudden stroke of ill fate.   He
thought himself a martyr, an innocent exile from a world to
which he belonged by right; and he frequently felt sobs of self-
pity mounting in his throat. "[30]   Earlier, when he saw his
three-year-old son at Ellis Island, he "began to regard him,
with his mother, as one great obstacle dropped from heaven,
as it were, in his way" (pp. 75-76).

     Jake is not in love with Mamie, but with the image of
himself as a "Yankee" or an "American feller," an image
sustained by the impression that he is an attractive blade to
Mamie and the other working girls who attended "Professor"
Joe Peltner's ghetto dancing academy.   Maggie too is victimized by a false estimate of herself and her world.   She is
enthralled by the glitter of the tawdry music halls to which
Pete takes her and believes literally in the "transcendental
realism" of the Bowery melodramas, which celebrated the
"hero's erratic march from poverty in the first act, to wealth
and triumph in the final one" (p. 71).   Trapped by inadequate
romantic conceptions of life, Maggie and Jake fall victim to
a world which will not come around to them.   They attach
themselves to false ideals and to false lovers.   Pete and
Mamie are their deliverers, avatars of the bright night world
outside.   Pete, Maggie's "knight," swaggers into the Johnson
flat and

> As Jimmie and his friend exchanged tales descriptive
> of their prowess, Maggie leaned back in the shadow.
> Her eyes dwelt wonderingly and rather wistfully upon
> Pete's face.   The broken furniture, grimey walls, and
> general disorder and dirt of her home of a sudden ap-
> peared before her and began to take a potential aspect.
> Pete's aristocratic person looked as if it might soil
> [p. 47].

This passage can be compared to one in Yekl in which Mamie,
overdressed, struts into Jake's tenement flat.   Just as Maggie sees Pete as her champion, Mamie represents to Jake the
possibilities of a larger, freer world, a world to which he had
once belonged but from which he was unjustly banished:

> Her perfume lingered in his nostrils, taking his breath
> away.   Her venomous gaze stung his heart.   She
> seemed to him elevated above the social plane upon
> which he had recently ... stood by her side, nay upon
> which he had had her at his beck and call; while he

was degraded, as it were, wallowing in a mire, from
which he yearningly looked up to his former equals,
vainly begging for recognition. An uncontrollable desire took possession of him to run after her, to have
an explanation, and to swear that he was the same
Jake and as much of a Yankee and a gallant as ever
[pp. 112-113].

Thus while Pete steps into the Johnson tenement flat
to announce to Maggie what the world might hold for her,
Mamie calls on Jake to remind him of what he has had and
lost. Perhaps Maggie is less to be blamed than Jake. It
can be argued that she had little real choice, but to Jake
too "environment is a tremendous thing." He is ensnared in
a world whose borders are the tenement and sweatshop.
Alone, lonely and bored, he had sought out and found--before
the arrival of his family--some glitter in the night world of
the ghetto, and now with his "greenhorn" wife and a son who
hardly knows him on the scene, he misses desperately the
glitter.

When Cahan's novel opens, Jake is already enmeshed
in Mamie's sleazy world and unwilling to send for his wife.
He is the recent immigrant who flaunts his claims to being
an American by aping the most raffish manners of his adopted
land. In much the same way that the opening scene of Maggie (Jimmie's valiant struggle for the "honor" of Rum Alley)
sets the ironic tone of that book, the first chapter of Yekl establishes the pattern for Cahan's novel. Clean-shaven, unlike
his bearded fellow-workers, Jake sits at his sewing machine
in an East Side sweatshop loudly boasting about his knowledge
of American life. He argues the superiority of Boston over
New York and speaks knowingly of John L. Sullivan's career
and prize-fight betting. In contrast to Bernstein, the presser,
who studies English from a book propped up against his machine, Jake learns his English from life, which to him means
boxing, baseball and the dancing academy. To the "ladas" of
the ghetto he plays the role of gallant, feeling no compulsion
to let it be known that he has a wife and child in Russia waiting for him to send money for a boat ticket. In the land
where a Yekl can become a Jake, Gitl and the past come to
mean less and less to him. A statement Larzer Ziff has
made about Crane's story applies as well to Cahan's: "What
Maggie is is the result not of the action of her environment
on a plastic personality, but rather the reaction of that environment to the proposals made to it by her pretensions and
her longings. [31]

The proposals made to the environment by both protagonists, it should be pointed out, are not identical.   Maggie and Jake seek freedom from intolerable confinement, but
the kind of freedom each seeks is different.   Whereas Maggie wants only to escape the endless squalor and brutality of
her existence at home, Jake wants to escape his "greenhorn"
status.   He is searching--though in the wrong places--for an
American identity and not simply an end to his poverty.   Maggie Johnson belongs to an Irish-American family and lives in
an Irish enclave in Manhattan, but the fact of her "Irishness"
is in no way crucial to the story.   Jake's conflict, on the
other hand, is directly related to the fact that he is an East
European Jew and a recent immigrant, living culturally on
the very margin of American society.   Jake is a man who
has sold his birthright for a distorted version of Americanization.   What the immigrant Jew loses in his attempts to become Americanized is a theme which occupied Cahan throughout his fiction, and which is given its fullest expression in
The Rise of David Levinsky (1917).   As a novel about immigrant acculturation, Yekl deals with a subject which became
increasingly popular with writers as the vast presence of
South and East European immigrants made itself felt in the
last decade of the century.

More significant, though, than the difference in the
precise focus of the two short novels is the realization that
at the height of the popularity of the romantic tenement tale
they brazenly defied the conventional attitudes which characterized these tales.   In these two novels poverty is not ennobling,
women not inviolable, men not always hard-working, stoical
and uncomplaining.   Poverty does affect character and not for
the best.   Moreover, in these works there is no middle-class
narrator between us and the slums, no kindly guide leading
us through the exotic netherworld of the city, interpreting for
us, moralizing, justifying.   Instead of the romantic slum
tale's predictably and superficially ironic revelations of the
nobility of the downtrodden, these two books achieve an irony
which is both more profound and more fundamental in the opposition between their protagonists' deluded, romantic self-
images and the reality demonstrated in their actions.

Later in the nineties Cahan wrote a group of short
stories in which he again dealt with the confusion, ironies,
and contradictions attendant on becoming an American.   Only
after the new century began, however, did other first-generation urban immigrants begin to articulate in imaginative literature the lessons of their acculturation.   Meanwhile, another

group of writers--some of whom were the sons of earlier-
arriving immigrants--were discovering engaging literary possibilities in the immigrant ghettos. Drawing on the conventions of the slum fiction tradition and on familiar ethnic type-
casting, they provided a gallery of sympathetically if shallow-
ly drawn portraits of the newest immigrant as he hovered between two worlds.

IV

OLD WORLD IN THE NEW:
THE LITERARY DISCOVERY OF THE GHETTO

Although large-scale immigration from South and East
Europe began in the early eighties, it was not until the following decade that the presence of the newest arrivals was
reflected in fiction. Seldom does the East European Jewish
or Italian immigrant appear in the fiction of the eighties; the
immigrant is represented almost exclusively in this decade
by the Irish and German (including the German Jew). Only
gradually did the more recent immigrant groups find their
way into imaginative literature, and only after the new century began did they become anything like familiar figures.

William Dean Howells took note of the "new" immigrant in A Hazard of New Fortunes (1890), a novel which
dramatizes, through its narrator Basil March, the author's
own move to New York in the late eighties. March, like
Howells, has come to New York from Boston to take on an
editorial job. Specifically, the novel is concerned with March's
shift in perspective from the city as spectacle--as a fresh,
exciting region for local color--to the city as social force,
as symbol of what he calls the "economic chance world"--
visible evidence of the ruptures in American society brought
on by chaotic, unregulated industrial growth.

March discovers New York by foot and by the new elevated rail lines. In the house-hunting scenes which dominate the
early pages of the novel, the Marches, unfamiliar with New
York's neighborhoods, walk through noisy, squalid tenement
districts, garbage-lined slum streets, and teeming immigrant
ghettos on their way to elegant apartment buildings enticingly
advertised in the newspapers. They discover on their daily
excursions the ragged, unplanned patchwork of the city. "They
came to excel," Howells notes, "in the sad knowledge of the
line at which respectability distinguishes itself from shabbi-
ness," and they "found that there was an east and west line

beyond which they could not go if they wished to keep their self-respect. "[1] They wander onto Washington Square, where March has his shoes shined by a scruffy Italian boy, and Howells satirizes their self-satisfied air and smug reaction to the scene around them. They regard "the picturesque rag- gedness of Southern Europe with the old kindly illusion that it existed for their appreciation and that it found adequate com- pensation for poverty in this" (I, 67). March is fond of rid- ing the elevated trains and studying the faces of the swarms of Italian immigrants on their way to and from work on the construction gangs at the end of the line. He "found the va- riety of people in the car as unfailingly interesting as ever" and he "preferred the East Side to the West Side lines, be- cause they offered more nationalities, conditions and charac- ters to his inspection" (I, 241). His interest in the immi- grant is essentially a literary one, but as he discovers the conditions under which the Italians are compelled to work, his conscience is stirred.

One of March's guides in his discovery of social in- justice is Berthold Lindau, the only immigrant who has a speaking part in the novel. Lindau is not, however, one of the "new" immigrants whom March had been finding on his voyages through the city, but a German who emigrated in the fifties, settled in Ohio, and fought in the Civil War, losing an arm in the struggle against slavery. His radicalism is not imported, but the product of a fierce democratic and egalitarian idealism soured by the gilded age. To the disil- lusioned veteran, Negro servitude in the South had simply given way to white wage slavery in the North. Sympathetical- ly drawn, the character of Lindau may have been inspired in part by Howells' reaction to the injustice suffered by the eight radicals arrested after the Haymarket Square bombing in May 1886. The eight were convicted though no direct evi- dence linking them to the violence was produced at the trial. There is a connection between Lindau's losing his job as translator for the journal Every Other Week because his po- litical views infuriated the journal's reactionary owner and the fate of the Haymarket Eight, as Howells saw their case. Still, Lindau's views, the novel makes clear, are not Howells'. Beyond a generalized sympathy for and condescend- ing approval of Lindau, there is little real empathy or iden- tification with him or his aims. Howells' emotional attach- ments were far stronger when they involved his own class.

Larzar Ziff in his chapter on Howells in The American 1890's quotes a statement about the author by one of his

contemporaries, Robert Underwood Johnson, the associate
editor of Century Magazine. The passage is worth quoting
again:

> One might have expected that the man who pleaded for
> the lives of the Chicago anarchists would have done
> more in fiction to present the claims of the working
> men and the proletariat. The fact of it is, perhaps,
> that his sympathy came from the kindness of his heart
> and from his conclusions in his study, rather than
> from close contact with the laboring classes in their
> everyday life. He was not a slumming novelist. [2]

Howells was neither a "slumming" novelist nor a ghetto novelist. His portraits of urban immigrants, however charitably
drawn, are distanced and shallow, and reflect his own inner
conflicts and ambivalent feelings when it came not only to the
foreign-born but to the unsettling social issues of the day. [3]

In the tenement tale collections of the nineties, the
glimpses we get of the recently-arrived Southeastern Europeans are no less superficial than those in Howells' novel.
Italians and East European Jews appear alongside their German and Irish slum neighbors in the stories of James Sullivan, Jacob Riis, Brander Matthews, and Isaac Kahn Friedman,
but the portraits are hardly distinct. James Sullivan's Tenement Tales of New York features both Irish and Italian immigrants; he treats them much the same, though. "Slob"
Murphey, the penitent street arab, and Luigi Barbieri, the
self-sacrificing fruit peddler, are little more than exemplars
of the familiar unsung heroism of the poor. Barbieri is
killed rescuing a little girl from the path of an oncoming
truck. The story ends with a piece of dialog between two
neighborhood businessmen, one of whom is the rescued girl's
father: "'By Jove! there's another new Italian keeping the
fruit stand.' 'Ya-a-a-s,' drawled Mr. Bookkeeper, 'I wonder
what killed the last one--laziness or bad whiskey.'"[4] Sullivan
provides still another version of the tale--this time with a
Jewish immigrant--in "Threw Herself Away." Legrand
Brighton, brilliant young member of the East Side Chaucer
Literary Society marries a Jewish girl from the ghetto. The
Society condescendingly tolerates him, attributing his reluctance to speak of his wife to a recognition of error. When
he fails to appear for some time and is reported ill, a member visits him and finds him a dissolute drunkard living off
the earnings of an uncomplaining, hard-working wife. She,
the story reveals, has thrown herself away, not he.

While this kind of superficial irony, revealing hidden
depths of nobility and heroism in the immigrant, pervades the
fiction of Sullivan and most of his contemporaries, pejorative
stereotypes also appear. Throughout this fiction the reader
is confronted with the disparity between the attempt to reveal
the inherent virtue of the immigrant poor and the persistence
of traditional and derisive type-casting. Sullivan reveals this
negative side in the story "Cohen's Figure," which projects
the image of the coarse, vulgar Jewish clothing manufacturer
who delights in pawing the body of a beautiful model, a cigar
in his mouth and a "lascivious, brutal, gloating" expression
on his face. The Irish in Alvan Sanborn's two collections of
stories are sentimentally portrayed as loyal, generous, and
capable of rising to heroic heights, but alongside such virtues
he dramatizes their stereotyped vices--chronic intemperance
and explosive tempers. Mrs. Malloy in "Mrs. Malloy's Revenge" (Meg McIntyre's Raffle and Other Stories) brutally attacks a neighbor for suggesting that her daughter is anything
less than innocent, and in the ensuing brawl both husbands
and two policemen are required to separate the pair.

Irish tantrums may have been a source of humor in
some of the tales, but they also provide some of the most un-
pleasant scenes in the fiction. Drunk Irish parents who
scream and strike at each other in front of their cowering
children are familiar figures. The domestic violence in the
early pages of Crane's Maggie found its way into other novels
of the period. The mother and father of Effie Flynn, Cora's
friend in Edgar Fawcett's The Evil That Men Do, flail at each
other while in the next room a daughter lies dying of tubercu-
losis. The parents of Maud Dolan in Edmund Fuller's The
Complaining Millions of Men are another such couple, swing-
ing wildly and ineptly at each other until, exhausted by their
efforts, they fall on the bed in a stupor. The parents of Maggie O'Donell in Brander Matthews' story, "Before the Break
of Day," beat their daughter viciously, and then, like the
mother of Crane's heroine, self-righteously lock her out when
she "goes bad."

The domestic brutality of the Irish, however, could in
no way be compared to the deadly violence of the Italians in
the period's fiction. The Italians appeared only infrequently,
but when they did the specter of the stiletto, imported terrorism, and blood-lust usually hung over the picture. Brander
Matthews reserved his most vicious portrait of immigrant life
for the Italians in his Vignettes of Manhattan. Interestingly,
Matthews made a statistical study in the nineties of the

proportional representation of natives and immigrants in New
York City's institutions for criminals and paupers, and while
he found that the representation of immigrants in penitentia-
ries and poorhouses was considerably higher than their over-
all representation in the city, it was the Irish and not the
Italians who drove the figure up. [5] Still, in his story about
the Irish cited above, his real focus is not on the brutality
of the girl's parents but on the girl's courage in foiling a rob-
bery attempt, while his story about the Italian community offers nothing to balance or mitigate the sordidness of his
portrait.

    The story, "In Search of Local Color," tells of the
knickerbocker novelist Rupert de Ruyter, whose search for
urban local color leads him to "Little Italy." Accompanied
by his friend, the settlement worker John Suydam, he makes
the descent onto Mulberry Bend where he finds the Italians
true to type. The men are large, swarthy, tough, and quiet.
They sit and drink beer from old cans or play cards in tiny,
hot tenement rooms. Some wear knives in their belts. Some
are at work in front of sewing machines, their wives and
children working at their sides. Infants sleep amid the whir
of the machines:

> Rupert de Ruyter felt as though he were receiving an
> impression of life itself. It was as if he had caught
> a glimpse of the mighty movement of existence, inces-
> sant and inevitable.... The spectacle before him was
> not beautiful; it was not even picturesque; but never
> for a moment, even, did it strike him as pathetic. In-
> teresting it was, of a certainty--unfailingly interest-
> ing. [6]

In one dark tenement room a large, silent Italian, a layer of
mosaic tile from Naples, with "an eye like a glass stiletto,"
stands cooking macaroni over an oil lamp. Just as the pair
leave the Bend, the police arrive to arrest the Italian for
having just stabbed his wife to death.

    The image of the stiletto pervaded other portraits of
the Italian. "The Return," one of the stories in Isaac Kahn
Friedman's The Lucky Number, tells of a young Italian who
returns home to his mother's lodging house in Chicago's Little
Italy, after having been away for thirteen years. When the
mother does not recognize him, he decides to say nothing and
surprise her in the morning. Catching a glimpse of his bank-
roll, though, she enters his room during the night and at-

tempts to rob him. He awakens, and in the struggle she
kills him, only afterward discovering his identity.

Friedman's collection is an exhibition of immigrant
stereotypes. "Chauvinism at Devereaux's" is a humorous
story about a clever detective who takes advantage of French
jingoism to nab his man. In "Aaron Pivansky's Picture"
Friedman explores the familiar Jewish father-son conflict,
but instead of giving us the spiritual old-world father rejected
by his emancipated new-world son--the tragic conflict which
Lincoln Steffens and Hutchins Hapgood were describing--he re-
verts to the age-old Shylock stereotype for the father. The
son is the idealist, a self-taught painter who works late into
the night in his father's pawnshop painting a picture of sol-
diers observing Yom Kippur on a battlefield while shells ex-
plode in the background. When the miserly father recognizes
the commercial value of the picture, he sells it for twenty
dollars.

After the turn of the century literary interest in the
East European Jews increased. As the result of emigration
from East Europe the population of Jews in America quad-
rupled in the last two decades of the nineteenth century, and
in the first decade and a half of the new century Jews came
in even greater numbers. Some 500,000 Jews emigrated
from the Pale of East Europe between 1880 and 1900; another
one and a half million arrived in the 1900-1915 period. One-
third of East Europe's Jews had left their homeland. In New
York City alone, there were almost a million and a half Jews,
representing 28 per cent of the city's population, in 1915. [7]
But it was not only the size of what novelist Harold Frederic
called "the New Exodus" which made the Jewish ghettos so
attractive to writers. There was also the literary infatuation
with the Lower East Side shared by Lincoln Steffens, Hutchins
and Norman Hapgood. All three were fascinated by the rich
cultural life of New York's Jews and were communicating
their fascination to native readers. Steffens' Commercial Ad-
vertiser--with the Hapgoods and Abraham Cahan on the staff--
featured articles and stories about the Lower East Side, and
Hutchins Hapgood's celebration of the region, The Spirit of
the Ghetto, appeared in 1902. There was also the example
of Cahan, who in addition to writing sketches and feature
stories for the Advertiser, was contributing stories to Cosmopolitan, Everybody's, Century, and Scribner's. Still another
major reason for the profusion of tales and novels about Jewish immigrant life was the fact that many of the writers were
themselves Jews--not recent arrivals but the children and

grandchildren of German Jewish immigrants. Such writers
came to the ghetto with considerable sympathy but also with
some images and notions shaped by their American upbring-
ing.

If, as Leslie Fiedler has said, the task for the American-Jewish writer is to create Jewish character out of experience and against the grain of the popular image of the
Jew in the American imagination,[8] then these early explorers
of Jewish life in America were not prepared for the task.
The experience they wrote about was not their own, and they
relied, far too much, on popular conceptions and conventions.
The treatment of the ghetto follows, with some refreshing exceptions, well-worn paths. The romantic and sentimental
conventions inherited from the tenement tales of the eighties
and nineties dominate the portrayal, although in the best of
the tales, the beginnings of a distinctive American-Jewish
literary tradition emerge. Three separate but overlapping
literary interests are discernible: (1) a romantic fascination
with the bizarre, extraordinary or exotic qualities of ghetto
life; (2) an almost opposite concern with the hardships and
sacrifices of everyday life and the struggle to retain traditional ways in the face of unsettling and dislocating conditions;
and (3) an attempt to portray the humor inherent in the Jew's
marginal position in the New World. Some of the roots of
broad, farcical Jewish-American comedy can be found in this
fiction.

The inclination among writers to focus on the bizarre
and extraordinary aspects of ghetto life is evident in a number of works. Actor-playwright (of Yiddish theatre fame)
David Warfield, for instance, wrote a collection of stories in
conjunction with settlement worker Margherita Hamm, Ghetto
Silhouettes (1902), which parades an assortment of Jewish
gamblers, swindlers, con-men, and drunkards. In one story
a robber is convicted on the testimony of his wife, who re-
fuses to support his alibi--as she had in the past--when she
learns he has stolen the money to run off with another woman.
In another, a lawyer who swindled an East Side merchant is
exposed by the merchant's shrewd daughter, who opens a
cigar-stand in the lawyer's office building and patiently gathers
evidence against him. In still another, three East Side merchants, jealous of the enormous business done by Jobbelovsky's
ghetto bank, borrow huge sums of money, propagate a rumor
of the banker's overextensions in order to create a run, and
then proceed to purchase at great discounts the passbooks of
panicked East Siders. A few stories center on noble, heroic

Jews. In one a man rescues his ex-lover and her two children from a tenement fire started by the woman's dissolute husband. The husband--as expected--perishes in the fire, and the pair are free to wed. The tenement fire here, as in the romantic slum stories described in the last chapter, is the vehicle for revealing the heroism of the poor.

Perhaps the oddest fictional portrait of the East European Jew was A. H. Frankel's 1898 novel, In Gold We Trust, an eclectic and loosely constructed work which is something of a Dickensian novel of the innocent poor exploited by the sagacious rich, something of an allegory of the many faces of greed, and something of a vegetarian tract. The characters, all immigrants in the Jewish quarter of New York, form a gallery of grotesques, men enslaved to their greed, whose "stupid desire for excess" leads them into the most hideous crimes against their immigrant neighbors and their own families. The melodramatic plot consists of a number of episodes loosely strung together calculated to demonstrate the pervasiveness of man's cupidity, not simply to perpetuate the stereotype of Jewish greed. The army of the greedy are endowed with connotatively suggestive names: Wolf Zamzumewsky, wholesale clothing dealer who poses as a wealthy merchant in order to wed rich Jewesses, two of whom he drives to early graves; Micha Kalbi, the father of one of Wolf's victims, who lives to mourn the greed which led him to sacrifice his daughter; Zimri Lachmandritzky, pawnshop owner and banker, who flees to Europe with his clients' money; Balaam Amalik, promoter of land schemes, who swindles thousands of East Siders in a bunko land investment; Schmandritzki, the marriage-broker, or schachden, whose greed gets the better of his conscience as he procures wealthy girls for men he knows to be fortune hunters.

But if the immigrant community is thus infected with greed, the cause is not in the innate character of the Jew, and the cure is not the restriction of immigration. Frankel enters the immigration debate, maintaining that the immigrant simply follows the inclinations he finds here; he learns to ape the greed around him in the city. One of his targets in the book, in fact, is the immigration restriction movement, which was gathering momentum in the nineties. More than once he points out through his protagonist-spokesman Nathanael Disraeli the self-interest which lies behind the charges made by organized labor and by "the senator from New England" (i. e., Henry Cabot Lodge) that immigration lowers the working standards of native Americans. Immigrants, he maintains, have

supplied much of the "brawn and brain" which have built
America, and if the immigrant has become corrupted, it is
because the life around him is so.

The solution Frankel proposes is the Thoreauvian one
of simplification, of reducing needs.   The author of a vegetarian tract, "Thou Shalt Not Kill," he has his protagonist
Disraeli deliver long sermons on the evils of eating meat and
on the efficacy of establishing a rural, agricultural colony of
immigrants, a project realized at the book's end by Disraeli's
son Amiel.   The unnatural craving for meat--for the flesh of
fellow animals--is, to Frankel, a form of cannibalism and of
a kind with the greedy exploitation of man by his fellow.   Our
craving for luxury leads us to victimize animals and men
alike.   In the melodramatic unraveling of this incredibly dis-
connected and complicated plot, the exploiters one by one die
ignoble deaths and the virtuous succeed--if not in the older
then in the younger generation.   A deplorable novel, In Gold
We Trust nevertheless deserves consideration as a fascinating example of how far the tenement tale and the ghetto tale
strayed toward the bizarre.

Nathan Kussy's The Abyss, published almost two decades later, in 1916, is another bizarre portrait of the Jew in
America.   Sammy Gordon--a literary descendent of Dickens'
Oliver Twist--is a pious Jewish ghetto boy who after the death
of his mother runs away and is taken up by a band of thieves and
forced to beg on New York's Mulberry Bend in the 1880s.   Unlike Dickens' young hero, though, Sammy is never rescued by
a wealthy benefactor.   He is brutally treated by his captors--
even maimed so he can better play on the sympathies of people as he begs.   The "abyss" is the New York underworld of
the eighties and Kussy provides detailed pictures of the beer
dives, filthy hovels, and seven-cent flop houses which Riis
had complained about.   Although Sammy, who tells his own
story, keeps mentioning his "moral degeneration," he remains
through all his adventures the young innocent so familiar in
the slum fiction of the nineties.   Surrounded by crime, he
never succumbs to it.   Yet he is branded a criminal and this
keeps him from rising from the gutter.   Sammy's worst
crimes are begging and vagrancy, for which he serves a jail
term.   This gives Kussy a chance to attack a corrupt and
sadistic penal system.   Whatever reform impulse motivated
Kussy to write the novel in 1916, however, the long and loosely constructed narrative provides today only another example
of the sensational and outlandish treatment of the Jew in some
of the period's fiction.

At almost the opposite extreme from Frankel's and
Kussy's episodic novels are the tightly-knit tenement and
sweatshop stories of Rudolph Block.   Block, a New York reporter and editor associated with Hearst publications until
1940, wrote the thirty stories collected in Children of Men
(1903) under the name "Bruno Lessing."   Like Frankel's, his
characters are the immigrants of New York's Lower East
Side, but they are the sweatshop workers and sweaters--Jew-
ish clothing makers and Hungarian cigar makers--not the grotesque speculators and con-men of the ghetto.   Some of the
stories are as sentimental as Frankel's novel, but the sentiment derives not so much from emotional overindulgence as
from the attempt--so pervasive in the ghetto tale--to portray
the inherent goodness and nobility of the poor immigrant.
One of the stories, "A Rift in the Cloud," is preceded by a
Talmudic quotation which might apply equally to all of Block's
stories and to the larger number of tales considered in this
and the previous chapter:

> Though the sky be gray and dreary, yet will the
> faintest rift reveal a vision of the dazzling brightness
> that lies beyond.

> So does a word, a look, a single act of a human
> being often reveal the glorious beauty of a soul. [9]

The story which follows concerns a Hungarian cigar
maker, a lonely, solitary, expressionless man, "as uninterest-
ing a man as you could find," who spends his evenings drinking and weeping over gypsy music at Natzi's Cafe.   One evening, disappointed by the music he hears, he grabs the violin
away from a gypsy entertainer and plays a version of the
"Rakoczy March" which moves the Hungarian audience to tears,
after which he resumes his solitary drinking.   This is the unexpected "single act of a human being" which reveals to the
author "the beauty of a soul."

Such an act, demonstrating the immigrant poor's re-
sponsiveness to beauty, is central to a number of the pieces
in the collection, most notably the opening story, "The End
of the Task."   Braun and his fiancée Lizschen, who is dying
of consumption, work in a sweatshop where thirty sewing machines "whirred like a thousand devils."   One Sunday they
wander the city and discover in an uptown gallery a Corot
landscape valued at $3000.   The picture transfixes the woman;
in it she sees the sylvan past of her Russian girlhood.   When
that evening she is seized with violent coughing, Braun steals
the painting so that she may get some comfort from it.   She

dies gazing at it, and Braun the next day is arrested attempt-
ing to return the picture. "It had been a brief communion
with nature, but it had thrilled the hidden chords of her nature, chords of whose existence she had never dreamed before.... For that brief moment of happiness Lizschen was
to submit to a swift, terrible punishment" (pp. 15-16). The
"beauty of a soul" belongs not only to Lizschen but is mani-
fest also in Braun's unselfish, sacrificial act of love for the
dying woman. Another story concerns a sweatshop worker,
a hunchback, whose love for a woman in the shop leads him
to risk his life rescuing her and her lover, the boss, when a
fire engulfs the shop. Sometimes the act of sacrifice and
renunciation takes on more of the pathetic than the heroic, as
in the story of a rabbi's daughter who is in love with a gentile youth and who, unable to reconcile the conflicting claims
of her faith and her heart, ends her life in the East River.
In these somber and maudlin stories Block perpetuates the
conventions of nineteenth-century slum fiction. [10]

Sacrifice, renunciation, and the acquiescence to fate
are the recurrent themes in another collection of stories about
New York's Lower East Side immigrants, Herman Bernstein's
In the Gates of Israel (1902). Refreshingly, the familiar ghetto stereotypes are absent from these tales. There are no
cruel landlords or sweaters, idealistic young labor organizers,
or consumptive sewing machine operators. The situations,
moreover--with the exception of one story about a youth who
rescues the rival for his love from a burning tenement--are
less hackneyed. Few of the stories are concerned directly
with the problems of poverty, although the characters by and
large are poor ghetto Jews who discover their fate in obedience, duty, and acceptance of their cultural heritage. "Soreh
Rivke's Vigil," the best story in the collection, tells with
humor and affection of the desperate struggle of a cantor's
wife to stay awake all night in order to awaken her husband
and his choir in time for the morning holiday prayers. She
succeeds but then drops off to sleep and for the first time in
her life misses the prayers. "Have I, then, turned heathen
in America?" she moans at the story's end. [11]

In the following story (a sequel), "The Messenger of the
Community," the old cantor, deprived of his son, his position
in the synagogue, and his Landsmanschaft membership, dies
quietly and in dignity after reciting the Passover prayer from
his death bed. "The Awakening" deals with a Jew's discovery
of his birthright after thirty years of marriage to a Catholic
woman. On her deathbed she pleads with him to become a

Catholic, but instead of the dying woman's voice he hears the
deathbed voice of his father many years earlier pleading with
him to affirm his Jewishness always.   She dies without his
promise.   His Jewish faith has been awakened ironically by
the plea of his Catholic wife to renounce his birthright.

The conflict between parents and children--between
what Steffens called "parents of the middle ages ... and the
children of the street today"--was perhaps the central and
most persistent theme in this embryonic American-Jewish fiction.   The estrangement of the older and younger generation
could serve the writer as a metaphor for the tragic breakdown of traditional Jewish life in the face of New World temptations, or it could be used as a source of humor.   Both possibilities exist in Cahan's Yekl and in his story, "The Imported Bridegroom" (1898), and it is an indication of Cahan's
fertile imagination that he could see more than one possibility
in his material.   Herman Bernstein, two years after the publication of In the Gates of Israel, wrote an extremely melodramatic and maudlin novel, Contrite Hearts (1904), on the
theme of the estrangement and reconciliation of parents and
children.   Rudolph Block discovered the humorous possibilities
of the subject in his story "The Americanization of Shadrack
Cohen," which reveals how a pious old Jew, rejected by his
Americanized sons, regains their admiration when he demonstrates by taking charge of their affairs that piety is not incompatible with shrewd American business sense.

Henry Berman also dealt with the theme of alienation
and reconciliation in his 1906 novel Worshippers, one of the
few works in the period whose subject was the Americanized
middle-class Russian-Jewish community.   The heroine of this
novel is a Philadelphia woman, the wife of a successful and
assimilated druggist.   Bored with her bourgeois life and harboring the dream of becoming an actress, she runs off with
a famous Yiddish Socialist poet.   Her lover, it turns out, is
not the romantic, adventurous spirit she expected, but a prig-
gish, self-centered and stodgy creature, and so she returns
home to the husband who at least appreciated her.

James Oppenheim's Dr. Rast (1909) is a collection of
sentimental stories which, like those of Rudolph Block and
Herman Bernstein, focus on the "act of faith," on the Jewish
heart asserting itself in time of crisis and amid squalor.   The
volume brings together a number of Oppenheim's popular magazine stories of the idealistic East Side doctor who treats the
bodies and souls of his immigrant patients.   Born in

Minnesota, of German-Jewish parents, Oppenheim came to
know the ghetto as a student at Columbia and afterward as a
teacher and settlement worker on the Lower East Side. Birth,
death, and the diseases of the East Side--consumption, typhoid, and pneumonia--are the subject matter of the stories
and the events which give Morris Rast's life its meaning.
Rast battles daily with death and disease in the ghetto just as
he battles with the despair in his own heart and in the patients who depend on him. In their dependence on him he
discovers his own reason for existence: "To bring God out--
to take God down into the dust of things--to get God into the
day's work--the commonplace! He's here--He's in each one.
We must turn him on! The race is going out to glory--look
--look--."[12]

Beneath the filth and squalor of the ghetto Rast discovers goodness and humanity, and his periodic moods of de-
jection alternate with such passionate expressions of faith.
Like Hapgood, Steffens, Bernstein and Block, Oppenheim
idealizes the old ghetto men and women who cling to their
Old World faith and denounces the children who reject the
ways of their fathers. An East Side daughter in "Groping
Children" is able to attend medical school because her parents and sister work long hours in a sweatshop. She enter-
tains vague dreams of romantic experiments and the glorious
science of the future while her sister dies of consumption.
Ashamed of her parents and blind to her sister's symptoms
as she has been to her parents' sacrifices, she is a foil to
Rast, who as a doctor dedicates himself to "the bruised hearts
and broken souls of the ghetto." A dedication to science, on
the other hand, which is not divorced from the immediate
needs of the ghetto, is the mark of the Oppenheim hero, as
he reveals in the story of a colleague of Rast, who bears a
resemblance to Sinclair Lewis' Max Gottlieb; in order to test
an antitoxin needed in the ghetto, the doctor puts his life on
the line by inoculating himself.

While Bernstein, Block, and Oppenheim were dealing
melodramatically with the Jews of New York's Lower East
Side, Myra Kelly and Montague Glass, both foreign-born, were
discovering the humor inherent in the material. Miss Kelly
was born in Dublin but spent most of her brief life (1875-
1910) on the Lower East Side, where her father had his medical practice and she taught for a few years in a ghetto school.
Glass, who was born in Manchester, England, was a New
York lawyer whose clientele included a number of small Jewish clothing manufacturers. From the immigrant life they

came to know in their work--the ghetto classroom and the
fiercely competitive garment trade--they drew the material
for volumes of popular stories.

In introducing the second of three volumes of collected
magazine stories,[13] Wards of Liberty, Miss Kelly candidly
acknowledged the difficulty of recording the lives of immigrant children from the outside: "The deepest can never be
written out by one of an alien race.   The lives being lived in
those crowded streets are so diverse, so different, in end
and aim, that no mere observer can hope to see more than
an insignificant vista of the whole, seething, swarming mass
of hope, disillusion, growth and decay."[14]   The stories are
indeed limited by the "insignificant vista" they provide into
the complexities of the acculturation process and by the condescending tone of the author, but the best of them have a
cleverness and a wit that come as a relief after some of the
somber, melancholy, and mawkish versions of immigrant life
that so frequently appeared in the fiction.   With Myra Kelly
immigrant ghetto fiction moves a step away from the conventions and formulas of late nineteenth-century slum fiction and
toward a lively involvement with the problems of cultural interaction.

Her recurrent subject is the humor inherent in the disparity between the Old World ways the ghetto children bring
to their first-grade class and the sympathetic, native gentility
of their teacher, Constance Bailey, whose task it is to Americanize them.   The public school on the East Side is the meeting place of Old World and New, and Miss Bailey finds, as
her author had, that her task in Room 18 is not only to teach
skills but to introduce new values and concepts alien to her
charges.   The children are portrayed as being in some ways
wise beyond their years but gently innocent and picturesque in
their tattered clothing and dirty faces.   The author makes
capital of the ignorance, fears, and superstitions of the East
Side.   In the story "Slaughter of the Innocents," for instance,
the school is invaded by angry, hysterical mothers who see
the school's campaign to perform adenoid operations on the
children as a Czarist-inspired plot--a rumor, it turns out,
which had been perpetrated by the East Side doctors.   The
most interesting story in the collection, "A Soul Above But-
tons," concerns the schooling of a nine-year-old "sweater."
Having inherited his father's basement sweatshop, "the Boss"
decides to enroll in school in order to learn how to read and
thus be able to join the union and get finishing work instead
of just buttonholes.   Once in the classroom, the boy introduces

the spirit of labor to his fellows.   He demands wages for his
tasks and better working conditions.   He tries to organize a
strike among the first-graders and, unable to gain support,
flees the school, hurling the epithet "scab" at his classmates.
The maxims of the schoolroom are too far removed from the
realities of the dog-eat-dog life "the Boss" has had to endure
in his nine years.

          Miss Kelly avows that her purpose in writing these
stories is to contribute to the sympathetic understanding of
the cultural differences between Americans and immigrants.
"If I have succeeded even to a degree in making others see
what I have seen," she wrote, "I shall have contributed something to the quickening of intelligent interest in the poor and
unfortunate of an alien race..." (pp. ix-x).   Misunderstand-
ings between teacher and pupils and between parents and their
children who take home--sometimes in distorted versions--
the lessons of the classroom cause the conflict in a good number of the stories.   In "The Touch of Nature," from Little
Citizens (1904), her first collection, Miss Bailey's attempt to
instill the virtue of kindliness leads to young Morris Mogilew-
sky's feeding a stray cat the family's sparse breakfast and
his unharnessing a horse--an act which puts him in the hospital.   Leah Yanowsky in "The Uses of Adversity" (Little
Citizens) speaks only halting English but romantically names
the twin brothers under her charge Algernon and Percival.
Unable to manage the incorrigible twins, she coaxes them to
associate with boys who have chicken pox and measles, knowing that the charity hospitals will take care of them while she
secures a little freedom.   In "Love Among the Blackboards,"
also from Little Citizens, three of Miss Bailey's boys see her
in the company of a young man and fear they will lose their
revered teacher if she marries.   One boy--unaware that his
teacher is Christian--warns her that her suitor "could be a
Krisht."   They attempt to buy the man off with eleven cents
and an offer to substitute the teacher across the hall.

          The literary territory Montague Glass made his own
was not the ghetto but the area just outside its walls.   His
characters are not immigrant children making their first confusing contacts with American culture but the rising breed of
Jewish clothing merchants who live "uptown."   Glass's best-
known stories deal with the business and personal adventures
of the cloak-and-suit partners Abe Potash and Morris Perlmutter, the one conservative and suspicious, the other venture-
some, trusting, and gullible.   Potash and Perlmutter stories
were enormously popular in Saturday Evening Post installments,

and following their initial collection in book form (Potash and Perlmutter, 1909), the stories continued to enjoy a vogue for more than two decades. [15]

The stories are constructed largely of banter between the two partners or between one of the partners and a competitor. To a large extent they depend for their comic effect on colorful quasi-Yiddish linguistic features superimposed on the English. Sol Liptzin in his study The Jew in American Literature described the language of Glass's characters as "a picturesque English behind which a Yiddish substratum peered through."[16] Glass exploits the stereotyped Jewish penchant for hyperbole or exaggeration and such supposedly Yiddish-derived syntactical peculiarities as placing verbs at the end of sentences and misplacing modifiers. All of these are contained in the following passage: "I got my stomach full with Pincus Vessell already, and if Andrew Carnegie would come to me and tell me he wants to go with me as partners together in business in the cloak and suit business, I would say No, so sick and tired of partners I am."[17]

The stories depend also for their effect on extravagant comic plots and ironically contrived situations, all with clear ethical implications. The partners are able to recoup their losses to an unscrupulous competitor or customer through a stroke of fate or luck. A deus ex machina may appear in the form of an unexpected piece of information enabling them to cancel a shipment of goods to a bankrupt customer or to beat a villainous competitor to a large order. Sometimes in their haste to outsmart their competition, they outsmart themselves. In one installment "Mawruss" is in such a hurry to entertain an out-of-town woman buyer before his competitor gets to her, he picks up the wrong woman at the hotel and lavishes a large sum on her before he realizes his mistake.

In the Potash and Perlmutter stories, Montague Glass brought to popular fiction the folklore of the Jewish clothing merchant, the sweatshop worker risen to petty manufacture, dizzy at the height he has attained, haunted by fears of bankruptcy, fiercely competitive, suspicious, and distrustful. Brash and often rude, he is nevertheless drawn with compassion and affection. This is a stereotype of the Jewish clothing merchant which persists to the present time in popular novels and plays. In the early years of the twentieth century Glass put on record in fiction a new phase in the life of the Jewish immigrant--his emergence from the ghetto and entry into the American world of business. Yet while the insecurity of the

newly-risen merchant comes through clearly, the high cost of
becoming an American--the traumas associated with giving up
one set of cultural values for another--is not part of Glass's
story.   It would remain for Abraham Cahan to reveal the
spiritual price of American success for the Jewish immigrant
in his novel about another rising cloak-and-suit merchant,
David Levinsky.   Perhaps the difference is that Cahan sought
to write a serious novel about acculturation, while Glass found
a sure-fire comic formula early in his career and kept it up
for decades.   Perhaps, too, the difference is that Cahan, a
Russian Jew who came penniless to America, knew first-hand
the dilemmas posed by assimilation while Glass, born in England of wealthy parents, never faced such dilemmas.   In any
case it was Glass who was lauded by American audiences
while Cahan's fiction went largely unnoticed until recent years.

     Many of the authors of the tales described in this chap-
ter were immigrants or the children of immigrants, yet they
were not themselves products of the ghetto life they chose to
write about.   Their stories only occasionally got beneath familiar surface impressions.   In a few we are given sensitive
and incisive portraits of first-generation life on the culture
island--some of the stories by Block and Bernstein, for ex-
ample--but for the most part the writers seemed content to
retrace the familiar ground explored by the tenement tale authors of the nineties, focusing on the exotic, comic, squalid,
or heroic potential of the material.   This is not to suggest,
however, that firsthand, daily contact with the ghetto is a
guarantee of or even a requisite to the realistic portrayal of
immigrant life.   Crane was not a product of the Bowery yet
managed to cut through the romantic overlay which gilded the
treatment of the urban poor in fiction.   Conversely, some of
the first-generation ghetto immigrants who chose to write about
their own experiences in novels and autobiographies glossed
over the psychological complexities of acculturation, either because of their own limitations as writers or because their desire to justify the assimilability of the immigrant was stronger than their desire to record the life they actually lived.   In
such works, which are the subject of a later chapter, propaganda was an important motivation.

     While justifying immigrant assimilability was not a major
concern in the fiction described in the present chapter, the portraits taken as a whole are quite sympathetic.   Despite the per-
petuation of ethnic stereotyping--particularly of the Irish and
Italians--the stories generally stress the virtues of the newcomer and should be credited with contributing to America's sympa-

thetic social and literary awakening to its submerged immigrant population. The tales of the Jewish ghetto, moreover, in focusing on the strained relations between parents and children, and the inner conflict between old-world ties and new-world enticements, laid the thematic groundwork for much of the American-Jewish fiction of the twentieth century.

V

SONGS OF THE SWEATSHOP:
THE IMMIGRANT LABOR NOVEL

As late as 1884 it was possible, as John Hay had
shown in his novel The Breadwinners, to write a labor novel
in which the workers bore Anglo-Saxon names, but as the
century drew to a close, the industrial laborer in fiction, as
in life, became more closely identified with the South and
East European immigrant.   The subway construction gangs
Basil March confronts on his rambles in New York in Howells'
A Hazard of New Fortunes (1889) are largely Italian; and in
Ignatius Donnelly's Caesar's Column (1889) the "Brotherhood
of Destruction"--the proletarian mob which destroys the Plutocracy (and all American civilization)--is headed by a man
named Caesar Lomellini.   In the nineties, as the horrendous
working and living conditions of the newest immigrants were
reaching native audiences through the reports of Jacob Riis,
Jane Addams, Lincoln Steffens and dozens of lesser-known in-
vestigators, many young writers eager to expose more of the
shame of the cities made their own investigations, turning
their findings into novels.   Some were drawn to immigrant
labor through their involvement with socialism; others were
drawn to socialism through their involvement with immigrant
labor; while still others rejected socialism altogether and
argued in their fiction the "more American" solution of trade
unionism.

Essentially a product of the progressive movement and
a reflection of its basic aims and assumptions, the immigrant
labor novel of the period 1890 to 1915 ran a parallel course
to the period's muckraking journalism.   Like the journalism,
the fiction was written by middle-class and native-born writers and combined a meticulous concern for documentation and
authenticity with a considerable amount of sensationalism.
Most of the novels were fictionalized treatments of recent cataclysmic labor struggles--notably the Homestead, Pa. , steel
strikes; the Chicago Haymarket riot; the Chicago "Packing-

town" strikes; and the "Great Revolt" of immigrant working
women in New York's garment district. Typically, the novelists made painstaking studies of the events they reported, although they frequently colored their reports with their own
rage and their flair for the bombastic. Upton Sinclair spent
seven weeks living among the immigrant workers in Chicago's
meat-packing industry to document the conditions he reported
in The Jungle. Frank Harris came from England to America
in 1907 for the sole purpose of studying the trial record of
the Chicago Haymarket anarchists, convicted twenty years
earlier. The following year he produced, in what he termed
"an angry burst of fury," his account of the events in The
Bomb. A number of writers, among them Isaac Kahn Friedman, Edward King, Albert Bullard, and Ernest Poole, served
long apprenticeships in the ghetto as settlement house workers, labor organizers, and investigative reporters.

     "Proletarian fiction" of the 1930's is rooted firmly in
the earlier immigrant labor novel. The themes and structural designs which surface in the depression decade fiction
had clear antecedents in the pre-World War I labor novel.
The urban immigrant provided an ideal proletarian hero for
the novelists. Aside from the obvious fact that in terms of
numbers he most broadly represented the worker in urban
America, he could be portrayed convincingly as one who came
to America in search of freedom, who fled the tyranny of the
Old World and brought with him to the new an idealistic notion of what democracy ought to be. The disparity between
expectation and actuality could--and was--played up by the
writers. Exploiting the disenchantment of the immigrant was
a characteristic device in immigrant proletarian fiction.

     Related to this is the recurrent "conversion" pattern--
common to the 30's proletarian novel--in which the protagonist
is converted to the cause of organized labor. Jurgis Rudkis
in Upton Sinclair's The Jungle (1906), Yetta Rayefsky in
Arthur Bullard's Comrade Yetta (1913), and several of the
Hungarian steelworkers in James Oppenheim's stories Pay Envelopes (1911) are prime examples of exploited immigrants
who organize against their oppressors. Native-born heroes
and heroines who are drawn to the immigrant labor movement
appear even more frequently. The protagonists in Isaac Kahn
Friedman's By Bread Alone (1901), James Oppenheim's The
Nine-Tenths (1911), Florence Converse's The Children of
Light (1911), and Ernest Poole's The Harbor (1915) are examples of middle-class Americans who undergo political
awakenings.

The immigrant labor novel, like progressivist literature generally, is seldom radical in outlook. Reform not
revolution is most typically argued. Violence as a solution
to labor inequities is seldom condoned, and only infrequently
is the complete transformation of the system argued. Socialism is often enough advocated but it is a gentle, pacifistic
form to be achieved gradually and piecemeal. Immigrant
anarchists and radicals are portrayed characteristically as
sinister, deranged, and wholly irrational figures, who, like
their enemies, the ruthless capitalists, obstruct real labor
reform. The anarchist, whose radicalism is often seen as
imported, serves as a foil to the true proletarian hero, who
stands for peaceful solutions to labor warfare.

Contrary to the stereotype of the alien radical perpetuated in the most sensational of these novels, the real-life
experience of the urban immigrant tended to foster conserva-
tism and the acceptance of authority. The struggle to organize ghetto workers was a long, hard one. Historically excluded from participation in government (which was simply
the taskmaster) and bewildered by a complex new social order, the immigrant at first shied from the organizers. Another inhibiting factor was the initial hostility of the American
labor movement to the south-eastern European immigrant work
force. This led to the establishment of immigrant unions, but
such organizations failed to recruit much support. The sizable
number of immigrants who planned to return to their homelands
after a few years found it more convenient to tolerate conditions
than participate in costly strikes. The Jews, who had to remain,
tended, nevertheless, to see their sweatshop labor as temporary,
until they could learn English and get better jobs. And so, reluctant to strike, they relied on longer hours at "piece work" to
earn a living wage. [1]

As sweatshop conditions worsened in the late eighties
and early nineties, and as the fiery young unionists and socialists of the ghetto made themselves heard, Jewish participation
in the labor movement intensified. In 1888 the United Hebrew
Trades was established with Abraham Cahan and Morris Hillquit as prime movers. The organization was highly efficient
in creating unions among the many sweated trades on the Lower East Side and drawing these unions together in a federation.
Employing "walking delegates," the UHT managed to organize
one after another of the garment trades. The largest Jewish
immigrant employer then was the ladies' cloakmaking industry.
When the non-unionized cloakmakers went out on strike in
1890, the UHT sent a young organizer, Joseph Barondess, to

lead the strike and unionize the workers. Through Barondess'
efforts, the cloakmakers won their strike and with nearly
3000 members became the largest of the unions affiliated with
UHT. [2] Barondess was one of the most interesting, enigmatic,
and controversial of the labor leaders the Jews were to produce.   The New York press slandered him by falsely identifying him as an exiled Russian aristocrat, an anarchist and
revolutionist.   Later he was imprisoned for twenty-one months
(before a pardon was granted) on a technical charge of extortion when he collected for his union "damages" from a manufacturer following a strike settlement. [3] Barondess, the "king
of the cloakmakers," arrived in New York in 1888 and held a
number of jobs in and out of the sweatshop before gaining
prominence as a labor leader.   The respect he was ultimately to receive in America is suggested by his being appointed
to the New York Board of Education in 1910.

Despite the increased activity of Jewish labor in the
nineties, it was still difficult to achieve solidarity among workers.   For one thing, those workers who saw their positions
as stopgaps remained apathetic.   For another, ideological dis-
sension hampered the growth of unions.   The United Hebrew
Trades, for instance, split between radical members who regarded it as a political organization, a weapon in the warfare
with capitalism, and the more moderate and practical members like Cahan and Hillquit, who regarded it simply as a federation of unions.   Only after the turn of the century, when
the needle trades came into the sphere of Samuel Gompers'
American Federation of Labor, historically antipathetic to the
immigrant, did immigrant labor solidarity emerge.   Only, in
other words, when the immigrant labor movement entered the
mainstream of the American labor movement did it succeed.
Tied to the AFL, the UHT grew from 5000 members in 1909
to 250,000 in 111 affiliated unions in 1914. [4]

The earlier antipathy of American labor to the immigrant was grounded in the belief that the unskilled newcomer
by working for less pay was replacing the native worker and
preventing the rise of wages and the improvement of conditions.   Moreover, he was used frequently as a strike-breaker.
Terence Powderly, leader of the secretive and ritualistic
Knights of Labor in the eighties, argued that the immigrant
was the tool of unscrupulous business interests, herded here
en masse to force wages down by competition.   The immigrants, he wrote, had been "used as the club with which employers struck down the independence of the American laborer....   [Their] influence on the labor market is so degrading

and baneful, that they are everyday reducing the conditions of
the American workman to a parallel with their own."[5] Powderly, the son of Irish immigrants, in opposing the foreign
workman and urging immigration restriction, found himself in
the rather peculiar position of agreeing on a major political
issue--though for different reasons--with patrician exclusionists like Henry Cabot Lodge, Francis Walker, and Henry
Adams.

     Some of the bitterest immigrant labor struggles took
place in New York's sweated garment industry, which employed several hundred thousand workers. By far the most
dramatic, and for novelists the most popular, strike was the
1909 general strike, the so-called "Uprising of the Twenty
Thousand," which was but one battle in the protracted "Great
Revolt" of sweatshop workers. The walkout attracted national
attention. College girls and society women marched with the
strikers, and noted attorneys defended the arrested pickets.
The greatest strike in New York's history took place as
60,000 garment workers walked out at an appointed hour,
shutting down the cloak industry. In the lengthy negotiations
which followed, labor was represented by Louis Brandeis and
the prominent socialist attorney Meyer London.[6]

     Domestic garment work, the largest and most charac-
teristic occupation of the city's immigrants, was the subject
of the earliest of the urban immigrant labor novels, Edward
Smith King's Joseph Zalmonah (1893), a rather crude melodrama patterned after the stormy career of Joseph Barondess.[7] The plot of Joseph Zalmonah pivots on the struggles
of the young, idealistic labor leader to organize Jewish sweatshop workers of New York's Lower East Side. In a flashback
we are told that Zalmonah had been forced to flee Russia,
leaving behind his wife and infant child, when he had been observed reading Marx. After a few years as a victim of New
York's "sweaters' dens," he had turned his efforts to the organization of ghetto labor, founding the United Hebrew Trades.
Zalmonah has two adversaries in the novel. At the one extreme are the "bosses" and the "system," represented by the
clothing manufacturer Freier and his lieutenants, the "sweaters"--themselves victims of the system. At the other extreme are the "socialists," headed by the fanatical, insane
Rudolph Baumeister. In his attempt to lionize his Barondess-
figure and to propagandize the cause of labor unionism, King
thoroughly villifies capitalists and socialists alike. Baumeister
is called a socialist in the novel, yet he is in reality the
stereotyped wild-eyed foreign anarchist bent on destroying

American society. He is portrayed as the deranged product
of years of persecution and poverty. Whatever collective
ideology he may once have embraced has since been perverted
into an obsession to destroy his tormentors. His madness is
both fact and metaphor in the novel. King attempts allegori-
cally to identify Baumeister and his co-worker, the seduc-
tress Bathsheba, with the army of Satan. Baumeister tries
to win the frustrated Joseph (who is identified with Christ) to
his cause with the promise of power, while Bathsheba tempts
the hero sexually. To underscore the satanic role Baumeister plays, King has him appear before Joseph writhing on the
floor like a serpent in an epileptic seizure. His madness is
revealed in his every speech and act. In one scene he sets
fire to a tenement house in an attempt to destroy his wife
and child who have followed him from Europe and stand in
the way of his revolutionary aims.

     King wholly distorts socialism by failing, in the novel,
to distinguish it from violent and destructive anarchism. His
socialists are products of personal defeat who turn their frustrations outward into hatred for all society. Bathsheba, in
league with Baumeister, is similarly a convert to "socialism"
through personal frustration. She had run away from a genteel, middle-class home in Russia with a violinist who in
America proved a dull husband and a mediocre, usually out-
of-work theater musician. "With the loss of her illusions,"
King tells us, "had come an immense and overpowering disgust, which gradually transformed itself into a fixed hatred
for society and all its institutions." Revolution became to
her "a charming relief from the deadly monotony of life in a
dreary street in an obscure quarter...."[8] Bathsheba is the
dark, seductive, "Oriental" Jewess so familiar as a type in
western literature. To resist her sexual offerings is one of
Joseph's trials, as it was the trial of saints to resist volup-
tuous dreams. Although she plays only a minor role in the
novel's ideological struggle, she emerges as the work's most
interesting character, the only one to show any development
or change. Early in the novel she appears to Joseph as Baumeister's tool to win him over to anarchism, but as the novel
progresses she becomes a thoroughly human and pitiful woman tortured by her passion for the labor leader.

     At the opposite pole from the socialists are the capi-
talists--the large manufacturers and the sweaters. The latter
are petty tyrants, malicious and cruel taskmasters. Themselves poor Russian Jews and victims of the system, they
dwell most often in the foul sties where the clothing is pieced.

Forced to underbid their competitors to get the cut goods,
they survive only by "sweating" the more recent immigrants
who work for them. They cut the wages of the workers without warning, knowing that should the workers walk out there
are plenty of unemployed "greenhorns" waiting to replace
them. In collusion with the large manufacturers they engage
in periodic lockouts to break the will of discontented laborers
and in slow seasons close the shops and disappear without
paying the workers, reappearing later under different names
in different locations. Simon, King's sweater-figure, is not
unlike the insane Baumeister in the sub-human state to which
he has been reduced by the system. He bears a family resemblance to Dickens' Fagin as well:

> What tremendous activity pervaded the little company
> of twenty-five men, women, and children! Gazing on
> it with his merciless eyes, the sweater felt a pride
> in the talent for organization which it manifested. In
> this Inferno he made his fortune; every click of the
> machine meant profit for him. ... To see men and
> women worn to exhaustion by grinding toil was so
> common a sight for the sweater, that he no longer ap-
> preciated the horrible indignity, the immense pathos
> of it [pp. 154-155].

Simon is a cog in the well-oiled machine of the clothing firm of Freier and Monach. He is one of thousands of
small subcontractors on the East Side who depend upon the
large manufacturers and conspire with them in the systematic
harassment and enslavement of the work force. Freier is
portrayed as the familiar opulent, flashy, uptown German
Jew. An immigrant of an earlier day, he has risen to wealth
and can maintain his position only by the economic strangulation of those below him. King describes him as "a huge,
brawny man, elaborately dressed, with a rolling shirt collar
and a profusion of jewelry, which gave him the air of a trav-
eling theatrical manager." It is Freier who instigates the
lock-outs in the shops and who shrewdly engineers Joseph's
arrest and imprisonment on a spurious extortion charge.
When the labor leader demands and receives a one-hundred-
dollar damage fee to be paid to the union as part of a settlement ending a strike and lock-out, Freier writes a check pay-
able to Joseph, making him appear culpable of extortion.

The betrayers of the ghetto Jews are thus themselves
Jews--Baumeister, the "socialist"; Simon, the sweater; Freier, the manufacturer. Each preys upon those below him.

Behind all the evil is the sweating system itself, which has destroyed the souls of the bosses as it has crushed the bodies of the workers. The system is King's real target in the novel:

> The sweater's Hell! Would it never be swept out of existence? Was there any excuse for its toleration in this new land of plenty, where fortunes are made in a single year, and where labor could think and say whatever it pleased? Was there not a sweater's Hell in more than one of the great American cities? What had these poor exiles done that they should be compelled to starve and freeze in winter, and starve and roast in summer, and to become the prey of typhus when their puny frames were exhausted? [p. 347].

Novelists were indeed discovering the "sweater's Hell" in other cities and in other industries. Upton Sinclair discovered one in Chicago's "Packingtown" in 1904 and the following year produced a novel which explored more relentlessly the inferno of immigrant labor than had any novel before or since. In his autobiography (American Outpost), Sinclair revealed how he became involved with the immigrant workers of the city's meat-packing industry and how he came to write The Jungle. Fred D. Warren, editor of the socialist journal Appeal to Reason, impressed with the young novelist's Manassas, urged him to do for wage slavery what he had done for chattel slavery and advanced him five hundred dollars for serial rights to the new novel. Sinclair picked the stockyards because his sympathy had been attracted to the 20,000 yard workers who had just lost a strike against the "Beef Trust." He had already written a manifesto to the workers ("You have lost the strike, and now what are you going to do about it?") which appeared in Appeal to Reason on September 17, 1905, and he was already in touch with the socialists among the workers:

> So, in October, 1904, I set out for Chicago, and for seven weeks lived among the wage slaves of the Beef Trust, as we called it in those days....
>
> I sat at night in the homes of the workers, foreign-born and native, and they told me their stories, one after one, and I made notes of everything. In the daytime, I would wander about the yards, and my friends would risk their jobs to show me what I wanted to see. I was not much better dressed than the workers, and found that by the simple device of carrying a dinner-

> pail I could go anywhere. When I wanted to make
> careful observations, I would pass again and again
> through the same room. [9]

The novel was serialized in Appeal in 1905 and in February
1906 Doubleday, Page, and Co. brought it out in book form
after the cautious publishing house, which a few years earlier
had virtually suppressed Sister Carrie, sent an investigator
to the yards to verify Sinclair's findings.

   The Jungle is a muckraking exposé both of the exploitation of the industrial workman and the foul conditions of animal slaughter and meat preparation.   It is also a socialist
conversion and propaganda novel; its final chapters are weight-
ed down with a rather heavy load of collectivist message.   It
is easy to forget, however, that The Jungle is also a novel
of the urban immigrant experience in America.   Jurgis Rudkis and his family are recent immigrants, and the fact of
their immigration has a great deal to do with their exploitation as laborers.   They have been lured to America by the
enticements of the packers' agents, and in their bewilderment
and unfamiliarity with America and their ignorance of English,
they easily became the packers' victims.   Socialism brought
Sinclair to the yards.   He was not at first interested in the
immigrant as such.   Once in the yards, though, he realized
that if his story were to record the life of the yards faith-
fully, it must also be the story of the exploited immigrants
who lived and worked there.   The germ for the novel--he
was to recall in his autobiography--came from a Lithuanian
wedding he had witnessed.   I quote the following passage from
his autobiography because it stresses, if we take Sinclair at
his word, the centrality of the immigrant to the initial conception of the novel:

> At the end of a month or more, I had my data, and
> knew the story I meant to tell, but I had no charac-
> ters.   Wandering about in 'Back of the Yards' one
> Sunday afternoon I saw a wedding party going into the
> rear room of a saloon.   There were several carriages
> full of people, and I stopped to watch, and as they
> seemed hospitable, I slipped into the room, and stood
> against the wall.   There the opening chapter of 'The
> Jungle' began to take form.   There were many char-
> acters--the bride, the groom, the old mother and
> father, the boisterous cousin, the three musicians,
> everybody [pp. 155-156].

Sinclair had little of the local colorist's interest in
the "exotic" customs of the immigrants, but the fact that the
Lithuanians he had been observing in the yards brought with
them to America customs and ideals from the past and
dreams for the future which contrasted sharply with the new
life they found increased for him the pathos of their condition
and reinforced his theme. Throughout the novel Sinclair
stresses the Rudkis family's attempt to preserve the stable,
peasant values of the past in the face of industrial dislocation
and dehumanization. The contrast between the rural, peasant
past of the Rudkis family and the urban, industrial present is
central to the novel's meaning. It is the values and customs
of the past which give their lives significance. The wedding
scene which opens the novel, patterned after the Lithuanian
wedding Sinclair had observed in the yards, reveals this
theme. For the Rudkis family, just arrived from the Old
World and tied to the foul yards, the wedding is too expensive, but it is a link with the past which they must preserve
at all costs.

New World experience intensifies Old World ties. The
immigrants of Packingtown clung to the past not only because
it was all they had, but because they discovered in the symbolism of the Old World new meanings relevant to their present
situation. The performance of the veselija at the wedding is
one such ritual from the past which acquires added significance in the present:

> Bit by bit these poor people have given up everything
> else; but to this they clung with all the power of their
> souls--they cannot give up the veselija! To do that
> would mean not merely to be defeated, but to acknowl-
> edge defeat--and the difference between the two things
> is what keeps the world going. The veselija has come
> down to them from a far-off time, and the meaning of
> it was that one might dwell within the cave ana gaze
> upon shadows, provided only that once in his lifetime
> he could break his chains, and feel his wings, and be-
> hold the sun; provided that once in his lifetime he
> might testify to the fact that life, with all its terrors,
> is no such great thing after all, but merely a bubble
> on the surface of a river, a thing that one may toss
> about and play with as a juggler tosses his golden
> balls, a thing that one may quaff, like a goblet of red
> wine. Then having known himself for the master of
> things, a man could go back to his toil and live upon
> the memory of his days. [10]

The Jungle follows the degradation of its protagonist
as a wage slave and then his awakening and conversion to
socialism. Jurgis Rudkis has come to America from Lithuania in a party of twelve who share his dream of a better
life. America becomes the broken promise. Wages are higher but so are costs, and one cannot be sure of steady employment. Jurgis has to pay graft to keep his job and is
mercilessly "speeded" and, as a result, injured. His wife
is forced into prostitution. His son is drowned in a stagnant
pool in front of the wretched shack he has been swindled into
buying. Upon the single family are piled all the atrocities
of the yards Sinclair had witnessed or heard about. The
family become not typical but composite figures, representing
the degradation of all the workers. Jurgis Rudkis is the immigrant destroyed by the meat-packers and their henchmen,
the police and the political bosses. Early in the novel, when
he first sees the slaughter of hogs at Durham's, he exclaims:
"Dieve--but I'm glad I'm not a hog"; it is the burden of the
rest of the novel to demonstrate that he is just that.

The history of Packingtown, like the history of the
"new" house, is one of successive waves of immigration. As
each new immigrant group arrived, it provided cheaper labor
for Durham's and replaced the previous group in the yards,
just as each new coat of paint on a house erased the evidence
of its former inhabitants. Packingtown was settled first by
Germans, skilled butchers brought over by the owners. Then
came the Irish who were followed in turn by the Bohemians,
Poles, Lithuanians, and Slovaks, as the packers' agents
reached deeper into Europe for replacements: "The people
had come in hordes, and old Durham had squeezed them tighter and tighter, speeding them up and grinding them to pieces
and sending for replacements" [pp. 78-79].

The Irish, who were the exploited workers of Packingtown a generation or so earlier, now control the yards, and
in this sense the conflict in the novel is between "old" immigrant and "new." Mike Scully, "who even bossed the mayor,"
is the ward heeler who guarantees election results in the district and instantly naturalizes foreign workers in order to buy
their votes. Pat "Growler" Callaghan is the judge "who held
two offices at once before he was old enough to vote" and
who with his "contempt for foreigners" imprisons Jurgis for
striking Connor, the Irish boss who had raped Jurgis' wife.
These are the men who rose to power, Sinclair tells us,
"when the whole city of Chicago had been up at auction."
They control the garbage dumps, the workers' shacks erected

over them, the houses of prostitution, the saloons, and all
the jobs of Packingtown.

If it was the immigrant of an earlier age who provided
the forces of corruption in Packingtown, it was from the most
recent immigrant, the victim of the corruption, that regeneration in the form of socialism was getting its strength and
inspiration.   Jurgis gets his lessons in socialism from the
Polish Jew Ostrinski, who brought his ideology with him from
the Old World.   A pants-finisher in a ghetto sweatshop, Ostrinski explains to Jurgis the system which governs domestic
piecework and which applies as well to Packingtown labor:

> The workers were dependent upon a job to exist from
> day to day, and so they bid against each other, and
> no man could get more than the lowest man would con-
> sent to work for.   And thus the mass of the people
> were always in a life-and-death struggle with poverty.
> That was 'competition' so far as it concerned the wage-
> earner, the man who had only his labor to sell; to
> those on top, the exploiters, it appeared very dif-
> ferently, of course--there were few of them, and they
> could combine and dominate, and their power would
> be unbreakable.   And so, all over the world two
> classes were forming, with an unbridged chasm be-
> tween them--the capitalist class with its enormous
> fortunes, and the proletariat, bound into slavery by
> unseen chains [pp. 372-373].

The Jungle ends with Jurgis' conversion to socialism.
The final pages are filled with speeches and lectures Sinclair wanted his readers to hear.   It is a disappointing ending to a novel otherwise rich in concrete experience.   The
problem is not so much accepting Jurgis' conversion, which
comes with the suddenness of a religious awakening.   Rather
it is in the all too sudden shift from a novel of action to one
of talk.   The density of revealed experience in the first part
gives way abruptly before a dreary harangue.   The failure to
fuse fictional with political statement, the concrete rendering
of life with abstract statement about life, is pervasive in
"ideological" fiction of all stripes and is endemic as we shall
see to novels written by immigrants advocating one or another
formula for cultural assimilation.   The message too often in
such novels becomes something apart from, and not integrally
contained in, its medium.

It should also be said, however, that in contrast to

the stereotyped, irrational, anarchistic "socialists" who appear in lesser novels, Sinclair's socialists are sane, reasonable, and human.   The familiar "sinister alien" figure, the murderous and suicidal bomb-throwing revolutionary found in the works of writers like Edward Smith King and Isaac Kahn Friedman has no kinship with Sinclair's socialist heroes.   In Friedman's By Bread Alone (1901), the crazed foreign radical appears in the figures of the Frenchman La Vette and the Russian Jew Sophia Goldstein--ruthless saboteurs who, like King's Rudolph Baumeister, obstruct the peaceful labor struggles of the novel's hero.

Friedman's novel is set in Marvin, a company steel town on the outskirts of Chicago, although the events were patterned on the Homestead, Pa., strikes.   Blair Carrhart, Friedman's idealistic young hero, has left the ministry to work at the mill.   After a series of wage cuts and a shutdown of the plant (perpetrated to manipulate stock prices), he leads the workers, mainly immigrants, out on strike. Like Joseph Zalmonah, King's hero, Carrhart must fight two enemies, the Pinkerton "detectives" (or strike-breakers) brought in by the owners, and the anarchists who attempt to assassinate Henry Marvin and blow up the plant.   (Alexander Berkman attempted to murder Henry Clay Frick at Homestead; in 1901, the year the novel appeared, President McKinley was assassinated by Leon Czolgosz.)   Sophia Goldstein, who leads the attack on the mill, has come to Chicago after fleeing from St. Petersburg to New York.   It is she who instigates the assassination attempt on Marvin.   Her confederate La Vette, a chemist in the plant, commits suicide when he realizes that if he blows up the mill he will kill Evangeline Marvin, the owner's daughter--and the hero's fiancée--with whom he has fallen in love.   This kind of melodrama, which characterizes Friedman's earlier works, Poor People and The Lucky Number, are serious enough flaws in the novel, although certainly common to the period and to the subject. On balance the novel has the real virtue of dramatizing concretely, vividly, and with abundance of detail, the harrowing conditions of immigrant labor in a major American industry. This is the novel, to Walter Rideout, "with which the history of the radical novel in the present century truly begins."[11] Carrhart rejects the violence of the anarchists, and with Evangeline leaves Marvin, committed to the ideal of a Cooperative Commonwealth to be obtained without recourse to violence.

In placing the blame for violent, subversive labor

activity on "sinister aliens" who imported their anarchism
and exploited the ignorant but honest immigrant workman,
Friedman, like King, was placing the blame where many
Americans wanted and expected it placed. Such was the case
in a number of novels which dealt directly or indirectly with
the period's most celebrated anarchist incident, the Chicago
Haymarket Riot of 1886. When police attempted to suppress
a meeting of workers agitating for an eight-hour day in Haymarket Square on May 4 of that year, a bomb suddenly exploded in the crowd, killing a policeman and injuring sixty
other people, mostly strikers. In the ensuing riot six other
policemen were to lose their lives. It was never proved who
threw the bomb, but eight of the leading labor agitators--
seven of them immigrants--were arrested and subsequently
convicted. Four were hanged, one (Louis Lingg) committed
suicide in prison, and three were given life sentences. Despite the protests of hundreds of prominent Americans who
argued that the men were being convicted for their opinions,
not their acts, Illinois' Governor Oglesby refused to commute
the sentences of the condemned men. Six years later Illinois' new governor Altgeld pardoned the three surviving
prisoners and denounced the trial.

The oblique reference to the incident in Howells' A
Hazard of New Fortunes has already been mentioned. It appears more directly in Robert Herrick's The Memoirs of an
American Citizen (1905). The protagonist, Van Harrington,
serves on the jury which convicts the "Eight." He is chosen
because, as an up-and-coming young businessman, he is considered a "safe" jurist, one whose capitalist sympathies
could be counted on. After the trial he is rewarded by his
employer, Henry Dround. The event is a stepping stone in
Van Harrington's march to wealth and power. Another example of the novelistic use of the event is Charlotte Teller's
The Cage (1908), which deals with a woman whose Hungarian
socialist husband aids the Haymarket anarchists.

The fullest and most interesting treatment in fiction of
the incident, The Bomb (1908), came from the pen of the
Irish-born writer Frank Harris. At the time of the trial
Harris was editing the Evening News of London. Accounts
which reached England were largely one-sided and prejudiced
against the anarchists. George Bernard Shaw circulated a
petition for commutation of the convicted men's sentences,
but most liberal Englishmen remained silent. Harris' own
journal had, like many English journals, taken an editorial
stand against the "Eight," though Harris himself had remained

publicly silent until The Bomb appeared some twenty-one
years after the trial.   Angered by the trial record, which he
had been reviewing largely through newspaper reports in
America, he became convinced that the hearing had been a
sham and claimed to have dictated most of his novelistic version of the incident to a secretary in a single night. [12]

Ostensibly a defense of the "Eight," the novel nevertheless clearly implicates some of the anarchists in the planning stages, particularly Louis Lingg, whom Harris identifies
as the man who built the bomb.   He makes Rudolph Schnaubelt the actual thrower of the bomb.   Schnaubelt, in real life
a radical German immigrant and brother-in-law of Michael
Schwab, one of the "Eight," was a prime suspect for the police.   He was reported to have been on the speakers' platform with the other leaders when the bomb exploded.   Twice
arrested for questioning and released, Schnaubelt fled Chicago
before the trial. [13]   The novel is in the form of a first-person confessional by Schnaubelt written years later from his
home in Bavaria where he is dying of consumption.   He recalls in the opening chapters the degrading construction labor
he had been forced to submit to in his early days in America,
first in the air-filled caissons under the Brooklyn Bridge,
then at road construction--work handed out, he learned, by
Tammany politicians who shared the spoils of the rich contracts with the labor contractors.   He then had gone west to
Chicago where he became involved in radical journalism and
met the eight men who were to be arrested and convicted
after the bomb exploded.

Schnaubelt's greatest find in Chicago was Louis Lingg,
who built the bomb in his tenement laboratory.   Lingg is portrayed in the novel as a serious, intense, brooding German,
totally committed to the exploited workman and given to passionate outbursts.   He is an eloquent speaker, but, more important, he is committed to radical action.   "The submission
preached by Christ is the one part of his teaching I am unable to accept," he tells a socialist Verein meeting, and in
his tenement laboratory where he lives with Ida Miller, the
woman he has rescued from prostitution, he quietly builds the
bomb he plans to use.

Much of the book is devoted to Lingg's ideas--his passionate idealism coupled with his equally passionate dedication
to terrorist activity to bring the capitalistic oligarchy to its
knees; his sometimes lucid, sometimes crazed pronounce-
ments; his fierce hatred for capitalists and their agents, the

police.   Others of the "Eight" are less thoroughly individual-
ized.   Albert Parsons, the only native-born American of the
group, editor of the socialistic journal, The Alarm, is a
skillful rhetorician, a practical, pragmatic fighter for moderate reform, a man with whom the fiery Lingg has little patience.   August Spies, who edits Chicago's Arbeiter Zeitung,
is, in contrast to Parsons, idealistic and emotional, a man
who "really believed in the possibility of an ordered socialist
paradise on earth, from which individual greed and acquisi-
tiveness should be banished, and in which men should share
the good things of the world equally. "   George Engel is portrayed as an emotional, sentimental man who works in a toy-
shop and weeps at reports of strikers felled by police.

        Schnaubelt writes for the Arbeiter Zeitung and the
Herald in Chicago.   He attends socialist Verein meetings
where with the "Eight" he not only takes part in abstract
ideological debates, but confronts some of the direct victims
of capitalism.   He meets a Herr Leiter who at the age of
twenty-six had been blinded by a factory boiler explosion and
dismissed without compensation.   He hears about cases of
lead poisoning in paint factories and "phossy jaw" (jaws de-
cayed when the fumes from the phosphorus used in making
matches enter teeth cavities).   He goes to a strikers' meeting where the speaker, Samuel Fielden, one of the "Eight, "
is clubbed by policemen for challenging an order to get off
the stand and dismiss the meeting.   Another of the "Eight, "
Adolph Fisher, a communist reporter, comes to Fielden's aid
and is also brutally clubbed.   When Schnaubelt attempts to
publish his account of the incident in the Herald, his editor
will not print it.

        The strike at the McCormick Harvester and Reaper
factory on Chicago's West Side sets the stage for the climac-
tic Haymarket scene.   The plant is situated in the midst of
the German, Polish, and Bohemian quarters of the city, and
nine-tenths of the workers are foreigners.   The firm replaces the strikers, with the result that fighting breaks out
among strikers, scabs, and police.   After one such battle in
which police shoot into the mob, killing seven and wounding
dozens, the Haymarket meeting is called in protest.   If the
police interfere, Lingg decides, the bomb will be thrown.
Schnaubelt, who is yet little known to the police in Chicago,
volunteers to throw the bomb and then, according to plan, escape to England under a false name.   In the novel the meeting is not held in the Haymarket but one hundred yards away
on Des Plaines Street, between Lake and Randolph Streets.

The principal speakers, Spies, Parsons, and Fielden, are
placed on a truckwagon in front of a crowd of between two
and three thousand.   When the police move in, Schnaubelt
throws the bomb and makes his escape.   Lingg and the other
seven are arrested and convicted.

News of the arrests and trial comes to Schnaubelt in
England.   It had been a sham trial.   Unable to obtain evidence, the police had turned to the leaders of the anarchist
and socialist press.   Evidence had been manufactured in the
form of weapons--a whole arsenal--discovered in the apart-
ments of the "Eight."   Newspaper publicity had prejudiced
the trial before it began.   The jury had been stacked.   The
trial had begun only six weeks after the arrests, too soon to
erase public hysteria.   In his cell, Lingg, meanwhile, committed suicide by exploding a bomb in front of his face, fulfilling his earlier prophesy that he would be his own execu-
tioner.   Everything in the novel is subordinated to the fanatical heroism of Lingg, who hovers fully conscious for days
between life and death without uttering a groan, his flesh in
strips and his lower jaw gone.

Lingg, the fanatic, not the equivocal Parsons or the
overemotional Spies, emerges as Harris' superman-hero.   To
have made Schnaubelt the thrower of the bomb seems to have
been a compromise.   It allowed Harris to repudiate the findings of the court, to demonstrate that the "Eight" were convicted for their radical views, not their acts, and at the same
time to illustrate the truth of what Schnaubelt, early in the
novel, following his own degrading labor experiences in New
York, tells the editor of the Yiddish Forward: "I told him
that manual labor is so hard, so exhausting in the American
climate, that it turns one into a soulless brute. ...   The conditions of manual labor in the States are breeding a prole-
tariat ready for revolt. "[14]

Schnaubelt, in the novel, is not one of the Chicago
anarchist group, and except for his association with Lingg
and Spies not intimately connected with the "Eight."   Yet like
them he is a man whose mind has been tortured by what he
has seen of the cruel exploitation of labor and the brutal suppression by police of labor meetings.   Harris carefully documents the abuses of wage slavery, and while he repudiates
bomb-throwing and terrorism as solutions, he maintains a
pro-anarchist sympathy throughout.   Schnaubelt has been driv-
en to a crazed, desperate act by the shock to his nervous
system of what he has seen, heard, and experienced in a few

years in America.   However, although Harris makes the
bomb-throwing the act, ultimately, of a single man and not a
conspiracy among the "Eight" and although he documents the
systematic and brutal suppression of labor which stands behind the event, he nevertheless raises again in fiction the
specter of the "sinister alien," the crazed, foreign anarchist-
figure.

    The Bomb, published in London, received praise from
a variety of sources in England and America when it appeared.   Arnold Bennett called it "the finest of realistic novels" and Emma Goldman labeled it the "Bible of Anarchism."
The strongest praise, though, came from George Bernard
Shaw, who called Harris the "Homer of Anarchism" and maintained that "he has lifted the Chicago Anarchists out of their
infamy, and shown that, compared with the Capitalists that
killed them, they were heroes and martyrs."[15]   Yet the book
was attacked by some of those closest to the Chicago group
for implicating some of the "Eight" in the planning stages.
The principal opponent was the widow of the executed Albert
Parsons.   According to one accepted anarchist belief the police themselves threw the bomb to justify strong reprisals
against the troublesome agitators.   To those who held this
view, Harris' version was, of course, unacceptable.   While
Harris absolved the "Eight" of any conspiracy, the blame for
the act was placed uncomfortably close.

    Three years after Harris' novel appeared, James Op-
penheim published a collection of stories, Pay Envelopes, and
a novel, The Nine-Tenths, which also drew on the period's
cataclysmic immigrant labor struggles.   The eleven stories in
Pay Envelopes, reprinted from The American, Everybody's,
Forum, Metropolitan, Pearson's, and Success, vary in subject and setting but focus chiefly on the exploited Austro-
Hungarian steel mill workers in Pennsylvania's "Hunkeytowns,"
the industrial arena which Isaac Kahn Friedman explored in
By Bread Alone a decade earlier and which came into national
prominence with the Homestead strikes.   In the Nine-Tenths,
Oppenheim turned to two recent events in New York immigrant labor history, the 1909 massive walkout of sweated East
Side garment workers and the infamous 1911 Triangle Waist
Company fire, in which 146 workers, mostly girls, were
trapped and burned to death.   (Zoe Beckley's novel A Chance
to Live (1918) also dealt with the Triangle fire.)   Oppenheim
reverses the order of the two events in his novel: it is after
the disastrous fire that the workers hold mass meetings and
plan the walkout.

The stories in Pay Envelopes are every bit as sentimental as those in his earlier Dr. Rast stories, but in their
concern with immigrant labor conditions they document a step
in Oppenheim's passage to political radicalism.   He is no
longer content to record the heroic adventures of the idealistic East Side doctor as he battles the diseases of the ghetto.
But while the subject has changed, the same pervasive and
almost mystic optimism is evident.   The proletarian heroes
of Pay Envelopes are lifted from their misery and desponden-
cy by a sudden and exhilarating recognition of complicity with
their fellow workers, a discovery which comes to them as a
blinding illumination of their involvement and participation in
the lives of others.   The "conversion" is political only in the
broadest sense.   Like the heroes of his fellow midwesterner
Sherwood Anderson, whom he anticipates, Oppenheim's heroes
"enter into the lives of other people," finding that state "beyond desire."

The story "Slag" illustrates this gratuitous conversion
--gratuitous in the sense that what precedes it in the story
fails to prepare the reader or provide adequate causation for
the shift.   We can understand Jurgis Rudkis' conversion to
the vision of a Cooperative Commonwealth given Sinclair's
detailed and harrowing portrayal of the conditions at Packingtown, but with Oppenheim's heroes the conversion is uncon-
vincing both because there has been too little objective and
concrete rendering of life at "Hunkeytown" and because the
ideals they so optimistically embrace are so vague and amor-
phous.   Jo, the Austro-Hungarian hero of "Slag," works
twelve hours a day at the foot of a blast furnace.   He is bitter and resentful at what America has made of him.   In
Hungary he was a poor peasant, but his struggles were with
the soil and with the weather, not with oppressive foremen
and bosses.   He was engaged with elemental forces.   He was
conscious of the wind, the sun, the stars, and these gave
his life meaning.   In America he works indoors, fronting the
full heat of molten iron, exploited by foremen and forced to
live with fourteen other men in two tiny rooms.   The result
is to destroy--or rather force into exile--his humanity.   The
New World, he feels, has turned him into "slag"--the waste
matter remaining after the pure iron has been drained off.

When he suspects, falsely, that his foreman is making
love to his wife, he strikes out with a knife, blindly venting
his rage against a whole system which has imprisoned and
degraded him.   Later, overcome by shame and guilt at his
misplaced aggression, he is encouraged to enroll in a night

school for immigrants. Here, suddenly, he discovers another America: "It made him feel queer about the heart.
Was it possible in this terrible country anyone wanted to help
him? It made him feel like choking. He gave a low laugh.
Was he being shown a new America--a place of hope and of
light--yes, a place of love? Was he something better than
slag in the eyes of his new country?"[16] This kind of abrupt
and dramatically unjustified conversion from despair to hope
marks the conclusion to a number of the stories and clouds
the whole issue of industrial exploitation with which the
stories begin. In "Joan of the Mills" Oppenheim tells the
same story, except that his worker-hero Ignatz Plavier is
transformed not by the discovery of an America that recognizes his worth and dignity, but by the vision of worker solidarity in the face of capitalistic tyranny.

Plavier, like Jo, came to the New World brimming
with hope, but found America the broken promise. He recalls nostalgically his peasant life in Hungary where he was
poor but happy. Then came the steamship agents and the al-
luring immigration circulars. He beheld "the dream of all
the world ... the land of freedom called, the land of the future, the land of his children." But from Ellis Island he is
tugged and hurtled by boat and train to the mill outside Pittsburgh where "his strength, grown out of the soil and under
the sun, was worth just ten dollars a week." Typhoid has
killed his wife. Wages are cut; those who complain are fired;
company spies check all attempts to organize. Yet the 6000
workers do strike and, persuaded to join the strikers by an
idealistic young woman, Plavier discovers in the collective
action of the workers a new faith in America, based on
brotherhood and democracy. Like Jo, he finds a meaning to
America which runs deeper than exploitation. For Plavier it
is not so much a political or ideological awakening as an
emotional recognition of group identity with the 6000 through
their shared hope for a better future and their willingness to
act together to realize it. He watches the strikers march by:
"It was the brute giant in motion--a tapestry of many colors--
strange foreign faces--the stolid Slavs, the fiery Italians, the
eagle-like Russians, the stolid Germans. It was like Ellis
Island marching by" (p. 170). He listens to the fiery
speeches and

> suddenly Ignatz knew in his heart that he was no long-
> er a separate soul, no longer lonely and apart; but
> that the great soul of man had absorbed him; he en-
> tered into the larger manhood; he felt himself a part

of a throng of humanity; a sense of brotherhood, divine
and lovely, stole into him; he could have shaken hands
with every man in the crowd; cried with them, laughed
with them, died with them" [p. 176].

It is this type of emotional, sentimental and vaguely
socialistic transformation that comes also to Joe Blaine, the
hero of Oppenheim's novel The Nine-Tenths. The owner of
a small print shop, Joe is striken with guilt when a fire
which broke out in his eighth floor shop--the result of cotton
waste set aflame by a carelessly tossed cigarette--spreads to
a neighboring factory and sixty girls, mostly Bohemian and
Russian Jewish immigrants, are trapped and killed. The papers are filled with angry editorial denunciations of the lack
of concern for industrial safety, and Joe, not legally culpable, vows to make amends. After attending a mass meeting
of working women at Carnegie Hall and listening to the passionate speech of an immigrant girl, he becomes aware for
the first time of the "division of humanity" into capitalists
and workers and experiences a vision of future brotherhood
which is as blinding and apocalyptic as those which come to
the worker-heroes of Pay Envelopes: "He heard the music
of that Hymn of Human Victory, which from millions of
throats lifts on that day when all the race is woven into a
harmony of labor and joy and home and great unselfish
deeds. "[17]

Joe moves to a basement flat in Greenwich Village,
where he edits a labor journal, The Nine-Tenths, studies the
conditions of sweatshop labor, and leads the garment workers
out on strike. Like Dr. Rast, Joe finds beauty, nobility,
and heroism beneath the filth of the ghetto. Sally Heffer,
the girl who gave the speech in Carnegie Hall, joins Joe in
organizing the strike of shirtwaist makers. Together they in-
spire the "Uprising of the Thirty Thousand" New York working girls. Two other women play important roles in the
novel--Myra Craig, Joe's fiancée, a delicate and genteel
schoolteacher who overcomes her initial antipathy to immigrants when she encounters the harassment of women strikers by paid strike-breakers, and Rhona Hemlitz, a seventeen-
year-old picket who is arrested on a trumped up charge of
striking a "detective" (i.e., a strike-breaker). Most of the
later chapters of the novel are devoted to Rhona's trial and
imprisonment. She is herded into a crowded, foul-smelling,
ice-cold jail, not allowed witnesses in her defense, and sentenced off-handedly to five days in a workhouse by a judge
whose anti-labor prejudices are clearly revealed.

While the events of the novel should lead, it would
seem, to a hardening of Joe's position, Oppenheim has him
retreat at the novel's end from his radical stance.   His love
for Myra and a confrontation with a now-bankrupt employer
of women garment workers combine to produce a softening
of his position.   The bankrupt man, Joe learns, had been as
generous with his employees as conditions allowed, but the
strike ruined him.   The economic world, Joe concludes, is
more than a black and white struggle between greedy capitalists and exploited workers.   There are infinite gradations of
right and wrong.   Joe and Myra--like Blair Carrhart and
his fiancée Evangeline Marvin in Friedman's By Bread Alone
--dedicate themselves to continue to work for the brotherhood
of man, but the final vision of the novel is blurred.   As in
his other works, the ending is more religious in tone than
political.

The 1909 "Uprising of the Twenty Thousand" (which
Oppenheim upped to thirty thousand) provided the background
for other immigrant labor novels.   Florence Converse used
the incident in The Children of Light (1912), which like Oppenheim's novel concerns a native-born American who goes
to live and work among New York's immigrants and helps
organize the strike.   Miss Converse's heroine, Clara Emery,
is a wealthy heiress with a passion for St. Frances who goes
to New York and with her two cousins founds a settlement
house, publishes a socialist journal, The Torch, and gets increasingly involved in the labor troubles of immigrant working girls.   Unlike Oppenheim, Miss Converse explores in
some detail the internecine warfare among the labor forces--
the rival Women's Trade Union League, the socialists, and
the anarchists.   Clara aligns herself with the socialists and
stands in firm opposition to the violence perpetrated by the
anarchists (including an attempt to derail a speeding train
carrying three to four thousand Italian "scabs" rushed in by
the employers).   The novel ends with the massive strike patterned after the "Uprising."

The real inspiration for the general walkout came at
a mass meeting of waist-makers at Cooper Union on November 22, 1909.   Labor leaders Abraham Cahan, Benjamin
Feigenbaum, Meyer London, Samuel Gompers, and Mary
Dreier (president of New York's Women's Trade Union League)
had addressed the crowd when suddenly an inspired teen-aged
working girl, Clara Lemlich, rose from the audience and delivered an emotional strike plea in Yiddish, following which
the assembly voted overwhelmingly for a general strike. [18]

The incident, which appears in The Nine-Tenths, seems to
have furnished Arthur Bullard the germ for his novel of the
"Uprising," Comrade Yetta (1913), which he wrote under the
name "Albert Edwards." Bullard, a socialist, edited with
Ernest Poole, Leroy Scott, and Charles Edward Russel the
Socialist daily, The Call. The Clara Lemlich figure in the
novel is Yetta Rayefsky, a young sweatshop vest-maker who
early in the novel attends a dance given by the Women's
Trade Union League, headed by Mabel Train (the novel's
Mary Dreier), for the benefit of striking skirt-finishers. Inspired by the speech of the radical unionist Walter Longman,
which asserts that Jews are being crushed because they re-
fuse to fight back, she suddenly delivers her impassioned
plea:

> What he says is true. We Jews don't fight for Free-
> dom like we ought. Look at me.... I'm--yes, I'll
> tell you. I'm speeder in my shop. I'm sorry. I
> didn't think about it. Nobody ever told me what it
> meant before. If there's a union in my trade, I'll
> join it; I'll try not to be a slave. I can't fight much.
> I don't know how. I guess that's the real trouble--
> we're not afraid--only we don't know. I aint got no
> education. I had to stop school when my father died.
> I was only fifteen. But I'll try harder for those that
> are fighting.... [19]

Like most of the other novels in this genre, this is
the story of the degradation, awakening, and conversion of the
protagonist. The awakening, signaled by her impromptu
speech before the labor ball, occurs early in the novel.
Much of the balance of the work consists, as it does in Florence Converse's novel, of a contrast between the three ideological claims which appeal in different ways to the heroine--
the claims of AFT trade unionism represented by Mabel
Train and the WTUL, the IWW-type radical industrial unionism represented by Walter Longman, and doctrinal socialism
represented by the attorney and editor Isador Braun.

The early chapters document Yetta's sweatshop experiences. She is the daughter of a scholarly bookseller who
brought her to America after a pogrom in Russia left his wife
and son dead. On her father's death when she is fourteen,
Yetta goes to work in Jake Goldfogle's tenement sweatshop.
The sweater-figure is not presented here as the petty tyrant,
literally imprisoning his help, as he was in Joseph Zalmonah,
but as a rather pitiful, impoverished young Russian Jew who

grew up in the ghetto and who is as much under the lion's
paw as his workers:

> He had 'got wise' young, with the wisdom of the
> gutter, which says you must be either a hammer or
> an anvil, preyed upon or preying....
>
> Hundreds of men throughout the city, in the differ-
> ent garment trades, were in exactly the same position.
> Ground between the gambling nature of their contracts
> and insufficient credit, the fear of ruin in their hearts,
> they had been driving the rowels deeper and deeper
> into the flanks of the animals who worked for them--
> on whose backs they hoped to win the gilded goal of
> success. But revolt from such conditions was inevita-
> ble. Strikes were constantly occurring. This fear
> was the worst of Jake Goldfogle's nightmares [pp. 29-
> 30].

Before the general strike, spontaneous walkouts on the
Lower East Side were frequent but unorganized and futile.
All but the smallest sweaters could afford to wait until the
workers were "starved back to the machines." Bullard de-
picts the initial reluctance of Jewish clothing workers to
strike. With the general strike dozens of sweaters, Goldfogle among them, are immediately forced to shut down. The
manufacturers and the larger sweaters hire "greenhorns" to
keep the machines going and "detectives"--often thugs--to keep
angry pickets away from the scabs. In one scene Yetta
strikes a hired "detective" from behind when he attacks a
woman picket. She is arrested and sentenced to ten days in
the workhouse. This gives Bullard, who had served on various municipal prison commissions, a chance to promote one
of his pet subjects, the need for prison reform. The incident
is similar to the one in Oppenheim's The Nine-Tenths in
which Rhona Hemlitz is arrested and imprisoned on the same
charge. In Nathan Kussy's The Abyss (1916) the immigrant
youth Sammy Gordon is arrested for vagrancy and exposed in
prison to a sordid variety of criminals. To the reformers
of the age, one of the worst features of the prison system
was that it subjected youthful offenders to the influence of
hardened and incorrigible criminals. Bullard dealt with the
penal system in an earlier novel, A Man's World (1912).

Another of Bullard's reform targets was prostitution,
which in the novel is seen as a product of the sweatshop.
Girls who spent the long day bent over machines for less
money than it takes to live with any comfort were easily led

into more abject slavery by the East Side "cadets," who
scavenged the sweatshops for attractive girls, offering them
money, clothing, and leisure.   Like prison reform, the prostitution issue was a frequent one in the reform and socialist
novels of the period.   The two issues were not unrelated:
it was in prison that girls were often introduced to the influence of prostitutes.   "White-slave traffic" was presented as
another product of capitalistic exploitation.   The fullest treatment of the subject in the novels of the period is Reginald
Wright Kauffman's The House of Bondage (1910), in which the
"social evil" is linked directly to capitalistic oppression.   In
Comrade Yetta, the heroine's cousin Rachel Goldstein is
drawn into prostitution, and Yetta too would have been a victim of the glib "cadet" Harry Klein, but is rescued when the
speech by Walter Longman at the labor ball convinces her
that her role is to fight against the system.

Although Yetta is roused from her lethargy by the industrial unionism of the fiery Longman, she gives her final
allegiance to socialism and Isador Braun.   First, though, she
goes through a period as a "walking delegate" and organizer
in Mabel Train's Women's Trade Union League.   The WTUL,
which achieves its practical, moderate reform goals by organizing one, then another of the women's sweated trades, is
supported largely by volunteer women from the upper classes,
some of whom are pictured as reveling in the daring plunge
into the slums.   Mabel Train herself is a product of the upper class who had come under the influence of liberal economics at the University of Wisconsin and left college to organize New York's working girls.   The New Woman stereotype, she is intellectual, reserved, and completely dedicated
to her cause.   In Yetta she recognizes a "firebrand" whose
ungrammatical speech has its effect on the purses of the
league's sponsors.   Yet the teas and meetings have the effect
of hardening Yetta's class consciousness, of making her recognize the width of the gulf separating the working girls and
these women who assuage their consciences with their pocket-
books; and with this recognition Yetta's interest in trade unionism wanes.   "Their cry, 'A little less injustice, please,'
seemed timid to Yetta."   More and more she responds to the
other pole of unionism, Walter Longman's brand of IWW radical industrial unionism.

Longman, an iconoclastic and eclectic thinker who does
research in Assyriology at Columbia University, has little patience with either the gradualism of Mabel Train or the cold
and sterile logic of the socialists.   Progress comes about

only through active struggle with the forces which enslave
man.   The social system is enforced by violence and can be
overcome only through violence.   Because strikes are usually
aimed at union representation or increased wages in a particular trade, Longman regards them as futile.   Each union
seeks its own demands.   What is needed is a general strike
based on "an ideal which is shared by every workingman."
Trade unions are a quaint anachronism in the age of giant
machine industry.   Large industrial unions--like those of
IWW persuasion--are bound to replace them.   Longman mixes
his politics with an optimistic evolutionary faith.   He likens
the working class struggles against the giants of industry to
the instinctive struggles of life forms to survive, to the push-
ing through from lower to higher forms, to the awakening of
man to new complexities.   "All evolution has been the history
of life struggling for liberty," he tells Yetta.   Progress in
man is the awakening to the "common sense of life" and the
struggles to obtain a decent life.   It is not an orderly progress, but one marked by accident, chance, false starts, and
spontaneous revolts.

To Yetta, who has come to politics not through the
study of economics, biology, or ideology, but through the experience of a working girl, industrial unionism has a strong
emotional appeal, but near the end of the novel she rejects
this solution as she had rejected trade unionism, recognizing
that its attraction had been a "blind and dangerous impulse."
The position she finally adopts is Bullard's own, the pacifistic socialism of Isador Braun; and after a long battle with
typhus takes the cold edge off Braun's intellectualism, she
marries him.   Together they edit the socialist daily, The
Clarion, a fictional counterpart to The Call, which Bullard
helped edit.   The appeal socialism has for Yetta is that it
binds together all workmen--industrial workers, farmers,
craftsmen--who work for wages and are victimized by industrial consolidation, trusts, and unchecked capitalism.   Her
convictions are strengthened near the end of the novel when
she encounters her old sweater, Jake Goldfogle, working as
a peddler.   Ruined by the general strike, he had been forced
back to the sewing machine where he worked until a belt
came loose, blinding him in one eye.   As Oppenheim's hero
Joe Blaine has discovered, the bosses, too, are victims of
the system they help perpetuate.

Comrade Yetta epitomizes the immigrant labor novel.
Coming as it does at the very crest of the "new" immigration
wave, it treats the most energetic phase of the protracted

labor struggle in the most characteristic of urban immigrant occupations. The novel explores, moreover, the ideological poles of the labor movement in the second decade of the twentieth century--Gompers' AFT, IWW radical industrial unionism, and socialism. Bullard's sympathies, like Sinclair's, Oppenheim's, and Converse's, lie with socialism, a socialism far different in its reasoned and temperate approach from the insane, anarcho-socialism presented in the earliest of the immigrant labor novels, Edward Smith King's Joseph Zalmonah.

In the two decades which stand between King's novel and Bullard's, immigrant labor made significant strides. Taken collectively, the immigrant labor novel traces the evolution of the immigrant work force from its initial ignorance, bewilderment, and apathy to a period of intense activism to the eventual joining with the American labor movement. Taken individually, each of these novels recapitulates the broader pattern of immigrant labor progress. Each focuses on a group of exploited immigrant workers who after a period of ignorance and inertia join with other workers to challenge their oppressors. The collectivist solutions proposed by the novelists are seldom either radical or violent. Only rarely --Frank Harris is a case in point--do the novelists retain any sympathy for anarchism or terrorist activities. The immigrant anarchist, like the predatory industrialist, is seen as an obstacle to genuine labor reform.

Like the ghetto tales described in the last chapter, the immigrant labor novels were written for the most part by native-born Americans, sympathetic observers who gained their knowledge of the ghetto from their experience as reporters, settlement workers, or labor organizers, and who learned, as Riis and Hapgood did, to turn their observations into fiction. No less sentimental than Riis and Hapgood in their depiction of the submerged immigrant, they went beyond the scope of the ghetto tale both in giving their fiction an ideological grounding and in exploring the role of the immigrant in the history of the American labor movement. Their subject was not the flavor, the charm, or the exotic features of life within the walls of the ghetto but the larger life outside those walls, the life of the Industrial City, in which native and immigrant, older and newer American confronted each other.

Marred too often by stereotyped characters--by stock villain-types like the cruel and malicious sweater, the parvenu German-Jewish industrialist, the irrational and sinister anarchist--by melodramatic story lines, by oversimplified and doctrinaire solutions, and by vague visionary messages, these novels nevertheless recall a vigorous phase of the immigrant's, and urban America's, period of adjustment. More than this, in focusing on the political initiation of the exploited urban worker, his awakening to collectivist ideology, they provide much of the foundation for the proletarian novel in America which was to peak in the thirties. The immigrant in these early labor novels provided an ideal proletarian hero not only because he most broadly represented the industrial laborer in the American city, but because, as Oppenheim and Sinclair had shown, he brought with him an idealized conception of democracy and was, consequently, soon made aware of the gulf between the promise of America and the actuality.

America as a broken promise is a theme which recurs in this fiction and in the fiction written by the immigrants themselves. Immigrant novelists generally were not so concerned with the exposé of industrial labor conditions as with the problems of personal adjustment to the New World, but like the native-born explorers of immigrant labor, they frequently drew attention to the contrast between the real and the imagined America. The immigrant's portrait of America --and his own adjustment to it--will be the subject of the remaining chapters of this book.

VI

"THEY WERE AMERICANS BEFORE THEY LANDED":
THE PROCESS OF ACCULTURATION
IN THE IMMIGRANT NOVEL

The chapter title is a quotation from Marcus Lee
Hansen's The Immigrant in American History (1940), a volume of essays which emphasized the receptivity of European
immigrants to American ideals.   Hansen was concerned chiefly with immigrants to rural America, but his optimistic vision of the newcomers' entering confidently into the national
life found expression as well in autobiographies and novels
written by urban immigrants in the opening years of the twentieth century.

Such autobiographies and novels were attempts to put
on record the immigrants' own experience of discovering and
adjusting to America.   These books have value for us today
both as documents testifying in personal terms to the acculturation experience and as pioneer efforts to portray America
in fiction through non-native eyes.   The South and East European immigrant was the American city's most conspicuous
element at the turn of the century, and yet his presence was
hardly noticed by most of our major native-born writers of
fiction.   It is possible to argue--as Howard Mumford Jones
did--that our national literature by 1900 had become that of
a minority culture. [1] When, as the new century advanced, the
immigrant added his voice to native fiction, poetry, drama,
and autobiography, a real breakthrough had been achieved.
American literature was on its way to becoming a cosmopolitan, pluralistic enterprise, broadly representative of the
varied elements of the population.

And yet, when we come to read these novels by first-
generation immigrants, we are forced to make some qualifi-
cations.   Just as we have seen--in Chapter II--that the literary explorers of the slums in the nineties were unable fully
to escape long-established literary conventions of slum por-

traiture, the urban immigrants who first recorded their experience in English language fiction were caught up in already-
established native patterns of depicting the foreign-born. Cultural assimilation--some degree of which had to precede the
fiction--included the assimilation of native attitudes and assumptions about immigrants. Their own absorption into American society and their receptivity to native ideals limited
their vision as writers at the same time that it gave them
the language skills requisite to writing American fiction. As
a result, the novels written by the first generation urban immigrants are a blend of convention and insight. Hackneyed
plots which belong to the traditional native success story formula co-exist with some fresh and intimate perspectives on
the hazards of cultural uprooting.

When the urban immigrant began to write novels in the
language of his adopted land--and it was only rarely that he
was able to do so in the first generation--it was both natural
and inevitable that his subject should have been his own adjustment to America. Having the leisure to write fiction
meant having achieved some measure of success in America,
and, as might be expected, the process the immigrant novelist characteristically described was one of assimilation and
accommodation with the dominant culture. We are given most
often an account of his own interpretation of "Americanization," a concept which could mean either the shedding of Old
World customs and the absorption of native habits or the
broader fusion of Old and New World cultures. Rarely did
cultural pluralism, or "cosmopolitanism," play a part in the
fiction written by the first generation immigrant, except as
an idea to be rejected: the writer's own experience had
moved in an opposite direction.

Like so many of the immigrant autobiographies which
appeared during the period, the novels written by immigrants
had a hopeful message to preach. In a period characterized
by the mounting distrust of foreigners and the suspicion that
the newer arrivals from Eastern Europe were unassimilable,
these novels were optimistic affirmations of immigrant assimilability. There were exceptions, of course--among them
Abraham Cahan's The Rise of David Levinsky and Sidney Nyburg's The Chosen People, which revealed the dilemmas and
frustrations of acculturation. For the most part, though, the
immigrant novel in the urban age is the story of successful
assimilation.

Before the twenties, this fiction was almost exclusively

the product of Jewish immigrants. Although the total number
of East European Jews to cross the Atlantic was only about
half that of the Italians--the largest of the "new" immigrant
groups[2]--the reasons behind Jewish emigration from the "Pale"
account to a large degree for the greater Jewish activity in
literature. Like other large groups from southern and eastern Europe, the Jews were motivated to emigrate for a variety of reasons, but to a greater extent than with other groups,
governmental oppression provided the spur. As political
refugees, East Europe's Jews brought with them a sizable
number of educated men and thus were able to achieve culturally in the first generation what other groups had to wait
until the second and third generations to achieve. The rela-
tive sparsity of Italian-American fiction before 1920 has to
do with the much more limited education of those portions of
the Italian population which emigrated. [3] Another reason, perhaps, for the greater bulk of Jewish-American fiction in the
first-generation, pre-1920 period is the fact that since the
Jews were fleeing political oppression there were among them
--in contrast to the Italians--very few "birds of passage."
There was no going home for the Jews, as there was for the
Italians, and for this reason the whole question of acculturation was a crucial one.

To some Jews acculturation meant simply sloughing
off Old World habits, customs, traditions, and language. To
others the process was a more complex and ambivalent interaction between two cultures. No better testament to the former exists than the autobiography of Mary Antin, The Promised Land, which created something of a literary sensation
when it appeared in 1912 and is read to this day in high
school classes as a paean to Americanization. The title is
by no means ironic. Like Jacob Riis's autobiography, The
Making of an American, it tells the story of the immigrant
child who through will and ambition enters the mainstream of
native life and achieves recognition and prosperity. Riis,
throughout his career as a police reporter and photographer
on New York's East Side, saw the clannishness of the recent
immigrant as a chief stumbling block to acculturation. Although he recognized that the tenement house and the sweatshop were major factors which contributed to the isolation of
the immigrant, his sympathies diminished in proportion to the
newcomers' obstinacy in clinging to Old World ways. The
Russian Jews were to him among the most recalcitrant of the
immigrants, standing "where the new day that dawned on Cal-
vary left them, stubbornly refusing to see the light."[4]

Mary Antin's autobiography is written in much the same spirit. The Promised Land tells of the girl who emigrated in 1894 at the age of thirteen from Polotsk, Russia, to Boston. In Russia she had been a stranger in her own land, a victim of Christian maliciousness, mischief, and persecution. In America she is made to feel at home and, encouraged to adopt the ways of her new land, is reborn as an entirely new person: "I was born, I have lived, and I have been made over.... I am just as much out of the way as if I were dead for I am absolutely other than the person whose story I have to tell.... My life I still have to live; her life ended when mine began. "[5]

The work was received enthusiastically. To the reviewers and to many readers it offered solid evidence that the newest immigrants could become good Americans, particularly if they arrived at an early age and were subjected to healthy American influences. A few readers, the patrician literary historian Barrett Wendell among them, objected to this and Miss Antin's other books and articles. In a letter written to a friend in England in 1917, Wendell complained, "She has developed an irritating habit of describing herself and her people as Americans, in distinction from such folks as Edith and me, who have been here for three hundred years. "[6]

The immigrant novelist whose works came closest to advocating the kind of assimilation Mary Antin and Jacob Riis were recommending was Russian-born Elias Tobenkin. In Witte Arrives (1916), he describes the Americanization of Emile Witte (born Wittowski), who emigrates as a youth from Russia and after attending a Western university becomes a commercial and artistic success as a journalist, while his father remains a peddler in America, too rooted in Old World ways to become Americanized. The course of Witte's career roughly parallels Tobenkin's own. The author came to America as a young boy, graduated from the University of Wisconsin in 1905, and went on to a career in journalism, working as a reporter for the Milwaukee Free Press, the Chicago Tribune, the San Francisco Examiner, and the New York Herald. His hero is a reporter on two Chicago newspapers and later in New York becomes a successful author of two books on American life and a series of magazine articles which articulate "America's Newest Problems." So thoroughly has Witte been made over that his articles on domestic issues, we are told, have an "Emersonian flavor" and most readers "would have placed the writer of such articles as none other than a scion of one of the oldest American families. "[7]

Witte seals his "arrival" at the end of the novel by marrying a gentile girl of wealthy New England stock after his Jewish wife dies. His transformation from bewildered alien to successful citizen seems much too facile but for the fact that, like Tobenkin, Witte grew up in the semi-rural West and not in the urban ghetto. He became Americanized not as Mary Antin had, by erasing the bitter memories of the past, but as Jacob Riis had, by channeling his writing talents into the mainstream of the middle-class American reform movement, by putting his journalistic skills to the service of broad, native, democratic ideals.

Although Witte's rural, midwestern boyhood is atypical of Jewish-American fiction (and life) of the period, the novel delineates quite clearly the major features of the urban immigrant novel, and its structural pattern can serve as a model. The pattern has three basic components or chronological stages which can be isolated: the initial embrace of everything American, coupled with the rejection of the father, who symbolizes the Old World; the subsequent recoil from the harsh actualities of America which shatter the joyful expectations; and, finally, the reconciliation, the adjustment, the "taking root."

Central to the initial phase is the generational conflict represented in Witte Arrives and in most immigrant novels as a total absence of communication between father (or father surrogate) and son. Witte reaches out to the promise of the New World, while his father remains mired in tradition, in but not of the New World. As we have seen, this generational split appeared frequently in native-drawn portraits of the immigrant. Observers of the ghetto like Lincoln Steffens, Hutchins Hapgood, and Jane Addams deplored the breakdown of traditional Jewish family life as a result of New World working conditions and the influence of the public schools and the streets. The drifting of immigrant children away from their parents was to them one of the tragic consequences of ghetto life. It could also be a source of comedy in literature. The prolific short story writer Rudolph Block portrayed the conflict with broad, almost farcical humor in "The Americanization of Shadrach Cohen," a story about a "greenhorn" father who, without abandoning his Old World piety manages to beat his Americanized sons at their own capitalistic game and thus win back their respect. Abraham Cahan in a much richer

story, "The Imported Bridegroom" (1898), found humor as
well as sadness in the conflict between parents and children.
James Oppenheim in his Dr. Rast stories--"Groping Children,"
for instance--treated this split far more solemnly, revealing
only contempt for immigrant children who rejected their parents.

The initial rejection of the parent and the embrace of
America by the immigrant hero is followed typically by a
period of bitterness or disillusionment, a recoil from an
America which fails to live up to its promise.   In Tobenkin's
novel, Witte, after graduating from a major midwestern university, takes a job as a Chicago reporter and is assigned to
"do up" for their pathos and human interest the city's immigrant quarters, the municipal lodging house, and the strike of
12,000 Polish and Lithuanian workers in the stock yards.
Witte becomes aware, for the first time, of "the fear that
stalked the greater part of Chicago" and "the caste lines that
unconsciously divided the city. "   Encouraged to "dive deep into the wells of misery," he discovers realities of slum and
immigrant life his rural past had not prepared him for, and
finding little chance in Chicago to report--without editorial
blue-penciling--what he has observed, he quits his job and
goes to New York where he eventually succeeds as a reform
journalist.

Witte's marriage to an aristocratic gentile girl marks
a third important stage in the immigrant hero's progress--
reconciliation.   Intermarriage--the act which would have
saved Henry Harland's Jews--is the most pervasive symbol
of reconciliation in these novels.   Leslie Fiedler wrote some
time ago of intermarriage "with its ambiguous blending of the
hope of assimilation and the threat of miscegenation" as a
principal theme in early Jewish-American fiction.   The Jewish writer, he suggested, defines his hero's approach to the
gentile American world in terms of a "sexual wooing"--the
Jewish Don Juan seeking to unite with the Christian maid. [8]
And although traditionally the barriers against intermarriage
have been easier to cross when the female partner is from
the outside or "forbidden" group (e. g. , the aristocrat marrying the lower-class woman), in the Jewish-American novel
this pattern is usually reversed: the immigrant male is as-
similated--or at least offers proof of his successful assimila-
tion--by marrying the native-born (and well-born) gentile female.

Witte Arrives was widely praised by the reviewers,

some of whom compared it to The Promised Land, which had
appeared four years earlier. Others read it--or misread it
--as an affirmation of the melting pot theory, ignoring the
implications of fusing contained in the metaphor. Edward
Hale wrote in The Dial that "the book does put into literary
form one of those experiences that may teach us about America," and H. W. Boynton said in The Bookman that "the main
picture of the ardent young alien becoming in a brief score
of years a loyal and thoroughgoing American is of a sort to
stiffen our faith in the melting pot." A reviewer for The
Nation, commenting a year and a half later on Tobenkin's
next novel, The House of Conrad, reminded readers of Witte
Arrives: "It was the story of the melting pot, of a young
Russian who came to this country in boyhood and made himself at least as American as the Americans."[9] Such re-
marks illustrate the looseness with which the term melting
pot was used during the period.[10] Although the metaphor of
intermarriage here would suggest cultural fusion, it is rather
a case of Witte's becoming thoroughly Americanized. His
own Russian-Jewish past has all but been obliterated.

The House of Conrad (1918) is in much the same vein,
emphasizing the father-son split in the New World and identifying success in America with the assimilation of native values.   The novel introduces three generations of an immigrant
family. Old Gottfried Conrad has come to America intending
to build a socialist "House of Conrad" based on the thought of
Ferdinand LaSalle, but his son rejects the vague ideals of his
father and becomes a labor leader--only to be victimized by
his union.   The grandson Robert, in turn, rejects the ways
of his father and "takes root" in America as an honest, in-
dependent worker.   The American spirit comes to mean in
Tobenkin's first two novels neither capitulation to materialism nor collectivism, but individualism, integrity, a social
conscience, cheerfulness, and optimism.   Neither book is a
study of the melting pot, if by that term we mean the blending of Old and New World cultures.   The shallow and com-
placent assimilation theme of The House of Conrad provoked
Randolph Bourne--an untiring foe of narrow Americanization--
to denounce the novel sarcastically in a review: "An insistent smugness, a note of the young and earnest immigrant's
proving to the wholesome and earnest native American how
very wholesome and earnest he can be, pervades this book."[11]

The movement in both of these novels is away from the
values of the father and toward the cultural standards of the
adopted country.   Because Tobenkin, like Mary Antin, arrived

in America while quite young, he absorbed native ideals with
less psychic friction than was the case with immigrants who
arrived as adults.   Obviously, the older the immigrant when
he arrives, the more unsettling and traumatic the process of
adjustment.   Immigration to Mary Antin and Elias Tobenkin
is seen as an escape from the past, a flight into freedom.
Missing is the traditional American attitude that Old World
culture is needed to enrich America, an attitude which found
expression in the late nineteenth and early twentieth centuries
in the settlement ideals of Jane Addams and the journalistic
sketches of Lincoln Steffens and Hutchins Hapgood.

     The term "melting pot" to describe the fusing of Old
and New World cultures on American soil was coined by the
English writer Israel Zangwill, who used it as the title for
his successful play about immigrant life in New York.   The
Melting Pot premiered in Washington, D. C. , in 1908 before
an enthusiastic audience which included President Theodore
Roosevelt.   Despite (perhaps because of) the romantic ex-
cesses of the play, it became a popular favorite on the American stage.   The play's optimistic theme of America as the
land of the future, its life continually being enriched by successive waves of immigrants, served as a reassuring counter-
weight to the stern warnings of xenophobic social critics.
For Zangwill, who had been a fervent Zionist and a prolific
author of novels and stories about East London ghetto culture,
the play marked a radical shift in thinking.   As a leader in
the Jewish Territorial Organization, he had sought to establish Jewish colonies not only in Palestine but in such places
as East Africa, Portugal, and England.   In a world filled
with race hatred, the Jew could survive as a people, he had
felt, only by maintaining a separate cultural and geographical
identity.   The Melting Pot reverses this stand.   Discouraged
with colonization efforts, Zangwill came to see America as
the best hope for the Jew.   He saw, moreover, that this hope
lay neither in maintaining a separate identity in America nor
in effacing the Jewish past, but in fusing Jewish and non-
Jewish cultures in the exhilarating New World environment. [12]

     Like Tobenkin's The House of Conrad, Zangwill's work
portrays three generations of an immigrant family which represent three stages of adjustment to--or relationship with--
the New World.   The play's hero, David Quixano, has fled
from Kishinev to New York following the pogrom in which his
parents had been massacred before his eyes.   Here he lives
in a tenement flat with his uncle and his grandmother.   The
grandmother speaks only Yiddish, observes every custom

and ritual of the Old World, and remains totally oblivious to
the New.   The uncle has developed an outward conformity to
the New World although he rejects any form of cultural fusion.
He occupies the middle ground between the grandmother and
David, who ecstatically embraces the new life he has found in
America.

Dedicated to the ideal of the melting pot, David com-
poses an "American Symphony" which will passionately pro-
claim his faith in the new land.   He is never allowed to forget the past, however; he carries as a reminder a Russian
bullet in his shoulder, is tormented by the memory of the
Kishinev massacre, and is given to hysterical paranoid outbursts.   The play's conflict arises when he learns that his
fiancée, a non-Jewish Russian immigrant, is the daughter of
the Czarist officer who led the Kishinev massacre.   By the
end of the play, though, his love for Vera and his almost
mystical vision of America as a land where ancient hatreds
can be put aside, prove stronger than the anguish of the past.
Standing with Vera on the roof of the settlement house where
his American Symphony receives its premiere, he expresses
his rapture as the final curtain falls:

> There she lies, the Great Melting-pot--listen!   Can't
> you hear the roaring and the bubbling?   There gapes
> her mouth--the harbour where a thousand mammoth
> feeders come from the ends of the world to pour their
> human freight. ...   Here shall they all unite to build
> the Republic of Man and the Kingdom of God.   Ah,
> Vera, what is the glory of Rome and Jerusalem where
> all nations and races come to worship and look back,
> compared with the glory of America, where all races
> and nations come to labour and look forward! [13]

At the almost opposite extreme from David's ecstatic
and even neurotic obsession with the melting pot is the cultural pluralism and separatism represented by the boy's uncle,
Mendel Quixano, who rigorously opposes his nephew's marriage with a Christian girl even before he knows of Vera's
past, arguing that the Jews have survived in captivity and in
Diaspora only because they have sustained a separate identity
and have refused to merge with the dominant culture.   Assimilation, he insists, would spell the death of the Jewish
people.   This position, of course, ironically reverses the
nativist contention that the assimilation of East European Jews
would spell the death of the Anglo-Saxon race in America.
The Jew, Mendel Quixano asserts, must always look back in

time to the roots of his faith, to "the call of our blood through immemorial generations." He tells his nephew: "Many countries have gathered us. Holland took us when we were driven from Spain--but we did not become Dutchmen. Turkey took us when Germany oppressed us, but we did not become Turks" (p. 102).

This position had considerable support among America's immigrant Jews. Those who had fled the pogroms of Russia came to America not to be fused into a different culture but in order to be free to retain old beliefs, customs, and cultural identity. Opposition to melting pot blending came not only from Orthodox Jews and Zionists, but from many of those immigrants who had reached maturity in Eastern Europe during the eighties and who retained the vivid memory of Czarist persecution. Such elders of the immigrant community were unwilling to give up their loyalty to Old World traditions which satisfied social and emotional as well as religious needs. [14] The American Hebrew, an important organ of the older, more assimilated German Jews, voiced the feelings of at least part of the ghetto when it said of Zangwill: "Certain it is that no man who has felt so distinctly the heart-beats of the great Jewish masses can be expected to be taken seriously if he proposes Assimilation as the solution of the Jewish problem. Not for this did prophets sing and martyrs die. "[15]

Opinion among "arrived" Jews was divided. Louis Marshall, president of the American Jewish Committee and one of the most influential Jews in American life, wrote that "the melting pot, as advanced by Zangwill, produces mongrelization ... [so] our struggles should be not to create a hybrid civilization, but preserve the best elements that constitute the civilization we are still seeking, the civilization of universal brotherhood. "[16] On the other hand, President Roosevelt's Secretary of Labor and Commerce, Oscar Straus, the highest ranking Jew in government, reportedly shared with the President an enthusiasm for the play's optimistic message of fusion. [17]

The conflict generated by the play raised fundamental questions about both the desirability and the possibility of cultural fusion for Jews--and by extension other immigrant groups--in the first generation. Zangwill has his hero conquer the bitterness of the past and prove it with a vengeance by marrying the "butcher's daughter," but for some of the other writers reconciliation was not so easy to come by. In

Ezra Brudno's The Tether, a novel which appeared in 1908--
the year Zangwill's play opened--the young immigrant hero
abandons his father in search of an American education and
an American wife, but his quest ends in frustration, a failed
attempt to return to the father, madness, and ultimately
death, "strangled by his tether." David Sphardi in this melodramatic novel is a reincarnation of Henry Harland's spiritual,
artistic Jew who yearns for love in the New World. Despite
the objections of his father, who sees secular education as
worthless and leading to a loss of faith, the boy manages to
complete four years at a Latin School and enter Harvard.
He meets and falls in love with the daughter of one of Boston's wealthiest German Jewish families. The Dunkelheims
have bought their way into the best urban society and jealous-
ly guard their newly achieved status, dreading to be identified with the Russian Jews who were crowding into the ghetto.
Mrs. Dunkelheim says, "It is the idea of their [society's]
looking down upon the Jews indiscriminately that is galling;
they don't seem to make any distinction between some poor
peddler in the slums and a prominent citizen--all Jews look
alike to them. "[18]

Brudno here is dealing with a subject which recurs ob-
sessively in Jewish immigrant fiction--the conflict between
"uptown" German Jews and "downtown" Russian Jews. We
have seen this conflict in fiction written by native-born observers of the ghetto, particularly in the labor novel--where
the German Jew is usually cast as the exploiting capitalist or
"sweater" figure. In novels written by Russian-Jewish immigrants the conflict is even more sharply delineated and leads
frequently to the ghetto hero's characteristic recoil from his
assimilationist position. Snubbed by Cora Dunkelheim, David
draws back to his father. Before long, though, he falls in
love with a gentile girl, Mildred Dalton. The pair run away
(her parents oppose the marriage as much as David's father
does), but faced with social barriers they cannot surmount,
they separate. The son, filled with guilt, self-reproach and
frustration, returns too late to his father: the brokenhearted
old man suffers a stroke and dies. David recites the memo-
rial prayer, joins the Zionist movement in atonement and
finally goes completely mad, unable to reconcile what he describes in his diary as "the misfortunes of possessing an
oriental heart with an occidental brain." David, in other
words, can intellectualize (and rhapsodize) about cultural fusion and the inconsequence of ethnic differences but emotion-
ally he is unable--and perhaps unwilling as well--to extricate
himself from the past. This conflict between fusion and

separation, future and past, drags him down.   No reconciliation between Old and New World is achieved.

Brudno's own life followed a quite different course.
He was born in Lithuania, emigrated as a boy, attended Yale
Law School, and practiced law in Cleveland, eventually be-
coming an assistant district attorney.   In an earlier work,
The Fugitive (1904), he presented a more typical and optimis-
tic, if not less melodramatic, fictional account of the Russian-
Jewish immigrant.   Much of this novel takes place in the Old
World--in a Polish shtetl (or village), in Vilna, and in Kiev.
Israel Rusakoff, the son of an Orthodox Jew falsely convicted
of the ritual slaughter of a Christian child, is adopted by a
Russian landowner who it later turns out--in one of the ironic
coincidences which plague this fiction--is the repentant betrayer of the boy's father.   When, though, Israel falls in love
with the landowner's daughter, Katia, he is expelled from his
comfortable quarters.   He wanders Russia in search of a
home and roots and becomes a student in a famous Yeshiva
where orthodoxy is practiced in its harshest and most medieval form.   The school is run by the fanatical Rabbi Brill and
his harridan wife, both of whom are constantly spying on the
students to make sure they are not being exposed to Haskala,
the broad secularized Hebrew culture movement spreading
through East Europe.

Israel comes eventually to America, fleeing both
Christian persecution and medieval Jewish orthodoxy, but in
the ghetto of New York's Lower East Side he finds still more
oppression, and his hope for a new life rapidly gives way to
despair.   To indicate the debasement of the European Jew in
the New World ghetto, Brudno uses the device--common in the
immigrant novel--of allowing characters from the protagonist's
Old World past to reappear in the New in different guises:
prominent Russian Jews, forced to flee following the 1881 assassination of the Czar, turn up as sweatshop workers; Talmudic scholars become Yankee "dandies" or "allrightniks,"
grotesque parodies of Americanization.   The usual metamor-
phosis places the Jew behind the sewing machine, tyrannized
by the German-Jewish sweater.   Mark Fetter, Brudno's villain figure, owns the sweatshop where Israel works, and when
the boy goes to the rabbi Dr. Fuchs, another German-Jew, to
plead for the exploited workers, he is rudely turned away.

Fuchs, the wealthy assimilated reform rabbi, and
Brill, the Old World orthodox rabbi, represent opposite ex-
tremes of Judaism, equally removed from the humanity and

compassion Israel searches for at the heart of his religion.
One is given over wholly to the materialism and secularism
of the New World, the other to the dogmatism and medieval-
ism of the Old World. To reconcile Old World and New,
Russian and German, Jew and Christian, becomes the youth's
mission. After a series of complications and twists, and a
deathbed reconciliation with his father's Old World betrayer
Bialnik (which adds still to the already overwrought plot)
Israel marries Katia, Bialnik's daughter, who with her father
has fled Russia. The marriage which has been forbidden in
the Old World is sanctioned in the New. As in Zangwill's
play, the union of the Jewish hero with his betrayer's daughter becomes a symbol of melting pot reconciliation and New
World rebirth. Beyond the degradation to which the immigrant is so often subjected in America looms the possibility
--absent in the Old World--of a coming together of the two
worlds.

        The fusion of Old and New World cultures is a recur-
rent theme in these novels. Edward Steiner's The Mediator
(1907) is another clear example. Steiner, like Tobenkin and
Brudno, was a Jewish immigrant (although he became a convert to Christianity) who attained considerable professional
success in America. A professor of sociology and theology
at Grinnell College in Iowa, he authored sociological studies
of immigration (including On the Trail of the Immigrant,
1906, and The Immigrant Tide, 1909), a collection of stories
about immigrants (The Broken Wall, 1911), a biography (Tolstoy the Man, 1905), and an autobiography (From Alien to
Citizen, 1914).

        The Mediator is strikingly similar in content to Brud-
no's The Fugitive. Both detail the Old World childhoods of
their protagonists, both present the flight to the New World
as a flight from forms of oppression imposed by both rigid
orthodox Judaism and Russian Christianity, both document the
degradation of ghetto sweatshop labor, and both end with the
hero's marriage to a Christian girl and his conversion to a
vague form of Christian socialism. Christ in both books is
the redeemer and unifier of Christian and Jew. The apocalyptic messages delivered by the two heroes at the end of the
novels can be compared. Brudno's "fugitive":

        Side by side the life of the Crucified and the life of
        my race among nations and the life of my father and
        my own strange life--in a vision they all presented
        themselves before me. And this vision, this revela-

tion, showed me the symbolism of my race, the symbolism of the Christ.   It showed me that the Crucified
was the symbol of His people as my father was of his
generation and I am of mine.   It showed me that not
the Pilgrims, not the Crusaders--none but the fugitive
race are the eternal bearers of the cross. [19]

Steiner's "mediator":

Some spot there must be, in that great desert of the
East Side, which his genius and his passion might re-
create an oasis that should prove a unifying centre for
Jew and Gentile--where, in short, a new race might
be born, which should know nothing of the ancient hate
and the ancient wrongs. [20]

Steiner's hero, Samuel Cohen, is, like Brudno's, a
Jewish boy raised among gentiles.   He is brought up by a
Catholic nurse and is so awed by the beauty and pomp of Ca-
tholicism that he enters a monastery to study for the priest-
hood.   When, several years later, he is witness to a bloody
pogrom committed in the name of Russian Christianity, he
abandons his vocation and sets out for America in search of
a new beginning.   Neither the rigid orthodoxy of his father
nor the hypocrisy of the church are paths he can accept.

Having been raised in a monastery and having fled with
the traumatic recognition of the gulf between Christian teaching and Christian practice, he becomes an evangelist on the
Lower East Side, proclaiming the true spirit of Christ to Jew
and gentile.   He is aided by the patrician philanthropist Mr.
Bruce, but the mission he sets for himself is a broader one
than the simple conversion advocated by Bruce.   The conflict
between the two men, which dominates the later chapters of
the novel, centers on the distinction between the rival inter-
pretations of Americanization, that is, one-sided assimilation
with the dominant population group as against the more liberal melting pot ideal.   Bruce seeks to Americanize the Jewish
immigrant by converting him to Christianity; Samuel Cohen
seeks to fuse the two faiths, preserving the highest ideals of
both.   Bruce resembles--and may in part have been modeled
after--missionary reformer Josiah Strong, who advocated
throughout his career Americanizing the immigrant by convert-
int him to Christianity.   While Strong warned again and again
of the perils of unrestricted immigration, his jingoistic faith
in America's divine mission to spread Anglo-Saxon Protestant-
ism to the "inferior races" of the world led him to advocate
even intermarriage.

Samuel Cohen marries Bruce's daughter at the novel's end, an act which signals his full entrance into American life, establishes his credentials as a cultural mediator, and proclaims the possibilities for New World regeneration. As in Witte Arrives, The Melting Pot, and The Fugitive, the marriage which has been forbidden in the Old World is sanctioned in the New. The union of the Jewish male with the gentile female--either an Anglo-Saxon aristocrat (Tobenkin and Steiner) or the daughter of the Old World betrayer (Zangwill and Brudno)--provides the symbolism for the reconciliation of Old and New World. Marriage to a Christian American is both the badge signifying the immigrant's successful "arrival" and the broader symbol of the possibilities for cultural fusion in America.

Lawrence Sterner's The Un-Christian Jew (1917) deals with another self-styled mediator, the rabbi Cordova, who becomes so disgusted with the exploitation of ghetto Jews by his own "uptown" parishioners--especially by the singularly obnoxious Simon Sachs, proprietor of Cosmopolitan Bargain Stores--he leaves the pulpit to establish a utopian community. "Quality Town" rejects both Judaism and institutional Christianity in favor of what the rabbi considers are the true teachings of Christ, which he is convinced will tie all men together. The plot becomes ridiculously and gratuitously bizarre when Sachs's daughter is abducted and spirited off to Russia to be sweated to death by one Tom Olson, whose sister met a similar fate in Sachs's sweatshop.

The most interesting response to the self-styled mediators of Ezra Brudno, Edward Steiner and Lawrence Sterner came in another novel about a rabbi who turns mediator written in 1917, the year of Sterner's book. In The Chosen People, Sidney Nyburg, a Baltimore lawyer and grandson of a Dutch Jewish immigrant, tells the story of Philip Graetz, rabbi of an affluent Baltimore synagogue, who conceives his divinely appointed mission to be the mediator between the Americanized, "uptown" German Jews of his own congregation and the recently-arrived "downtown" Russian Jews of the city's ghetto.

Nyburg's novel deals with the same clash between cultures in America as do the other immigrant novels, but there are some important differences. First, the pattern of the immigrant youth rebelling against his past in search of an American identity is reversed; here the protagonist is a successful second generation German Jew who rebels against his

assimilationist position in search of deeper roots.   Second,
the two worlds the hero tries to "mediate" are not those of
Jew and Christian but of German and Russian Jews in urban
America.   The clash between uptown and downtown is pervasive in the immigrant novel genre but in no other book is it
treated so relentlessly.   Third, and most important, the self-
styled mediator in this novel fails dismally in his mission.
Not only is Rabbi Graetz singularly unfit for his mission, but
the task itself is shown to be beyond the possibility of attainment by any single man.   What the world needs, Graetz
comes to learn in this apprenticeship novel, is not prophets
with their abstract pleas for justice and brotherhood ringing
in the wilderness but shrewd, pragmatic bargainers--tough-
minded realists, who, if they can not make the uptown Jew
love the downtown Jew, can at least keep the one from exploiting the labor of the other.

Graetz's teacher and foil in the novel is a tough, cynical labor attorney, David Gordon.   Unlike Graetz, a German
Jew who has come to Baltimore fresh from a midwestern
seminary, Gordon is a product of Baltimore's ghetto and a
man who has no religious ties or visions of a millenium.
Shrewd and experienced, he knows how to exploit the selfish
interests of the Jewish industrialists in Graetz's congregation
for the benefit of the Russian-Jewish workmen.   In the strike
which serves as the focus for the struggle between uptown
and downtown, Gordon is able to achieve a settlement favorable to the workers by outmaneuvering the industrialist Max
Hirsch, who has hired Gordon to stir up labor discontent
among the workers of a rival clothing firm, owned by Clarence Kaufman, another member of Graetz's congregation.   By
serving the devil, Gordon is able to do more for the ghetto
Jews than all of the rabbi's sermons.   The workmen make
progress in their struggle for decent wages and working conditions not because Graetz has convinced his congregation of
its selfishness, but because Gordon has marshaled an army
of workers willing to challenge the Jewish plutocracy.

Through his congregation Philip Graetz is ideologically
linked with the affluent uptown Jews, the employing class.
He is engaged to Ruth Frank, niece of Clarence Kaufman.
His spiritual conflict and his first recognition of the gulf which
separates his own congregation from the ghetto comes early
in the novel when he is called in the middle of the night to
Johns Hopkins Hospital to minister to a ghetto Jew who had
been struck by a car and who has requested a rabbi.   Graetz
rushes to the dying man only to find that he is unable to

understand a word of the man's Yiddish message. And the
old man, recognizing the rabbi's ignorance, hurls the defiant
"goy" at him, indicating that he thinks him no Jew at all.
The man dies before Graetz can summon an interpreter.
This very effective scene establishes the novel's central theme
of the failure in communication between uptown and downtown,
German and Russian, son and father. Graetz for the first
time recognizes the cultural distance between the two worlds.
He confesses to Gordon his sense of helplessness, and the
lawyer responds: "It wasn't only the Yiddish! You and the
Russian never could have understood one another, anyhow."[21]
Graetz seeks to make up for his failure, but everywhere he
turns he faces further scorn and criticism. He preaches a
sermon on the obligation of uptown to downtown Jew, incorpo-
rating his own hospital failure into the sermon, but his congregation is annoyed; he is making himself ridiculous and going beyond "good taste." Graetz then hires a Russian Jewish
student to teach him Yiddish and again finds himself rebuked.
He naively orders refreshments for his tutor and himself,
but the boy will not touch the non-Kosher food. Again the
rabbi, the traditional teacher, is put in the position of dis-
playing his ignorance in front of another Jew.

Later in the novel Gordon summarizes, in response to
Graetz's plea for help, the differences between the two worlds
of American Jews, differences Graetz's experiences have been
leading him to discover for himself:

> Your congregation likes to hear you talk about human
> brotherhood; the merest semblance to the real thing
> would horrify the women and enrage the men. The
> downtown Jews are Russian. The up-town Jews are
> American by birth, and German by descent. The one
> group is above the poverty line--employers mostly.
> The other group is on the border or below it, and
> they're employees. You and your crowd give some
> sort of an allegiance to a denatured Judaism. I and
> mine, so far as we have any religion left, are rigidly
> orthodox. So there you have a whole catalogue of
> reasons for hate. Your group has had the best of it
> so far,--easy lives, easy faith, easy education and an
> easy superiority.... They think our uncouth, immi-
> grant ways do the Jews in general, and particularly
> their comfortable selves, no good among the Christians.
> And now you come with bland words asking the upper
> dog to release his grip! If you try to force him, he'll
> turn around and bite you [p. 103].

To Gordon, the two worlds of Jews cannot be kept from fighting so long as they occupy opposite poles in a capitalistic, individualistic society. Gordon's own solution is Zionism, which he feels will bind all Jews together in the building of their own society. Like the cultural pluralists, Gordon believes that Jews can stay alive only by defining their deepest selves outside the value system of America. Whether they remain in America or establish colonies elsewhere, they must preserve their distinct cultural identity. At the opposite extreme are the uptown Jews of Graetz's congregation, who embrace the spirit of Americanization zealously and are embarrassed by the persistence of Old World traits in the Russian Jews. Graetz, standing in the middle, represents the futile attempt of a self-styled mediator to reconcile the enormous differences.

The conflict can be seen from another perspective--that of the political and economic polarization of the city. Graetz, like Howells' Basil March, finds himself caught in the middle of an economic struggle between the extreme ideologies of ruthless, materialistic individualism, represented by Clarence Kaufman, and radical and militant collectivism, represented by Israel Ginzburg, the fiery strike leader. Ginzburg, like Howells' Berthold Lindau (A Hazard of New Fortunes) and Harris' Louis Lingg (The Bomb), is persecuted for his opinions rather than his acts in another of the novelistic echoes of the Haymarket affair. And while Graetz wrestled ethically with the issues ("How could these men gain freedom without the right to organize,--yet what right had they to prohibit other men to fill their places in peace..."), Gordon was fighting. What Graetz learns through all his fumblings and uncertainties is that Gordon too had been doing God's work, and more effectively. Like Graetz, Gordon was on the payroll of the devil, but unlike the rabbi, he was able to use his position to better the workers' conditions.

The Chosen People was a needed antidote to the facile affirmations of Americanization and the melting pot that were offered by a host of immigrant and native-born novelists. Labor warfare between uptown German and downtown Russian Jews in Baltimore served Nyburg well as a vehicle for examining the broader conflict between the Old World and the New in urban America in the second decade of the twentieth century. Not a first-generation American, Nyburg was able to do what immigrant writers like Elias Tobenkin, Ezra Brudno, and Edward Steiner were unable to: portray realistically and with full regard for its complexities and ambiguities the relationship between one generation of immigrants and another,

between uptown and downtown, capital and labor, German and
Russian, American and European.   Only Cahan's The Rise of
David Levinsky, among pre-World War I fiction, surpasses
Nyburg's novel as a realistic study of the clash between im-
migrant generations and cultures in urban America.

Tobenkin, Brudno, and Steiner--immigrants who arrived as boys, matured outside the ghetto, and achieved material seccess in America--believed in the American dream
as fervently as did Jacob Riis and Mary Antin.   And while
they were critical of the labor conditions to which the new
immigrants were subjected in the American city, they allowed
their heroes to escape the ghetto only slightly scarred.   Immigrant fiction, like immigrant autobiography, has the advantage over historical studies of permitting us to view the immigrant experience from the immigrant's own eyes.   Yet in
most of the fiction the vision is distorted by the immigrant
writer's desire to celebrate and justify the assimilation process and by the conventional responses to immigration absorbed on the way to their own assimilation.   Their very success as transplants caused their failure as novelists.   The
heroes who parade through these novels are little more than
spokesmen for the Americanization and melting pot credos of
their authors.   As in some--but not all--of the immigrant
labor novels the message gets in the way of the fiction, statement overshadows action.   The complex issues of cultural,
generational and economic conflict were rarely faced head-on
in the urban immigrant novel of the first generation.   The
achievements of Nyburg's The Chosen People and Cahan's The
Rise of David Levinsky are even more remarkable considered
in this context.   These two novels, published within months
of each other, were frequently paired in reviewers' columns.
Their thematic parallels did not go unnoticed.

VII

SUCCESS AS FAILURE:
ABRAHAM CAHAN'S FICTION

In 1898, when Cahan was working for Lincoln Steffens
on the Commercial Advertiser, he wrote a sketch for that
newspaper which autobiographically contrasted a young man's
mental image of America before he arrived and the actualities he found upon arriving.   The immigrant is reminded of
the words of a German poet: America is a land where "the
birds had no song, the flowers no fragrance, and the men no
hearts."[1]   Nineteen years later in The Rise of David Levinsky, one of the characters, Tevkin, an Old World poet who
has turned real-estate broker in the New World, recites,
when asked by Levinsky why he no longer writes poetry, a
passage from one of his works, expressing the same sense
of spiritual emptiness in the New World: "Since the destruction of the Temple instrumental music has been forbidden in
the synagogue.   The children of Israel are in mourning.   Silent is their harp.   So is mine.   I am in exile.   I am in a
strange land.   My harp is silent."[2]

Throughout Cahan's novels and stories of Jewish immigrant life in New York City, the Diaspora, or dispersion,
a central and definitive historical fact in the Jewish experience, dominates the consciousness of the immigrant protagonists.   His heroes are painfully aware of their exile, and
whatever outer success they achieve in America, they are
never permitted to forget what they have lost.   This is Cahan's reply to the novels of acculturation with their glib, optimistic generalizations about cultural reconciliation and fusion.
Under the pressure of New World experience, Old World
values totter but never collapse entirely, for his protagonists
are both unable and unwilling to extricate themselves from
the grip of the past.   Yearning for the past becomes one of
the inescapable conditions--and indeed, positive forces--in
their lives.   "The gloomiest past is dearer than the brightest
present," Levinsky confesses (p. 526).   And even Jake

Podkovnik, Cahan's "Yekl," the flashy "Yankee" and most
vulgar of Cahan's Americanizers, sees his Old World past as
"a charming tale, which he was neither willing to banish
from his memory nor reconcile with the actualities of his
American present" (Yekl, p. 54). As Cahan's heroes outward-
ly assimilate into American life, they become increasingly
alienated from themselves. The outer self comes into conflict with an inner self which will not be stilled.

The result is loneliness, ennui, and guilt. In the no-
man's land in which Cahan's heroes reside, there are no enduring loves or happy marriages. There are no unions with
native-born aristocratic gentiles to symbolize melting pot fusion as we have had in the immigrant novels of Elias Tobenkin, Ezra Brudno, and Edward Steiner. Nor are marriages
or friendships from the Old World permitted to continue in
the New. Yekl divorces his Russian wife for the perfumed,
gaudy Mamie Fein, knowing too late that from the divorce
"he had emerged ... the victim of an ignominious defeat."
David Levinsky, despite his great wealth, is rejected by several women and remains single. The widowed Asriel Stroom
in "The Imported Bridegroom" (1898) is denied the old-age
dream of seeing his daughter married to a pious Talmudic
scholar. In Cahan's many other stories which deal with love
in the ghetto, only one, "A Ghetto Wedding," offers the prospect of a permanent, fulfilling liaison.

Contacts with the past are always unnerving for Cahan's
heroes. Yekl sends to Russia for his family but is embarrassed by his wife's appearance at Ellis Island and forces her
to remove the traditional wig which identifies her as a "greenhorn." Levinsky is always uncomfortable in the presence of
Old World figures. Throughout the book when faces from the
past reappear, he is unable to contend with his mixed feelings
of hostility and compassion. The faces remind him of all
that he has striven to eliminate from his mind--his near star-
vation, the brutal death of his mother at the hands of an anti-
Semitic mob, the bitter Czarist oppression--and yet he cannot
help identifying with these people and yearns for their company.

Fleeing from the past while simultaneously yearning
for it is the hopeless condition of all Cahan's heroes. They
can neither escape nor relive what has gone before. "You
can't go home again" is perhaps a truism, but in Cahan's fiction it is also true that one never really leaves home. Hunger, sexual deprivation, grief, and intense loneliness are the

baggage they carry to America and are unwilling to discard.
So they yearn for what they can not have, and the yearning
constitutes their deepest and truest selves.

The body of Cahan's fiction is small. After Yekl
(1896) came "The Imported Bridegroom" (1898), which was
bound with four of Cahan's earlier stories in a single volume;
several additional stories published between 1897 and 1902
when he was on the staff of the Commercial Advertiser; The
White Terror and the Red (1905), a novel about revolutionary
Russia; and finally The Rise of David Levinsky (1917), which
appeared earlier in serial form. Although he lived until
1951, he published no fiction in English after 1917. Imaginative literature always played a subordinate role in his active
career as labor organizer, socialist leader, teacher, translator, and editor--a career capped by his half-century long
editorship of the Forward.

The Forward had its genesis in 1897 when Cahan and
some of his East Side socialist allies--Morris Winchevsky
and Louis Miller among them--separated from the Socialist
Labor Party, then entering the orbit of the militant Daniel
DeLeon faction, and began publishing the daily in opposition
to the DeLeonist organ Abend Blatt. [3] A few months later,
however, Cahan, restless and dissatisfied, resigned in favor
of free-lance journalism. He was selling articles to the Sun,
the Evening Post, and the Commercial Advertiser when he
met Lincoln Steffens, who was then on the Evening Post staff.
The relationship was to be as opportune for Cahan as that
with Howells. Impressed with Cahan's sketches of the ghetto,
Steffens asked him to come along with him as a reporter
when he became the Advertiser's city editor. Steffens himself had been brought to the Advertiser by its new chief editor Henry J. Wright, who tried to steer the moribund newspaper away from its traditional anchorage in business news
and toward an involvement with contemporary social life. He
wanted a kind of "daily magazine" which would appeal to so-
phistocated, urban readers, avoiding both the sensationalism
of Hearst's Journal and Pulitzer's World and the low-key reporting of the Evening Post. Steffens, free to pick his staff,
sought writers like Cahan, young enough and enthusiastic
enough to find drama in the daily events of the city. Cahan's
first assignment--as Steffens' had been years earlier--was as
police reporter, working at the Mulberry Street headquarters.
Here he met Jacob Riis who, despite his aversion to Cahan's
socialism, taught him something about American-style journalism, particularly the need to "nose out" the news. [4]

Cahan remained on the Advertiser for five years, until 1902, when he left to take up again the editorship of the Forward. The Advertiser experience was invaluable for him. It enabled him to observe American life on a variety of levels. He interviewed President McKinley, William Cody, millionaire Russell Sage, Bishop Henry Cadman Potter (head of New York's Episcopal Church), the Russian anarchist Peter Kropotkin, Samuel Gompers, Theodore Roosevelt, "Boss" Richard Croker, and a number of other men in the national spotlight. Perhaps more important for Cahan's literary and journalistic development, he came into close personal contact with several bright, young writers, mostly Harvard graduates, whom Steffens had attracted to his staff. And as he learned from them about American life, they learned from him about ghetto life. Among Cahan's closest friends on the staff was Hutchins Hapgood, whom he introduced to the ghetto. "Hutch" was fascinated with the variety of life on the Lower East Side and soon began to turn out the sketches which he incorporated in The Spirit of the Ghetto in 1902. Through Hapgood's influence the Advertiser printed in translation the Yiddish poetry of Morris Rosenfeld. Hutch and his brother Norman, the Advertiser's drama editor, championed the East Side theater and wrote numerous articles on the Yiddish stage.

Writing years later in Types from City Streets, Hutchins Hapgood recalled the Advertiser experience. In contrast to other newspapers which sought "the unusual and the striking," and which featured events "interesting for the exceptional rather than for their typical character," the Advertiser, he noted, had the knack of "making the commonplace interesting." Steffens, he recalled, told his staff to write up what they saw and gave them a free hand to do it in their own manner, providing only that they told the truth. 5 Hapgood paid a very special tribute to Cahan, which suggests the depths of his respect for the immigrant writer, though he does not mention him by name:

> One of the reporters was a man in an extraordinary situation and of uncommon gifts. He was a Russian Jew, and had been an active socialist in Russia and this country, to which he fled for freedom's sake. There he learned the English language so idiomatically and well that he had written books and good ones in the language. He had the high ideals characteristic of his branch of the Jewish race; and, in addition, the passion, simplicity, and vehemence of the followers of Tolstoy in art and ethics. He formed a striking con-

trast to the young Harvard men; he gave them his point of view, and absorbed theirs; he taught them to understand something of the Great East Side of New York, of its picturesque human characters and customs [pp. 109-110].

Cahan came away from the Advertiser in 1902 with a clearer understanding of the sales technique requisite to mass media success. He was able to broaden the appeal of the foundering Forward by loosening up its structure and language and by including popular fiction and a variety of regular features like the "Bintel Brief" (Bundle of Letters) in place of theoretical socialist tracts. The newspaper even contained a section which printed photos of East Side husbands who had deserted their families along with descriptions of the situations of the abandoned families. Readers were requested to send in any information they had pertaining to the whereabouts of the wayward husbands. This and the "Bintel Brief" column were, of course, the daily's most popular features. Cahan brought more and more American life to the paper, interpreting from a mildly socialistic but non-dogmatic point of view American cultural, political, and social life. Howells' fiction was translated frequently, and Upton Sinclair's The Jungle appeared on its pages. The Forward actively supported the ghetto strikes, and its influence on ghetto readers more than once turned the tide for the unions. With Cahan as editor the Forward became America's largest-selling Yiddish daily.

While Cahan was reporting for the Advertiser, he was also writing articles and stories for other journals. In July 1898 he contributed an article to Atlantic Monthly arguing forcefully against the nativist position that the new Jewish immigrants were lowering American wage standards, importing subversive ideas, and swelling urban crime and disease rates. He pointed statistically to the relatively low crime and death rates among East Side Jews despite the fact that their tenement neighborhoods were as impoverished as those of other immigrant groups. He stressed the Jewish craving for education and personal betterment, citing the enrollment figures of the City College of New York as an example, and equated the active union participation of the East Side Jews with their desire for better living conditions and their willingness to fight for them. If the Jew becomes a socialist, he maintained, it is because conditions in America have made him one. The Jew's idealism, rooted in Scripture and in his piety, and the conditions under which he has been forced to live and work, have turned him into an active reformer.

A vigorous defense of the Russian Jew in America,
the article was a timely counterstatement in one of America's
leading journals to the mounting barrage of broadsides fired
from the Boston-based Immigration Restriction League. If,
however, we turn to the short fiction Cahan was writing at
the same time, we get a less idealistic picture of the immigrant Jew in America. As we have seen in the case of Jacob
Riis, journalism does not translate so easily into fiction.
Cahan was no propagandist in his fiction. His concern was
with the loneliness and alienation of the immigrant. The
ever-present character in the stories of these years is a man,
who, like Yekl, has drifted steadily and unconsciously away
from the beliefs and values of his youth until, awakening to
the bitterness of an empty existence, he seeks frantically and
too late to recapture what he has lost.

"The Imported Bridegroom" (1898), for instance, deals
with the aging Asriel Stroom, who has to stand by helplessly
while his dream of recapturing the past in the form of an Old
World bridegroom for his daughter is shattered. Stroom has
been in America for thirty-five years during which time he
has buried a wife, raised a daughter, and amassed a considerable sum of money. As the immigrant Jew who has attained the American dream of material success only to realize the hollowness of his achievement, Stroom is a prototype
of the kind of hero Cahan was to develop with much more
finesse and depth in David Levinsky. Contemplating his advancing age and the meaning of his life, Stroom feels a need
to rekindle his faith and so decides to visit his native Polish
village of Pravly. His triumphant return, however, is marred
by his having to share the spotlight with Reb Lippe, a successful local merchant who has just contracted the engagement
of his daughter to the town's young Talmud prodigy. Stroom
vows to have the bridegroom for his own daughter. How better, he reasons, can one assure himself a place in the world
to come than by taking on the support of a Godly scholar?
Does not the Talmud say, "He who supports a scholar of the
Law is like one who offers sacrifice"? And so Stroom, with
his wounded vanity and his dread of the unknown, decides to
invest in spiritual goods as all his life in America he has in-
vested in material goods. The American entrepreneur will
bargain for his real estate in the next world. He bids for
the bridegroom in front of the amazed townspeople, and, victory achieved (the young man is won over by the offer and
the prospect of going to America), he consoles Reb Lippe,
the loser: "You are going to stay here, so you can get another prodigy. But one cannot get such goods in America."[7]

Stroom, seeking his past in the Old World, brings back a piece of that world with him, but the goods are not exactly what his Americanized daughter, Flora, had in mind for a husband. The fifteen-thousand-dollar bridegroom with his earlocks, his Hebrew library, and his encyclopedic knowledge of the Talmud is not in keeping with her dream of an uptown doctor, a "refined American gentleman."

The irony of the story arises when the imported Talmudist, Shaya, like his benefactor years earlier, becomes in America a new man. He begins to read "gentile books" in the Astor Library, and Flora, encouraged by his new-found fascination for secular knowledge, conspires to turn him into the doctor of her dreams. This is the one contingency Stroom had not figured on: Shaya, who had been too Jewish for the daughter, becomes too "goyish" for the father. His discovery of America has led him away from his faith just as Stroom's had. The prodigy and the prodigal are alienated from each other because, ironically, they have followed the same path in the New World. Stroom thought he had found in Shaya his link to the past. Having forgotten most of his own Hebrew training, he now felt that the Hebrew world was one "in which he was now not without a voice." But you cannot transplant a piece of the Old World to the soil of the New, Stroom learns, and expect it to thrive as if in its original soil.

Nor can you mold a man into your own image of the ideal New World type. Instead of inhabiting "a world of physical and intellectual elegance into which she had dreamed to be introduced by marriage to a doctor," Flora finds herself on her wedding day in a smoke-filled tenement listening to her husband and a dozen other men, mostly immigrants, discussing August Comte's positivism. The Talmudist has not turned to medicine after all, but to philosophy. Once he has been led from orthodoxy, Shaya finds the step to secular philosophy a small one. This is the final irony. Both father and daughter have been denied their dreams. The bridegroom who had been nothing but a commodity to both of them turns out to be a man with some ideas of his own.

"The Imported Bridegroom" appeared in a volume with Cahan's four previously published English language stories. All of them converge on the same theme. To be the Jewish husband and father is what all the protagonists want, but conditions in America, their own shortcomings and shortsightedness, and the sheer perversity of fate conspire to make

things turn out otherwise.   In "A Providential Match," the
story which first attracted Howells to Cahan when it appeared
(translated from Arbeiter Zeitung) in Short Stories magazine
in 1895, he deals with the coarse "Yankee" type--the vulgar,
materialistic immigrant who would soon reappear as Yekl.
Rouvke Arbel as a boy had been a servant for a wealthy dis-
tiller in Kropovitz while secretly longing for his employer's
daughter.   After a few years in America he earns enough as
a furniture peddler to consider marriage, and hearing that
his old employer has become destitute, he contracts across
the ocean for the hand of the daughter.   It is to be a "providential match" which will benefit both men, and the daughter
reluctantly agrees.   But on board ship she meets her "providential match," a Russian student, and the perplexed Rouvke,
standing on the dock beside his hired carriage can think of
nothing to do but shout for the police as he watches the couple disappear in the crowd.

      Heyman, a sewing machine operator in "A Sweatshop
Romance" (also from Short Stories), is another of Cahan's
losers in love.   Fearing the loss of his job, he sits silently
while Beile, his fiancée, defies the unjust and imperious command of the boss.   Beile is fired on the spot and when Heyman summons up enough courage to visit her two weeks later,
he finds she is about to be married.   Cowardice has cost him
his love.   "Circumstances," the best of the shorter pieces in
the collection, also deals with a man beaten down by the circumstances of his sweatshop existence to the point that he
loses the woman he loves.   Boris Lurie, though, is a far
more commanding figure than either the crude "Yankee"
Rouvke Arbel or the cowardly Heyman.   Lurie had been a
fiery and idealistic law student in Russia.   Prevented from
practicing law by administrative anti-Semitism, however, he
emigrated to America with his wife.   Over the years the daily
drudgery of working in a button factory has turned him increasingly more sullen, indifferent, and unkempt until he
loses his wife's love to another man.   Ironically, it is Boris'
frantic effort to recapture something of his former self that
leads to the estrangement.   His ambition becomes his down-
fall as is so often the case with Cahan's heroes.   Boris convinces his wife to take in a boarder so that he may save
enough money to return to school and become a teacher.   Tanya, who to this point has idealized their life together and
wants no boarder to intrude on their privacy, finds in the immaculate and kindly boarder, Dalsky, the attention that had
gone out of her marriage.   Staring at the scar above the eye-
brow of her sleeping husband, she likens herself to Anna

Karenina, who "after having fallen under Vronsky's charm, is
met by her husband upon his return from St. Petersburg,
where the first thing that strikes her about him is the un-
couthness of his ears." Dalsky, anything but a Vronsky,
hastily exits from the flat when he realizes that Tanya is
drawn to him, but the damage has been done. Tanya decides
to leave her husband. And Boris, a shadow of the man she
married, crushed under the weight of New World circumstances and denied his opportunity to rebound, stands in an
empty flat at the story's end weeping for his lost Tanychka.
"Circumstances" was originally published in Cosmopolitan
(April 1897) and was the first story to follow Yekl, to which
it bears a similarity.

     "A Ghetto Wedding," reprinted from Atlantic (February
1898), is the final story in the collection and the only one in
which a man and woman end up together. Here too, though,
their dreams and the reality they face lie far apart. Goldie
and Nathan plan to marry, but unable to save enough money
for both a wedding and household furnishings, they decide to
spend all of their savings on a splendid wedding and count on
gifts to furnish their flat. But the ghetto is caught up in an
economic depression, and only twenty of the one hundred in-
vited guests show up. Heartbroken at first, the couple soon
awaken to the fact that after all they are still husband and
wife, and they leave the hall confidently to walk home to their
empty flat, "filled with the blissful sense of oneness, the like
of which they had never tasted before." The failure of their
scheme, the empty hall, the uneaten food, the deserted dance
floor, had been "too insignificant to engage their attention--
paltry matters alien to their new life, remote from the en-
chanted world in which they now dwelt."

     The irony, comic and often bitter, which runs through
these stories underscores Cahan's central concern with the
instability of the life of the immigrant Jew in America. Nathan and Goldie, leaving the empty wedding hall with the sense
of "there being only themselves in the universe" will presumably find stability in their life together. But they are exceptions to Cahan's obsessive portrayal of the failure of love in
the ghetto, a failure symptomatic of the immigrant failure to
fuse inner and outer identity, Old and New World selves.
Frequently, the object of love for Cahan's protagonists is not
a particular woman but a value or ideal associated in their
imagination with the woman. If they seek to escape their Old
World identity, they attach their desire to a woman who represents the values of the New World (Yekl abandons his wife for

the coarsely-Americanized Mamie Fein). If they achieve outward success in America, they find themselves lonely and
yearn for women who remind them of the Old World (Rouvke
Arbel, the rising American merchant, turns his thoughts back
to the Russian girl of his youth).

In the stories which followed the publication of The
Imported Bridegroom and Other Stories of the New York Ghetto Cahan expanded his range of subjects. He wrote stories
about the relationship between Jews and gentiles and even
wrote three stories concerned wholly with non-Jewish immigrants. It is as though Cahan were heeding, to some degree
at least, the words of Howells, who in his review of The Imported Bridegroom, asked whether the author, now that he
has mastered Jewish ghetto material, "will pass beyond his
present environment out into the larger American world."[8]
The stories which deal with the relationship between Jews and
gentiles focus usually on a Jew's crisis in faith as he confronts a non-Jewish world. In "The Apostate of Chego-Chegg"
(Century, November 1899), the story which immediately followed "The Imported Bridegroom," a Jewish immigrant woman married to a gentile Polish farmer suffers remorse for
her apostasy and agrees to run off with a Jewish man--al-
though a professed athiest--to London. At the last moment,
however, she recognizes her marital obligation and returns
to her husband, ironically becoming for Cahan more the Jew
by the recognition of familial ties than by escaping into a
nominal Judaism. Cahan reinforces the irony by making
Michalina's Jewish suitor a man who has gone from fanatical
orthodoxy to atheism. When we first see "Rabbi Nehemiah,"
he wears a long beard and symbolizes to Michalina the heritage she has abandoned. Later in the story--when he convinces her to run off with him--he is clean-shaven and claims
to have lost all faith, though in her eyes he remains a Jew
and a link with her past. Nehemiah, the intellectual who
has been transformed from rigid orthodoxy to atheism in the
New World, is a throwback to Shaya, the "imported bridegroom."

In Cahan's next story, "Rabbi Eliezer's Christmas"
(Scribner's, December 1899) both the fear and temptation of
apostasy are driven home with frightening realism to a bearded old man in the ghetto, the operator of a tobacco and book
stand. Two upper-class women, settlement workers, are attracted by the "pathos" in his eyes and offer him a twenty
dollar bill. When later that day the old man learns that it
is Christmas, he feels cheated and tainted by accepting the

gift. To him, "the paper now seemed to smell of the in-
cense and to have something to do with the organ sounds
which came from the Polish church in his birthplace." Yet
he desperately needs the money and so decides to return to
the women and ask them if the gift had been given in honor
of Christmas, phrasing the question so that they would see
his dilemma and answer no. They do sense his plight and
offer to take the money back and return it to him the next
day. Joyously he returns to his stand, his conscience tem-
porarily assuaged. Later that night the dilemma returns.
He knows that he has been deceiving his God and humiliating
himself. Still "the disagreeable little question" remains:
"Will the gentile lady pay him the twenty dollars?"

In the next year and a half Cahan wrote three stories
about non-Jewish immigrants. The first, "A Marriage by
Proxy" (Everybody's, December 1900), is a light piece about
an Italian barber who married "by proxy" a girl from the old
country. Disappointed in her husband, the newly-arrived
bride sets up separate housekeeping until the distraught husband wins her back by consulting a clever fortune teller.
"Dumitru and Sigrid" (Cosmopolitan, March 1901) deals with
an immigrant pair (he is Rumanian, she Swedish) who meet
when they are detained at Castle Garden. They eventually go
their separate ways but Dumitru cannot forget the lovely
Swedish girl. He becomes Americanized and successful, but
the memory of Sigrid haunts him. Like Rouvke Arbel and
Yekl, Dumitru is another of Cahan's new Americans caught
between a desire to assimilate and a hopeless yearning for
the past.

"Tzinchadzi of the Catskills" (Atlantic, August 1901)
is Cahan's most bizarre and fantastic story, yet thematically
also one of his most characteristic. Tzinchadzi is a former
Russian aristocrat who lives in the Catskill mountains and
earns money by selling trinkets to tourists--mainly bourgeois
Jews who were beginning to flock to the Catskill resorts.
Outlandishly dressed in a long coat gathered at the waist, a
white, conical fur cap, and a sabre dangling from his belt,
he is a figure from a faraway romantic world when the narrator, from the terrace of his hotel room, spots him on
horseback. Intrigued by the strange figure, he goes to visit
him in his forest hut and hears his story. Tzinchadzi in the
Old World had been in love with a "dark-eyed maiden,"
Zelaya, and won her over a rival by virtue of his superior
horsemanship in a race concocted by her father. But Zelaya
felt sorry for the loser and decided to marry him instead.

Tzinchadzi eventually wound up in America, roaming the hills
on horseback, brooding for his lost Zelaya.

Six years after the first meeting between Tzinchadzi
and the narrator the two meet again, this time quite acciden-
tally on a New York ferry. Tzinchadzi is dressed in a blue
serge American suit, a derby hat, and a starched shirt front
boasting a diamond in its center. He is beardless, considerably fatter, and has all the signs of prosperity. He tells the
narrator that he is now a merchant and real estate owner and
has changed his name to Jones. His heart, he says, is cured
of Zelaya, but he is not happy, "because I yearn neither for
my country nor for Zelaya, nor for anything else. I have
thought it out, and I have come to the conclusion that a man's
heart cannot be happy unless it has somebody or something
to yearn for. " To Tzinchadzi--as to so many of Cahan's
lonely immigrants--the attempt to escape from the past leads
only to empty and purposeless existence. At the end of the
story he tells the narrator, "If you want to think of a happy
man, think of Tzinchadzi of the Catskills, not of Jones of
New York. " Tzinchadzi--like Rouvke Arbel, Yekl, Asriel
Stroom, and Dumitru--loses more than he gains by becoming
an American success. With Rouvke, the first of Cahan's
"allrightniks," they are all left standing on the dock in their
starched shirt fronts watching helplessly as their visions of
happiness vanish in the crowd.

Zalkin, the wealthy clothing manufacturer in "The
Daughter of Avrom Leib" (Cosmopolitan, May 1900), is still
another version of the lonely immigrant parvenu. As the intellectual, former Talmudic scholar who has in America
achieved material success but remains painfully aware of the
spiritual cost of such success, he is the closest kin in Cahan's stories to David Levinsky. Nostalgically, Zalkin wanders the streets of the ghetto and drifts into East Side syna-
gogues. In one he is enthralled by the voice of the cantor
and strikes up a rich friendship with him. He proceeds to
fall in love with the cantor's daughter, who at first rejects
him. When her father dies, however, she agrees to marry
the man who had been so close a friend to her father. So-
phie is not in love with Zalkin, and it is not entirely clear
whether he really loves her or whether she is a link to the
past he seeks. In either case he comes out luckier in love
than David Levinsky, who continually falls in love with wom-
en he can not have.

Levinsky's very success has estranged him from the

things he most desires. His "rise"--like that of Silas Lap-
ham or Sister Carrie before him--is far too expensive. Material gain is purchased at too high a cost. The opening
paragraph of The Rise of David Levinsky summarizes the narrator's recognition of this fact. Looking back from his millionaire's perspective, Levinsky, in this confessional novel,
weighs his gain against the countervailing loss of identity and
integrity. He has achieved the American dream of success,
but the victory is hollow. His outer achievements have no
connection with his inner urgings:

> Sometimes, when I think of my past in a superficial,
> casual way, the metamorphosis I have gone through
> strikes me as nothing short of a miracle. I was born
> and reared in the lowest depths of poverty and I ar-
> rived in America--in 1885--with four cents in my
> pocket. I am now worth more than two million dol-
> lars and recognized as one of the two or three lead-
> ing men in the cloak-and-suit trade in the United
> States. And yet when I look at my inner identity it
> impresses me as being precisely the same as it was
> thirty or forty years ago. My present station, power,
> the amount of worldly happiness at my command, and
> the rest of it, seem to be devoid of significance
> [p. 3].

Levinsky's present life is without significance because
nothing in him has really changed. His character has been
formed by the hunger, loneliness, and deprivation of his boyhood in the Russian village of Antomir, and even amid his
wealth and power these conditions remain the constants of his
life. He had come to America to escape the privation of his
youth, to be able to study and learn free from grinding poverty and anti-Semitic persecution. In the ghetto of New York's
Lower East Side, though, persistent poverty forces the dream
of attending City College into the background, and, as opportunity presents itself, the glossier dream of American business success rises to take its place. He recalls how, as a
young manufacturer, he tried hard to erase the gestures and
speech peculiarities which identified him as a "greenhorn."
He remembers the "aristocratic camaraderie" he shared with
the gentile salesmen he met on Pullman trains. Dining and
talking politics with them, he was a "nobleman among noble-
men." "I throbbed with love for America," he recalls. And
yet, alone, he liked to "brood" over the past, which was
"very far and very near at once."

As if compelled to perpetuate the hunger, loneliness, and pain of his childhood, he falls in love with women who can not love him in return. Two of the women he loves are socialists, and to them his materialistic life in America is repugnant. He is attracted to women who remind him of the past, especially of his mother who was killed coming to his aid when he was attacked by a roving band of anti-Semitic youths. Levinsky has been habituated to sexual deprivation from his days as a Talmudic student in Antomir's "Preacher's Synagogue." He recalls how he had been tormented by thoughts of women while he stood swaying all day over the Talmud. From the pious old Reb Sender, a father-surrogate for the young Levinsky, he heard the Talmudic story of Rabbi Mathia, who pierced out his eyes to avoid the temptations of Satan, who appeared to him as a beautiful woman. "In the eyes of the spiritual laws that governed my life," he recollects, "women were intended for two purposes only: for the continuation of the human species and to serve as an instrument in the hands of Satan for tempting the stronger sex to sin" (pp. 42-43). In America Levinsky's sex life is limited to encounters with East Side prostitutes and a brief affair with the wife of a friend.

Levinsky came to America, as Cahan did, during the wave of terror which followed the assassination of Czar Alexander II in 1881. "Over five million people were suddenly made to realize that their birthplace was not their home," and to Levinsky, as to thousands of other Russian-Jewish youths, America had seemed a place of "fantastic experiences ... marvelous transformations ... just the kind of sensational adventure my heart was hankering for" (pp. 60-61). The discrepancy between expectation and actuality comes home to him on the day of his arrival. The American Jews he sees wear hats and stiff collars--luxuries in the Old World. They possess furniture "which would be a sign of prosperity in Russia." But his first glimpse of such furniture is on a sidewalk where it has been deposited by a landlord. Standing guard over the articles are a mother and two boys, while passersby are dropping coins in a saucer placed on a chair. A "greenhorn," Levinsky is taunted by earlier-arriving immigrants, and when he tries to stay overnight in the synagogue as he had done in Russia, he is told by an elder of the congregation, 'One does not sleep in the American synagogue. It's not Russia ... I wish I could take you to my house, but --well, America is not Russia. There is no pity here, no hospitality.... Alas, America has turned me into a mound of ashes" (p. 96).

Levinsky becomes a peddler in the New World, and under the weight of fierce competition and the influence of the "hawkers" around him, his idealism crumbles. He becomes aware of "certain unlovely traits that were unavoidably developing" in him and that "while human nature was thus growing smaller, the human world was growing larger, more complex, and more interesting" (p. 110). Inflexible as it is, the religious training of his past can not stand against the force of his altered conditions. "If you are a Jew of the type to which I belonged when I came to New York and you attempt to bend your religion to the spirit of your new surroundings, it breaks" (p. 110). On the streets of the East Side Levinsky, "intoxicated by the novelty of yielding to Satan," discovers "underworld women" and learns about the "politician parties," which seem to him "competing business companies," which rule the city and levy tribute from prostitutes, saloon keepers, and thieves. In Russia there had been no political participation; in New York the immigrant is introduced to politics by ward heelers eager to buy immigrant votes and sell favors and protection.

In night school he is introduced to Dickens and Thackeray, but Darwin and Spencer provide the chief stimuli to his emerging personality. As a young manufacturer faced with labor problems, he comes upon a Spencerian editorial attacking unionism and responds: "Why, that's what I have been saying all these days! The able fellows succeed, and the misfits fail. Then the misfits begrudge those who accomplish things" (p. 282). He recalls the intoxication he felt after reading Spencer's Social Statics: "I felt at the gates of a great world of knowledge whose existence I had not even suspected. I had to read The Origins of Species and the Descent of Man, and then Spencer again. Apart from the purely intellectual intoxication they gave me, they flattered my vanity as one of the 'fittest'" (pp. 282-283). The ex-Talmudist learns to cheat labor unions by drawing up phony contracts with "scabs"--paying them less by agreement than what their pay envelopes read--thus enabling him to undersell his competitors while guaranteeing year-round work for his men. When the Arbeiter Zeitung attacks him for "fleecing labor," Levinsky recalls how his vanity was flattered and how his visions of capitalistic glory soared. By circumventing labor unions and by copying the popular patterns of his competitors and producing his goods cheaper, he is able to build his clothing empire.

Levinsky, though, never becomes the soulless, vulgar,

greedy "captain of industry"-figure muckraking and progressivist tracts and novels were projecting. Money and power
remain unimportant to him, except as their attainment satis-
fies his sense of himself as a leader of men, as one of the
"fittest." Financial power represents empirical evidence of
his intellectual superiority, a superiority ground into his consciousness from his earliest days as a Talmud prodigy when
his teachers had taken him from door to door to display his
learning as an advertisement for their schools.

Levinsky never loses his Talmudic perspective on the
vanity of riches and the folly of those who flaunt their wealth.
Satiric attacks, directed at New York's parvenu class, largely but not exclusively Jewish, run through the novel. Levinsky is amused by the wealthy "slummers" who descend upon
the ghetto more for its local color and its supposed bohemian-
ism than for their professed motives of reform and philanthropy. He remembers a Houston Street cafe which special-
ized in serving expensive dinners to uptowners "who came
quite ostensibly to see 'how the other half lived' but who only
saw one another eat and drink in freedom from the restraint
of manners." To sympathize with ghetto strikers, he muses,
is clearly "within the bounds of the highest propriety ... as
correct as belonging to the Episcopal Church." Levinsky
spends a few days in the Catskill mountains, where in the
prestigious new Jewish resort hotels young--and not so young
--parvenu daughters seek husbands among the rising businessmen who come for weekends. He recalls the "after-supper
satisfaction" of the guests as they watch the sun go down and
remembers that one of the principal rooms of the hotel served
as a synagogue in the morning and a pinochle room the rest
of the day.

Levinsky persistently resists the allurements of the
nouveau riche and breaks off an engagement to a wealthy
young lady after his Catskill weekend. This is the closest he
will come to marriage. But while he cannot join the "riot of
prosperity," neither can he rejoin the class of East European
Jews who shared his background and came with him to America. His success and business methods have totally alienated
him from the ghetto. Unions are repugnant and socialists
are the "most repulsive hypocrites of all." Here Levinsky
and Cahan, character and author, are farthest apart. [9] Estranged from both large worlds of Jews in America, Levinsky
exists in a no-man's land and gropes blindly for personal
contact:

I had no creed. I knew of no ideals. The only thing
I believed in was the cold, drab theory of the survival
of the fittest. This could not satisfy a heart that was
hungry for enthusiasm and affection, so dreams of
family life became my religion. Self-sacrificing devotion to one's family was the only kind of altruism and
idealism I did not flout [p. 380].

Denied a family, he reaches out for friendship. On
the twenty-fifth anniversary of his arrival at Castle Garden
he invites his "ship brother," Gitelson, an East Side tailor,
to lunch, his heart full of nostalgia and sentiment. He wants
to talk of "our ship, the cap he had lost, of his timidity when
we found ourselves in Castle Garden, of the policeman I
asked to direct us. But Gitelson only nodded and grinned and
tittered" (p. 575). Slightly tipsy from the champagne and
feeling ill-at-ease among the Waldorf's obsequious waiters,
Gitelson seems unreachable and even irrelevant in Levinsky's
life. Contacts with the past are always painful. In one scene
he is unable--or unwilling--to leave a street car to offer aid
to a destitute man he sees on the sidewalk and recognizes as
a fellow student from his Russian boyhood. One of the operators in Levinsky's plant is a man he had known as a boy in
Antomir. He is an ardent socialist and leader in the cloak-
maker's union, but Levinsky, sentimentally, retains him.
When, finally, the man makes virulent anti-capitalistic speeches
to the workers, Levinsky dismisses him and a strike ensues.
Levinsky becomes to them the betrayer of his own people.

The conditions of his present life have made it impos-
sible for him to bridge the gulf to the past he yearns for,
yet, paradoxically, he is never far from that past. Loneliness, hunger, and alienation have been so firmly stamped on
his character since his boyhood, they seem the most authentic
parts of him. And while he cries on the one hand for an end
to his sorrows, the sorrows have their own kind of value.
Through his meteoric rise his inner identity has remained essentially unchanged. [10]

Predictably, the reviews of the novel were unfavorable.
To most reviewers, Levinsky was a gratuitous portrait of un-
mitigated corruption. The protagonist was the idealistic
young immigrant who traded a proud birthright for the worst
traits of his adopted land. He was the American "on the
make." His rise, The Nation's reviewer complained, was
"based from beginning to end on ruthless lying and trickery and
theft. And he tells the story of it all without a qualm,

pluming himself on having won his booty by means too despicable for his rivals. " The book was despicable, in other
words, because its main character was so. H. W. Boynton,
one of the period's most prolific reviewers, took essentially
the same position. In his review for The Bookman, he saw
it as "an unsparing interpretation of the predatory immigrant."
A few weeks later Boynton included the novel in his review
of the year's fiction for The Nation, in which he complained:
"The disconcerting thing is that we cannot make out whether
Mr. Cahan appreciates the spiritual obscenity of the creature
he has made: embodiment of all the contemptible qualities
an enemy of the Yiddish Jew could charge him with. " Like
most of the critics he contrasted it with Nyburg's The Chosen People, "an interpretation of the Jew in America shot
through with an idealism based on a proud faith in the destiny
of the race. " Only John Macy, writing in The Dial, recognized the ironies in Levinsky's "rise. " He hailed Cahan's
"benevolent impartiality" in letting his character speak for--
and impugn--himself and observed, as the other reviewers
did not, that Levinsky "never ceases to regard his visible
good fortune as poor compensation for the invisible things he
has missed. "[11]

In the end, neither the thorough Americanization pre-
scribed by Mary Antin, Jacob Riis, and Elias Tobenkin, nor
the cultural fusion urged by Jane Addams, Ezra Brudno, and
Edward Steiner are realizable states in Cahan's fictional
world. With The Rise of David Levinsky the novel of immigrant acculturation is no longer the story of easy faith.
David Levinsky, immigrant and entrepreneur, the penniless
refugee who amasses a fortune in that most characteristic
Jewish-American industry, finds emptiness at the end of the
American dream.

While all the immigrant novelists of the period described the disparity between the expectations and the actualities of America, only Cahan among them pursued the psychological implications of that disparity, its permanent cost to
the psyche. Only Cahan, among the pre-World War I, first-
generation immigrant novelists, refused to turn his heroes
into preachers or propagandists, refused to blink his eyes as
he faced the chasm which lay between Old World values and
New World experience.

AFTERWORD

The Rise of David Levinsky occupies a pivotal position in the history of American literature. It appeared at the very end of America's long period of unrestricted immigration and chronicles the later, urban phase of that period. At the same time it stands at the head of a long line of twentieth-century novels which would portray modern urban America from the eyes of the city's non-Anglo component. The novel's ambiguous mixture of material success and spiritual failure, its insistence on the high cost of assimilation, and its concern with the identity crisis bred by the Americanization process place it squarely in the forefront of twentieth-century "minority voice" fiction.

In the years following the publication of Levinsky several writers--first- and second-generation immigrants--carried forward Cahan's themes. Anzia Yezierska, the most important first-generation woman writer, arrived in America when she was fifteen in 1901 and produced between 1919 and 1932 several novels and stories about Jewish immigrant girls on New York's Lower East Side. In her story collections, Hungry Hearts (1920) and Children of Loneliness (1923), and in the novels, Salome of the Tenements (1923), Bread Givers (1925), Arrogant Beggars (1927) and All I Could Never Be (1932), she introduced a series of sensitive young heroines who hunger for American life, who like Cahan's greenhorns reach out from the ghetto for contact with the American world but remain unfulfilled and lonely. Central to her fiction--as it is to immigrant fiction generally--is the rejection of ghetto parents and the identification of success with marriage to an American born of a good family. One of her recurring stories is of the poor ghetto girl attracted to a refined, genteel and wealthy Anglo-Saxon male with whom she has only a brief romance. Shenah Pessah, who appears in the first two stories of Hungry Hearts, her first collection, is typical. An orphan brought over to the New World to work as a cleaning girl in her uncle's tenement house, she falls in love with John

Barnes, a university professor who has moved to the East
Side to study Russian Jews. Although Barnes is drawn to the
girl (attracted, as Shenah is, by the opposite qualities in the
other), he is unwilling to make a commitment. He kisses
her, awkwardly apologizes, and leaves abruptly.

By far the best story in the collection is "The Fat of
the Land," which the anthologist Edward O'Brien chose as
the top story of 1919. The story has neither a romantic interest nor a young heroine but deals, like so many of Cahan's
stories, with the high cost of material success in America.
Hannah Breinah, when the story opens, is a poor Delancy
Street mother complaining to a neighbor, Mrs. Pelz: "No-
body has pity on me.... Some mothers got luck. A child
gets run over by a car, some fall from a window, some burn
themselves, some get choked with diphtheria; but no death
takes mine away" (Hungry Hearts, p. 186). Life to Hannah
means hungry, dirty, squabbling children and unending toil.
Mrs. Pelz responds by telling her that when her children are
old enough to work, she "will have the fat of the land." The
prophesy comes true, and when we reach the last section of
this long story, Hannah is ensconced in a plush Riverside
Drive apartment, complete with dining service.

But Hannah in prosperity is still miserable. She
sneaks off to Delancy Street to bargain for fish from a peddler, smuggling her booty back to her apartment (bringing
food in is against the rules). "In that swell restaurant," she
complains, "is nothing but napkins and forks and lettuce
leaves. There are a dozen plates to every bite of food. And
it looks so fancy on the plate, but it's nothing but straw in
the mouth. I'm starving but I can't swallow their American
eating" (Hungry Hearts, p. 218). Like David Levinsky, Hannah is trapped between two worlds, unhappy on Riverside
Drive but too accustomed to physical comfort to return to the
ghetto.

Hannah's children have become phenomenally successful. Fanny is a Fifth Avenue milliner, Benny a famous playwright (the President attends the premiere of one of his plays),
Jake a rental agent, and Abe the owner of a large clothing
factory. The children about whom she had constantly complained have become ashamed of their mother's Old World
ways. "God knows how hard I tried to civilize her," Fannie
tells her brothers, "Delancy Street sticks out from every inch
of her" (p. 209).

The conflict between immigrant parents and their children and the obsessional second-generation drive to make it in America are central themes in the immigrant fiction of the 1920s. Samuel Ornitz's Haunch, Paunch and Jowl (1923), a confessional novel (published as an "anonymous autobiography") about a young man's rise from the ghetto to wealth and power, has some of the narrative flavor of Levinsky, but Ornitz's narrator has none of the misgivings of Cahan's. Meyer Hirsch rejects the Jewish education his parents offer him ("I can't swallow that bunk") for the more exciting life of the New York streets. From petty theft and gang warfare, he moves on to machine politics and extortion. Somehow he manages to complete law school and winds up a shyster lawyer and then a corrupt judge engaged in bribery and political favors. He ends where Hannah Breinah does--in a Riverside Drive apartment. Anzia Yezierska's lonely, unhappy, yearning immigrant and Samuel Ornitz's flashy, Americanized, and self-satisfied success-figure are the separated halves of Cahan's schizophrenic protagonists.

John Cournos' trilogy about a Russian Jewish youth growing up in America--The Mask (1919), The Wall (1921), and Babel (1922)--has a different outcome. John Gombarov, Cournos' autobiographical narrator-hero, comes of age on the streets of Philadelphia, a victim of both civic authority and street gangs, but instead of scrambling his way to American success, he escapes to England where, with considerable bitterness, he tells his story of an American childhood. Arthur Levy in Ludwig Lewisohn's somewhat autobiographical novel The Island Within (1928) is the New York-born son of German Jewish immigrants (Lewisohn was born in Germany). The parents are thoroughly Americanized and Arthur, hardly aware of his Jewish and immigrant heritage, marries a Protestant girl. Later, when he discovers that heritage, he separates from his wife and devotes his life to aiding Jews. Among other things The Island Within is a polemic against intermarriage (the symbol for cultural fusion in a number of earlier immigrant authors) and a plea for the assertion of ethnic and religious ties. Cournos and Lewisohn drew on their own lives to write of the contradictions and dilemmas of the immigrant son's coming-of-age in urban America. For both writers separation from the parent is a necessary step; for Lewisohn, looking forward to some third-generation writers, the movement is toward a reaffirmation of the immigrant heritage.

As the twenties gave way to the thirties, the themes of

intermarriage, rejection of the parent, and the second-generation drive to make it big gave way to the basic issue of
survival in the urban jungle.   Under the weight of the Depression, economic and political issues superseded the psychological ones of identity and assimilation.   Mike Gold's episodic
1930 novel Jews Without Money, a backward glance at his
own ghetto boyhood and a whole Lower East Side neighborhood
between 1900 and 1914, links ghetto fiction to proletarian fiction of the thirties.   Although the only direct reference to
socialist revolution comes in the last twelve lines of the book,
when Gold happens to hear "a man on an East Side soap box,
one night," the entire work is a bitter condemnation of an
economic system which enslaves the working class and is directly responsible for prostitution, violent crime, disease,
and the daily tragedies of the ghetto.

     Gold's work was followed by a number of others in
the decade of the thirties, some explicitly radical, some not,
about immigrant children growing up in the city.   Hyman and
Lester Cohen's Aaron Traum (a father-son collaboration) in
1930, Henry Roth's Call It Sleep (1934), and Isidor Schneider's
From the Kingdom of Necessity (1935) recalled Jewish boy-
hoods on the Lower East Side.   Roth's novel, by far the finest of the three, is in some ways a throwback to the ghetto
fiction of the twenties with its emphasis on the psychological
traumas of childhood, although it is often cited as a proletarian novel.   Since the novel's "discovery" in 1960 after being neglected for twenty-six years, it has enjoyed a strong
reputation.   The Cohens' novel is a rather sentimental and
idealized portrait of an immigrant youth's search for fulfill-
ment in America, including some episodes in which the hero
is a labor organizer in the garment industry.   Schneider's
work is the most radical of the three and, like Gold's, ends
with the hero's political awakening and identification with the
working class.   Daniel Fuchs's Williamsburg trilogy--Summer
in Williamsburg (1934), Homage to Blenholt (1936) and Low
Company (1937)--and Meyer Levin's equally massive novel,
The Old Bunch (1937), carry forward the immigrant children
in time and into new neighborhoods.   Both portray the coming-of-age in secondary areas of immigrant settlement--the
Williamsburg section of Brooklyn and Chicago's West Side.
Chicago was also the setting for James Farrell's study of lower middle-class Irish youth in the Studs Lonigan trilogy (1932-
1934).   Finally, as the thirties drew to an end, there came
Pietro DiDonato's Christ in Concrete (1938) and Richard
Wright's Native Son (1940), novels which violently and power-
fully portrayed growing up Italian and Black on the city's

streets. By 1940 ethnic and minority fiction were well-established in the American canon.

*   *   *   *   *

A half-century separates these depression-age novels
from the earliest urban immigrant fiction described in this
study, and while the focus has shifted over the years (from
the problems of initial contact to the dilemmas of assimilation and in the thirties, to economic issues and the politics
of survival), certain basic themes have remained constant.
Central to urban immigrant fiction is the clash between two
distinct cultural groups and the results of that clash. Meta-
phorically, the clash has been represented in a number of
ways--Old World parents set against their New World aspir-
ing children, uptown against downtown, capital opposed to labor, native-born against immigrant, older (German and Irish)
against newer (Russian and Italian) immigrant. The issues of
intermarriage and the survival of racial, ethnic, and religious
ties in the face of the collision of cultures--one basically
northwestern European and largely Protestant, the other southern and eastern European and overwhelmingly Jewish or Catholic
--played important roles in the fiction.

By far the most pervasive way of dramatizing the
clash between cultures in the fiction of the period was through
the conflict between parents and children. Almost every writer I have dealt with in this study, native-born or immigrant,
wrote of the generational conflict. To Lincoln Steffens, among
the most sympathetic of native-born observers of the ghetto,
the conflict was not simply between generations, but centuries
--between parents of the Middle Ages and children of today.
It was a tragic clash enacted every day in the ghetto. With
Hutchins Hapgood, James Oppenheim, and Jane Addams, he
sided with the immigrant parents who sought to maintain Old
World cultural and religious ties amid unsettling new conditions and deplored children who rejected the ways of their
parents. Urban reformers like Jacob Riis and Josiah Strong,
on the other hand, saw the rescue of the immigrant children
from the ghetto world of their parents as one of their most
important tasks. Among the dangers of the slum and sweatshop are that they perpetuate the separation of immigrant and
native and hinder the Americanization of the immigrant child.
For writers advocating assimilation, rejecting the father and
the values he represents and leaving behind the world of the
ghetto are, if sad, necessary first steps on the road to Americanization. For some of the writers--including most first-

generation immigrant authors--the final step, the one which
symbolizes full assimilation, is intermarriage.

Henry Harland, the earliest of the novelists I have
discussed, established the tone for much of the fiction to
come in his novels of Jewish life in New York in the eighties.
Through his bizarre and melodramatic stories, Harland was
preaching assimilation and intermarriage as the best course
for the Jew in America, a course he felt too few Jews were
willing, or able, to follow. Harland's fiction also reveals,
however, a local colorist's fascination with the flavor and
peculiarities of life in the immigrant community, and his work
reminds us that urban immigrant fiction is also an outgrowth
of the impulse toward regionalism, which peaked in the eighties. Setting aside the vital social issues which encouraged
the literary exploration of the ghetto, we should recognize its
development out of the local color movement--and, more directly, the urbanization of that movement in the tenement tale
vogue of the eighties and nineties. Behind much of the early
ghetto fiction of the nineties lies the literary appeal of the
faraway, the strange, the exotic.

And yet it is difficult to separate cleanly the varied
strands which went into the making of urban immigrant fiction: the local color impulse, the tenement tale and the long
history of slum fiction, urban realism, social reform. For
the early short story writers of the ghetto--Jacob Riis, Alvan
Francis Sanborn, James Sullivan, Rudolph Block, Julian
Ralph, Myra Kelly--the territory was attractive both as a
source of fresh, contemporary, urban material and of life far
removed from that most middle-class readers knew. Cahan's
early magazine fiction, published in the late nineties, has the
same split, but with Cahan and with most of the writers who
appeared after the turn of the century, local color interest in
the culture island is subordinated to a serious concern with
the problems of adjustment and cultural interaction.

What were to be the terms of adjustment? Would
(should) the newcomer shed his past (as Mary Antin did--or
claimed to), or would the immigrant's background play a part
in a developing new America? What is gained and lost by
becoming an American? And what would America gain or lose
by continuing to accept immigrants? These are some of the
questions the writers posed in the early years of the twentieth
century. Many were haunted by another question: what relation exists between the immigrant's expectation of America
and the reality he faced here? From the Renaissance on

immigrants were lured to the New World by the promise of
new beginnings on a new continent. The brochures put out
by steamship companies in 1900 echoed the chronicles of
some of the first Anglo-Saxon settlers of the New World in
proclaiming a vast territory offering unlimited opportunity for
the enterprising and energetic. To many of the immigrants
who arrived in the 1880-1917 period, settled in overcrowded
and unsanitary tenement houses in the city's immigrant quarters, and worked (if at all) amid the worst conditions imagi-
nable in sweatshops and factories, America was not the land
of new beginnings but of broken promises. This is a theme
which preoccupied some of the period's most sensitive writers, native-born and immigrant--Upton Sinclair, James Oppenheim, Sidney Nyburg, Abraham Cahan, Anzia Yezierska.

     For the author who wanted to point emphatically to the
disparity between the real and imagined America and drama-
tize the force of the collision between native and immigrant
cultures, the sweatshop was the perfect locale. Here the
two worlds met head-on. Here the immigrant made his first
contact with the American system, and here the clash between the two cultures (often between older and newer immigrants) was fiercest. In such works as Edward Smith King's
Joseph Zalmonah, Upton Sinclair's The Jungle, Arthur Bullard's Comrade Yetta, Frank Harris' The Bomb, James Oppenheim's The Nine Tenths and Pay Envelopes, and Sidney
Nyburg's The Chosen People the period's bitterest labor strug-
gles--struggles which inevitably pitted the newest Americans
against entrenched society--were reenacted. American fiction
had its earliest proletarian heroes in these works.

     The sweatshop, in addition to providing the precise lo-
cale for the clash between native and immigrant cultures, offered in a broader sense an apt symbol for modern urban labor. The system was marked by hierarchical organization;
reliance on machines and a temporary, unskilled labor force;
unstable and irregular work schedules; fierce competition;
strikes; layoffs; and lockouts. With women and children added to the labor force and the fact that much of the sweated
labor was performed in the already overcrowded tenement
flats of the workers, the traditional roles of the family unit
and functions of the home were radically altered. The immigrant novel thus not only documents the major labor warfare
of our recent past, but locates for us some of the origins of
the living and working patterns which characterize the modern
city.

Urban immigrant fiction in these years was largely
the work of native-born writers. Only a handful of first-
generation immigrants had the education, the leisure, or the
inclination to write imaginative literature in English during
the period of initial contact. Those who did, like those who
wrote autobiographies, tended to write optimistic and facile
accounts of their own acculturation. With the exception of
Cahan (and Yezierska in the twenties) their fiction reflected
their joyful, sometimes ecstatic embrace of America. The
pluralistic, cosmopolitan ideal which Horace Kallen, Randolph
Bourne, and some of the leaders of the immigrant community
were advocating found little expression in the fiction. Cultural pluralism was either ignored or raised as an alternative to be rejected. Immigrant writers differed as to what
form assimilation would or should take, but they never seriously questioned the virtue of assimilation. Now, with the
upsurge of white ethnicity in America--with what Professor
Michael Novak has called "the rise of the unmeltable ethnics"
--this strong affirmation of assimilation by first-generation
authors, particularly when set against the voices of influential immigrant leaders, seems strange. There are, however,
clear reasons.

For one, most of the immigrant authors whose works
I have discussed reached America when they were quite young,
came of age outside the ghetto, and went on to successful
careers. Their lives were hardly typical of the urban immigrant generation. For another, their own assimilation included the assimilation of native cultural ideals and literary
conventions as well as our most cherished and enduring national myth--success. Having achieved the American dream,
they believed in it and their novels were testaments to its
promise. Along with the greater number of immigrant autobiographies (not all, certainly) which came out of the period,
these novels deserve a place in the long tradition of American
success literature. Social criticism is not absent from the
novels. Elias Tobenkin, Ezra Brudno, and Edward Steiner
provide some vivid scenes of exploitative immigrant labor conditions, and the disparity between the expectation and the reality of America recurs as a theme. Their heroes, however,
after a period of revulsion from the harsh actualities of America, go on to a strong affirmation of New World possibilities,
often embarking on one or another vague scheme for reconcil-
ing native and immigrant cultures. Finally, at a time of increasing hostility to the "new" immigrant, these novels were
motivated, in part, by a desire to justify immigrant assimilability. The stumbling blocks to assimilation, as Jacob Riis

warned and as these novels dramatized, were not the inherited or cultural traits the newcomers brought, but the conditions they found here.

The eventual successful assimilation of the male immigrant heroes is signaled by their intermarriage--either with an aristocratic Anglo-Saxon beauty or the daughter of an Old World oppressor. The kinds of liaisons which had been forbidden in the Old World are permitted in the New. For Cahan and Yezierska, however, becoming an American is fraught with considerably more ambiguity and uncertainty. Their protagonists, too, seek New World mates, but they are denied. The failure of love for their young immigrants symbolizes the failed fusion of the old and new selves.

Urban loneliness, alienation, isolation--the themes of Cahan, Yezierska, and the immigrant authors who followed them--have become the standard themes. In the modern setting the victim or marginal figure has become the central, symbolic figure. The outsider is the insider in an age of anxiety. Separation and disconnectedness, the absence of love and of strong, fulfilling community ties--these have become the basic motifs of modern urban literature. Immigrant ghetto fiction, deplored (with some justice) for its sentimentality and banality in 1932 by Albert Halper in the essay cited at the beginning of the book, has helped shape the course of contemporary urban fiction. What Halper could not see then, and what we now can, is that in the generation ahead non-Anglo writers, black and white, like Richard Wright, Ralph Ellison, James Baldwin, Norman Mailer, Bernard Malamud, and Saul Bellow would stand at the very center of American literature. Immigrant ghetto fiction was not a dead end after all. Along with some of our earliest black novels, the immigrant fiction which has been the subject of this book helped clear the path to the present. Both chronologically and temperamentally the ghetto fiction of the years 1880-1920 bridges the last century with ours. American literature in these years began to reflect the tensions and strains of a multi-ethnic urban and industrial America.

In addition to opening up important new literary territory, these works--so uneven in quality and varying in tone--have value for us today as cultural documents, as concrete and personal responses to the experience of immigration and cultural clash, the breakdown of old certainties (for native and immigrant alike) in the face of the city's transformation, and the chaotic emergence of modern urban America. As we recover a part of our history through these novels and stories, we realize that we are not so far removed from the past they record as we sometimes think.

CHAPTER NOTES

CHAPTER I

1. A detailed summary and scathing critique of the methods and findings of the Dillingham Commission can be found in Oscar Handlin, Race and Nationality in American Life (Garden City, N. Y. : Doubleday (Anchor), 1957), pp. 74-110. The biases of the report are also discussed in Maldwyn Allen Jones, American Immigration (Chicago: University of Chicago Press, 1960), pp. 177-182 and ff.

2. Jones, p. 179. This book provides a very useful historical summary of the whole panorama of immigration into this country, stressing the continuous nature of immigration and rejecting the hard and fast distinctions between "old" and "new" immigration, except when they refer to place of origin. To document the shift in geographic source of European immigrants, the author cites figures: of the 788,000 immigrants who arrived in 1882, 87 per cent were from northwest Europe; of the 1,285,000 who came in 1907, 80.7 per cent were from southeastern Europe (p. 179).

3. Jones, pp. 208-209.

4. David Ward, Cities and Immigrants: A Geography of Change in Nineteenth Century America (New York: Oxford University Press, 1971), pp. 55-56. Ward provides a table showing percentages of urban settlement among all the major immigrant groups (p. 56).

5. Ward, pp. 105-109.

6. See, for instance, Jane Addams's description of the process in Chicago's immigrant quarter in Twenty Years at Hull House (New York: Phillips, 1910), p. 97. The residence pattern, of course, is related to the immigrant labor pattern. The newest arrivals typically occupied the lowest rungs on the job ladder, their presence making possible the upward movement of earlier-arriving immigrants.

7. John Higham, Strangers in the Land: Patterns of American Nativism, 1860-1925 (New York: Atheneum, 1966; paperback), pp. 63-67; Jones, pp. 252-257. Both authors make the important point that the period's nativism is not a product of "new" immigration, but existed, in Higham's words, through it. Only gradually was a distinction between immigrant groups made.

8. Oscar Handlin, The Uprooted: The Epic Story of the Great Migrations that Made the American People (New York: Grosset and Dunlap, 1951), pp. 275-277.

9. Henry Cabot Lodge, "The Restriction of Immigration," North American Review, 152 (1891), 27-36.

10. Francis A. Walker, "Immigration and Degradation," Forum, 11 (1891), 634-644.

11. Francis A. Walker, "Restriction of Immigration," Atlantic Monthly, 77 (1896), 822-829.

12. The Old World and the New (New York: Century, 1914). See also, "The Causes of Race Superiority," Annals of the American Academy of Political and Social Sciences, 18 (1901), 67-89. Vol. 87 of Century Magazine (1913-14) contains chapters from Ross's book.

13. "National Eugenics in Relation to Immigration," North American Review, 192 (1910), 59. See also, "Our Immigration Laws from the Standpoint of National Eugenics," National Geographic Magazine, 23 (Jan. 1912), 38-41.

14. Madison Grant, The Passing of the Great Race, 3d ed. (New York: DeForest Grant, 1944), pp. 86-92.

15. See, for instance, Terence Powderly. "A Menacing Irruption," North American Review, 147 (1888), 165-174.

16. Henry James, The American Scene, ed. by Leon Edel (Bloomington: Indiana University Press, 1968), p. 128. Subsequent page references will be indicated parenthetically.

17. Ignatius Donnelly, Caesar's Column (Cambridge, Mass.: Harvard University Press, 1960), p. 98. Subsequent page references are indicated parenthetically in the text.

18. P. 149. "He was, I should think, not less than six feet six inches high, and broad in proportion. His great arms hung down until his monstrous hands almost touched his knees. His skin was quite dark, almost negroid; and a thick, close mat of curly black hair covered his huge head like a thatch. His face was muscular, ligamentous; with great bars, ridges, whelks of flesh, especially about the jaws and on the forehead."

19. Owen Wister, "The Evolution of the Cow-Puncher," The Writings of Owen Wister, Vol. VI (New York: Macmillan, 1928), pp. xxii-xxiv.

20. Jack London, The Valley of the Moon (New York: Macmillan, 1913), pp. 15, 102-103.

21. Jack London, Mutiny on the Elsinore (New York: Mac-

millan, 1914), pp. 148-149. Subsequent page references are indicated parenthetically in the text.

22. Honore Willisie, "What Is an American?" Collier's, 50 (9 Nov. 1912), p. 14. The story is illustrated by John Sloan.

23. Catherine Metcalf Roof, The Stranger at the Hearth (Boston: Small, Maynard, 1916), pp. 314-315. Subsequent page references are indicated parenthetically in the text.

CHAPTER II

1. Josiah Strong, Our Country: Its Possible Future and Its Present Decay (New York: American Home Missionary Society, 1885), pp. 41-42. For a further expression of this view see W. M. F. Round, "Immigration and Crime," Forum, 8 (1890), 428-440.

2. Theodore Roosevelt, An Autobiography (New York: Scribner's, 1919), p. 169.

3. Lincoln Steffens, "Jacob Riis, Reporter, Reformer, and American Citizen," McClure's Magazine, 21 (1903), 419-425.

4. Jacob Riis, How the Other Half Lives (New York: Scribner's, 1892), p. 20.

5. Ray Lubove, The Progressives and the Slums: Tenement House Reform in New York City, 1890-1917 (Pittsburgh: University of Pittsburgh Press, 1962), pp. 117-125.

6. See Isaac Rubinow, "Economic and Industrial Conditions," The Russian Jew in the United States, ed. by Charles Bernheimer, (Philadelphia: J. C. Winston, 1905), p. 112.

7. For firsthand accounts of sweatshop conditions in New York, Chicago, and Philadelphia, respectively, see John DeWitt Warner, "The Sweating System in New York City," Harper's Weekly, 29 (2 Feb. 1895), 135-136; Florence Kelley, "The Sweating System," Hull House Maps and Papers (Chicago: Thomas Crowell, 1895), pp. 27-44; and A. F. Goodchild, "The Sweating System in Philadelphia," Arena, 11 (1895), 261-265.

8. Lucia True Ames [Mead]. Memoirs of a Millionaire (Boston: Houghton, Mifflin, 1899), p. 229. Subsequent page references are indicated parenthetically in the text.

9. Finley Peter Dunne, Observations by Mr. Dooley (New York: Harper and Bros., 1906), pp. 51-52. Subsequent page references are indicated parenthetically in the text.

10. Lincoln Steffens, The Autobiography of Lincoln Steffens (New York: Harcourt, Brace, 1931), p. 243.

11. In recent years Bernard Malamud, Philip Roth, and Saul Bellow, among others, have explored this theme. In the pre-1917 fiction which will be treated in this study, Sidney Nyburg's The Chosen People and Abraham Cahan's The Rise of David Levinsky are the best examples.

12. Louis Wirth, The Ghetto (Chicago: University of Chicago Press, 1928 and 1956), p. 205.

13. For suggestive discussions of these novels of Harland, see Leslie Fiedler, "Genesis: The American Jewish Novel Through the Twenties," Midstream, 4 (summer 1958), 23-27; Solomon Liptzen, The Jew in American Literature (New York: Bloch, 1966), pp. 91-95 and, most recently, Louis Harap, The Image of the Jew in American Literature (Philadelphia: Jewish Publication Society of America, 1974), pp. 455-471.

14. Milton Gordon, "Assimilation in America: Theory and Reality," Daedalus, 90(1961), 263-285. Gordon attributes the term to Stewart G. and Mildred W. Cole in their study, Minorities and the American Promise (New York: Harper and Bros., 1954), ch. 6.

15. Quoted in Ralph Henry Gabriel, The Course of American Democratic Thought (New York: Ronald Press, 1940), p. 45.

16. Oliver Wendell Holmes, The Autocrat of the Breakfast-Table (Boston: Phillips, Sampson, 1858), p. 21.

17. Herbert Spencer, Essays, Scientific, Political, and Speculative (New York: Appleton, 1891), pp. 471-472.

18. Jane Addams, "The Objective Value of a Social Settlement," Philanthropy and Social Progress (New York: T. Crowell, 1893). See, in particular, p. 35.

19. Jane Addams, "The Charitable Effort," Democracy and Social Ethics (New York: Macmillan, 1902), p. 32.

20. Jane Addams, Twenty Years at Hull House (New York: Macmillan, 1910), p. 246.

21. Hutchins Hapgood, The Spirit of the Ghetto (New York: Funk and Wagnalls, 1902), p. 5. Subsequent page references are indicated parenthetically in the text.

22. Norman Hapgood, "The Jews and American Democracy," Menorah Journal, 2 (1916), 203.

23. Steffens, Autobiography, p. 244.

24. Hutchins Hapgood, Types from City Streets (New York: Funk and Wagnalls, 1910), p. 22. Subsequent page references are indicated parenthetically in the text.

25. Philip Gleason, "The Melting Pot: Symbol of Fusion or Confusion?" American Quarterly, 16 (spring 1964), 20-46.

26. Horace Kallen, "Democracy versus the Melting Pot," The Nation, 100 (25 Feb. 1915), 220.

27. Randolph Bourne, "Trans-National America," Atlantic Monthly, 118 (July 1916), 86-97.

28. Vida Scudder, A Listener in Babel (Boston: Houghton, Mifflin, 1903), p. 74. Subsequent page references are indicated parenthetically in the text.

CHAPTER III

1. Ernest Poole's interview of Cahan, "Abraham Cahan: Socialist, Journalist, Friend of the Ghetto," The Outlook, 99 (28 Oct. 1911), 467-478, is useful as a brief biographical source. An account of Cahan's early career in New York can be found in Ronald Sanders, The Downtown Jews: Portraits of an Immigrant Generation (New York: Harper and Row, 1969), passim. The first part of Cahan's five-volume Yiddish autobiography has been translated and published under the title The Education of Abraham Cahan (Philadelphia: Jewish Publication Society, 1969).

2. Recent scholarship has corrected the earlier belief that Crane was working on Maggie in 1891 while he was a student at Syracuse. He was at that time writing a story about a prostitute, but it cannot be assumed that this story later became Maggie. For accounts of the errors in dating, see the introduction by James Colvert to Stephen Crane: The Bowery Tales, ed. by Fredson Bowers (Charlottesville: University Press of Virginia, 1969) and also the introduction by Donald Pizer to the facsimile of the 1893 edition (San Francisco: Chandler, 1968).

3. "New York Low Life in Fiction," New York World, (26 July 1896), section II, 18.

4. Stephen Crane: Letters, ed. by R. W. Stallman and Lillian Gilkes (New York: New York University Press, 1960), p. 102.

5. This tale was later included in the collection, The Imported Bridegroom and other Stories of the New York Ghetto (New York: Appleton, 1898). See Sanford Marovitz, "The Lonely New Americans of Abraham Cahan," American Quarterly, 20 (summer 1968), 205.

6. Rudolph and Clara Kirk, "Abraham Cahan and William Dean Howells: The Story of a Friendship," American Jewish Historical Quarterly, 52 (Sept. 1962), 27-57.

7. The Nation, 63 (2 July 1896), 15; Nancy Houston Banks, "The New York Ghetto," The Bookman, 4 (Oct. 1896), 157-158. For an English account of Crane in line with the above, see H. D. Trail, "The New Realism," Fortnightly Review, 68 (Jan. 1897), 63-67.

8. "During the first five years of Arena, we published over fifty carefully prepared contributions dealing with the problem of advancing poverty and its attendant evils." --Benjamin Orange Flower, Progressive Men, Women, and Movements of the Past Twenty-Five Years (Boston: New Arena, 1914), p. 120.

9. This estimate is O. H. K. Spate's in "The Growth of London, A. D. 1660-1800," Historical Geography of England, ed. by H. C. Darby (Cambridge, England: University Press, 1936), pp. 529-547.

10. Spectator, no. 403 (1712).

11. See also his pamphlet, Charity Still a Christian Virtue (1719).

12. Memoirs of a Millionaire (Boston: Houghton, Mifflin, 1889), p. 127.

13. Crumbling Idols (Chicago: Stone, Kimball, 1894), p. 72.

14. "The Bowery and Bohemia," Jersey Street and Jersey Lane: Urban and Suburban Sketches (New York: Scribner's, 1896), pp. 373-374. See the sketch "Jersey and Mulberry," pp. 3-31.

15. "In Search of Local Color," Vignettes of Manhattan (New York: Harper and Bros. , 1894), pp. 67-82.

16. The Honorable Peter Stirling (New York: Henry Holt, 1900), pp. 3-4.

17. Poor People (Boston: Houghton, Mifflin, 1900), p. 4.

18. Eric Solomon in the first chapter of Stephen Crane: From Parody to Realism (Cambridge, Mass. : Harvard University Press, 1966), discusses the influence of both nineteenth-century sentimental fiction and reform journalism on the body of slum fiction produced at the end of the century. Slum fiction, in treatment, seems closer to the former than to the latter, though the reform literature may have suggested the literary possibilities of the subject. Solomon's point in this chapter is that Maggie parodies both of these conventions.

19. Sanford Marovitz in "Howells and the Ghetto: The

Mystery of Misery," Modern Fiction Studies, 16 (1970), 345-362,
illustrates the writer-critic's ephemeral and rather shallow commitment to the denizens of the ghetto.

20. Harper's Weekly, 39 (1 June 1895), 508.

21. "Chimmie Fadden"; Major Max; and Other Stories (New
York: Lovell, Coryell, 1895), is a collection reprinted from
sketches which appeared in the New York Sun and San Francisco
Argonaut.

22. Robert Bremner, From the Depths: The Discovery of
Poverty in the United States (New York: New York University Press,
1956), p. 117; Frank Luther Mott, American Journalism: a History,
1690-1960 (New York: Macmillan, 1962), pp. 525-526.

23. The Poor in Great Cities (New York: Scribner's, 1895),
p. 92. See also William I. Hull, "The Children of the Other Half,"
Arena, 17 (June 1897), 1039-1050.

24. Introduction, Stephen Crane: The Bowery Tales, ed. by
Fredson Bowers (Charlottesville: University Press of Virginia,
1969), pp. ii-iii. Stephen Crane's Maggie: Text and Context, ed. by
Maurice Bassan (Belmont, Calif.: Wadsworth, 1966), provides a
selection from these and other reform writers.

25. Colvert, in the Introduction to Bowery Tales cited immediately above, dismisses the likelihood that Crane was influenced
by Zola's L'Assomoir as has been assumed by many literary historians, among them Lars Ahnebrink, xliii-xlvi. See Milne Holton,
"The Sparrow's Fall and the Sparrow's Eyes: Crane's Maggie,"
Studia Neophilologica, 41 (1969), 115-129, for a brief review of the
shifting critical perspectives on Maggie.

26. Marcus Cunliffe, "Stephen Crane and the American Background of Maggie," American Quarterly, 7 (spring 1955), 31-34.
In addition to this piece, those by Solomon, Colvert and Pizer cited
above all discuss the novel in the context of contemporary reform
documents.

27. Edgar Fawcett, The Evil That Men Do (New York: Belford, 1898 [1889]), p. 296. Subsequent page references are indicated
parenthetically in the text.

28. Quoted in Edwin Cady, "Stephen Crane: Maggie, A Girl
of the Streets," in Hennig Cohen, ed. , Landmarks of American
Writing (New York: Basic Books, 1969), p. 179. In the same letter
is the famous remark of Crane that "at the root of Bowery life is a
sort of cowardice. "

29. Maggie, A Girl of the Streets (New York: n. p. , 1893),
114. Subsequent page references to Maggie shall be from this first
(1893) edition and shall be indicated parenthetically in the text.

30. Yekl, A Tale of the New York Ghetto (New York: Appleton, 1896), pp. 93-94. Subsequent page references are indicated parenthetically in the text.

31. The American 1890's: Life and Times of a Lost Generation (New York: Viking, 1966), p. 192.

CHAPTER IV

1. A Hazard of New Fortunes (New York: Harper & Bros., 1890; 2 vols.), I, pp. 71-72. Subsequent page references are indicated parenthetically in the text.

2. Robert Underwood Johnson, Remembered Yesterdays (Boston: Little, Brown, 1923), pp. 355-56; quoted in Larzer Ziff, The American 1890's (New York: Viking, 1966), p. 40.

3. See his ambivalent and condescending portrait of ghetto Jews, "An East Side Ramble," in Impressions and Experiences (New York: Harper and Bros., 1896), pp. 127-149.

4. Tenement Tales of New York (New York: Henry Holt, 1895), p. 130.

5. "A Study of Nativities," Forum, 26 (Jan. 1899), 621-627.

6. Vignettes of Manhattan (New York: Harper and Bros., 1894), p. 73.

7. Moses Rischin, The Promised City: New York's Jews, 1870-1914 (New York: Corinth, 1964), pp. 20, 94.

8. "Genesis: The American Jewish Novel Through the Twenties," Midstream, 4 (summer 1958), 21-33.

9. Children of Men (New York: McClure, 1903), p. 43. Subsequent page references are indicated parenthetically in the text.

10. Block was a prolific writer of short stories about the ghetto and not all of them on so serious a note as those in Children of Men. Between 1905 and 1913 he wrote ghetto stories on a fairly regular basis for Cosmopolitan; in all, some 63 stories appeared. Some of the later ones were collected in the volume Lapidowitz the Schnorrer: "With the Best Intention" (New York: Hearst International, 1914). The stories are listed in David Fine's bibliography of immigrant ghetto fiction in American Literary Realism, 1870-1910, 6 (summer 1973), 183-185.

11. In the Gates of Israel: Stories of the Jews (New York: Taylor, 1902), p. 22.

12. Dr. Rast (New York: Sturgis and Walton, 1909), p. 239.

13. The three volumes are Little Citizens (1904), Wards of Liberty (1907), and Little Aliens (1910).

14. Wards of Liberty (New York: McClure, 1907), p. viii. Subsequent page references are indicated parenthetically in the text.

15. Potash and Perlmutter was followed in 1911 by Abe and Mawruss: Being Further Adventures of Potash and Perlmutter. Subsequent collections appeared introducing other clothing manufacturers, but the treatment was largely the same. Glass found a successful formula and stuck to it. His stories were dramatized for the stage, where they played to large audiences. When he died in 1934, he was working on radio adaptations.

16. The Jew in American Literature (New York: Bloch, 1966), p. 117.

17. Potash and Perlmutter (Philadelphia: Altemus, 1909), p. 7.

CHAPTER V

1. Gregory Weinstein in his eloquent immigrant memoir, The Ardent Eighties (New York: International Press, 1928), complained of the Jews' failure to support The Leader, a cooperative newspaper edited by the exiled Russian nobleman Sergey Schevitch. The urban laborer, he noted, does not consider himself a "class" but a temporary worker.

2. Ronald Sanders, The Downtown Jews: Portraits of an Immigrant Generation (New York: Harper and Row, 1969), pp. 91-95.

3. See Weinstein's account of the incident; pp. 142-146 of The Ardent Eighties. His account corresponds closely with Edward King's treatment in the novel, Joseph Zalmonah.

4. Moses Rischin, The Promised City: New York's Jews, 1870-1914 (New York: Corinth, 1964), p. 256.

5. Terence V. Powderly, "A Menacing Irruption," North American Review, 147 (1888), 169.

6. Rischin, pp. 243-257.

7. Edward Smith King is frequently confused with another Edward King, a Scottish-born friend of Abraham Cahan, and follower

of Auguste Comte's positivism, who lectured to the Lower East Side, worked in settlement houses, and organized the Central Labor Union. The author of Joseph Zalmonah is an American-born journalist and novelist. For an account of his life and career, see Milton Hindus, "Edward Smith King and the Old East Side," American Jewish Historical Quarterly, 64 (June 1975), 321-330. Gregory Weinstein presents a sympathetic first-hand portrait of King in The Ardent Eighties, pp. 40-42, 77-78, and 165-174.

8.   Edward Smith King, Joseph Zalmonah (New York: Lee and Shepard, 1893), p. 320.   Subsequent page references are indicated parenthetically in the text.

9.   Upton Sinclair, American Outpost (New York: Farrar, Rinehart, 1932), p. 154.   Subsequent page references are indicated parenthetically in the text.

10. Upton Sinclair, The Jungle (New York: Doubleday, Page and Co. , 1906), p. 14.   Subsequent page references are indicated parenthetically in the text.

11. The Radical Novel in the United States (New York: Hill and Wang, 1956), p. 13.

12. A. I. Tobin and Elmer Gertz, Frank Harris: A Study in Black and White (Chicago: Mendelsohn, 1931), pp. 153-154; E. Merill Root, Frank Harris (New York: Odyssey, 1947), pp. 164-165.

13. Henry David, The History of the Haymarket Affair (New York: Russell & Russell, 1958), pp. 264-271, 508-514.

14. The Bomb (London: John Long, 1908), p. 48.

15. George Bernard Shaw, Preface to "The Dark Lady of the Sonnets," The Collected Works of George Bernard Shaw (New York: Wise, 1930), vol. 13, p. 212.

16. James Oppenheim, Pay Envelopes (New York: Huebsch, 1911), p. 127.   Subsequent page references are indicated parenthetically in the text.

17. James Oppenheim, The Nine-Tenths (New York: Harper and Bros. , 1911), p. 51.

18. Rischin, The Promised City, p. 247; Sanders, The Downtown Jews, p. 400.

19. Albert Edwards [Arthur Bullard], Comrade Yetta (New York: Macmillan, 1913), p. 83.   Subsequent page references are indicated parenthetically in the text.

CHAPTER VI

1. "American Literature and the Melting Pot," Ideas in America (Cambridge, Mass.: Harvard University Press, 1944), pp. 185-204.

2. Between 1881 and 1917 some four million Italians came to America as compared to two million East European Jews. Moses Rischin, The Promised City: New York's Jews, 1890-1914 (New York: Corinth, 1964), p. 20; Harvey Wish, Society and Thought in Modern America: A Social and Intellectual History of the American People from 1865 (New York: McKay, 1962), pp. 242, 248.

3. For discussions of Italian-American literature see Olga Peragallo, Italian American Authors and Their Contribution to American Literature (New York: S. F. Vanni, 1949), and Rose Basile Green, The Italian-American Novel (Teaneck, N.J.: Fairleigh Dickinson University Press, 1974).

4. Jacob Riis, How the Other Half Lives: Studies Among the Tenements of New York (New York: Scribner's, 1892), p. 112.

5. Mary Antin, The Promised Land (Boston: Houghton, Mifflin, 1912), p. xi.

6. Letter of 31 March 1917, Barrett Wendell and His Letters (Boston: Atlantic Monthly Press, 1924), p. 282. Quoted in Thomas Gossett, Race: The History of an Idea in America (Dallas: Southern Methodist University Press, 1963), p. 305.

7. Elias Tobenkin, Witte Arrives (New York: Stokes, 1916), p. 293.

8. "Genesis: The American Jewish Novel Through the Twenties," Midstream, 4 (summer 1958), 27-28.

9. "Recent Fiction," The Dial, 61 (21 Sept. 1916), 194; "Witte Arrives," The Bookman, 44 (Oct. 1916), 183; "Dreams and the Main Chance," The Nation, 106 (14 March 1918), 295-296. For other reviews of Witte Arrives see New York Times Book Review, 27 Aug. 1916, 334; and "Witte Arrives," The Nation, 103 (28 Sept. 1916), 304-305.

10. See Philip Gleason, "The Melting Pot: Symbol of Fusion or Confusion?" American Quarterly, 16 (spring 1964), 20-46. The article is referred to in Chapter II.

11. "Clipped Wings," The Dial, 64 (11 April 1918), 358-359.

12. Maurice Wohlgerlertner, Israel Zangwill (New York: Columbia University Press, 1964), pp. 176-177.

13. The Melting Pot (New York: Macmillan, 1908), p. 199. The curtain falls after this speech on an image of the torch of the Statue of Liberty; "My Country, 'Tis of Thee" is heard in the background. Subsequent page references to the play will be indicated parenthetically in the text.

14. Solomon Liptzin, Generation of Decision (New York: Bloch, 1958), pp. 175-176.

15. Quoted in "Mr. Zangwill's New Dramatic Gospel," Current Literature, 45 (Dec. 1908), 672.

16. Charles Reznikoff, ed., Louis Marshall: Champion of Liberty (Philadelphia: Jewish Publication Society of America, 1957), p. 809.

17. Current Literature, loc. cit., p. 671. The play was discussed widely among Jewish leaders. For a summary of other opinions see "What the Jews Think of Zangwill's Play," Literary Digest, 37 (31 Oct. 1908), 628-629. For reviews and articles see The Bookman, 30 (1909), 324-326; The Nation, 79 (Sept. 1909), 240; Survey, 23 (Nov. 1909), 168-169; Munsey's, 42 (Nov. 1909), 258; Literary Digest, 39 (Sept. 1909), 440. The play continues to elicit discussion: see, most recently, Neil Shumsky, "Zangwill's The Melting Pot: Ethnic Tensions on Stage," American Quarterly, 27 (March 1975), 29-41.

18. Ezra Brudno, The Tether (New York: Lippincott, 1908), p. 107.

19. Ezra Brudno, The Fugitive: Being Memoirs of a Wanderer in Search of a Home (New York: Doubleday, Page, 1904), p. 387.

20. Edward Steiner, The Mediator (New York: Fleming H. Revell, 1907), p. 285.

21. Sidney Nyburg, The Chosen People (Philadelphia: J. B. Lippincott, 1917), p. 76. Subsequent page references will be indicated parenthetically in the text.

CHAPTER VII

1. Abraham Cahan, "Imaginary America: How a Young Man Pictured It," New York Commercial Advertiser, Saturday Supplement, 6 Aug. 1898. Reprinted in Moses Rischin, "Abraham Cahan and the New York Commercial Advertiser, 1897-1900: A Study in Acculturation," Publications of the American Jewish Historical Society, 43 (Sept. 1953), 15-17.

2. Abraham Cahan, The Rise of David Levinsky (New York:

Harper and Bros. , 1917), p. 458. Subsequent page references are indicated parenthetically in the text.

3. Ronald Sanders, The Downtown Jews: Portraits of an Immigrant Generation (New York: Harper and Row, 1969), pp. 179-180, 205-207.

4. Lincoln Steffens, The Autobiography of Lincoln Steffens (New York: Harcourt, Brace, 1931), pp. 311-312. The best recent accounts of Cahan's Advertiser experience are contained in the Rischin article cited above and in Sanders, pp. 211-218.

5. Types from City Streets (New York: Funk and Wagnalls, 1910), p. 96. Subsequent page references are indicated parenthetically in the text.

6. Abraham Cahan, "The Russian Jew in America," Atlantic Monthly, 82 (July 1898), 128-139.

7. Abraham Cahan, The Imported Bridegroom and Other Stories of the New York Ghetto (Boston: Houghton, Mifflin, 1898), p. 45.

8. "American Letter, Some Books of Short Stories," Literature, 3 (31 Dec. 1898), 628-629.

9. For a different interpretation see Louis Harap, The Image of the Jew in American Literature (Philadelphia: Jewish Publication Society of America, 1974), pp. 514-524. Harap views Levinsky as a "thinly disguised Abraham Cahan," pointing to parallels between Cahan's career and Levinsky's. Cahan's conflict between his socialist convictions and his need for success and recognition was transferred, according to Harap, to the character of Levinsky.

10. My discussion of The Rise of David Levinsky follows the general lines of Isaac Rosenfeld's essay, "America, the Land of the Sad Millionaire," Commentary, 14 (Aug. 1952), 131-135. For different approaches see the Harap book cited above and David Singer, "David Levinsky's Fall: A Note on the Liebman Thesis," American Quarterly, 19 (winter 1967), 696-697. Beginning with the thesis of Professor Charles Liebman that East European Jewish immigrants to America were not, in the main, orthodox Jews as is commonly assumed, Singer attempts to demonstrate that Levinsky had rejected his Old World piety long before emigrating and that such gestures as cutting his earlocks in America are not to be interpreted as signs of his loss of faith but of his desire for cultural assimilation and social acceptance. For a sensitive recent account of Cahan's career and a discussion of his fiction, including his short stories and the earlier, magazine version of Levinsky, see Ronald Sanders, cited above. Sanford Marovitz, "The Lonely New Americans of Abraham Cahan," American Quarterly, 20 (summer 1968), 196-210, is a thoughtful article. For additional material on Cahan see the bibliography compiled by Marovitz and Lewis Freed, "Abraham Cahan: An Annotated

Bibliography," American Literary Realism, 1870-1910, 3 (summer 1970), 197-243.

11. "Glimpses of Reality," The Nation, 105 (18 Oct. 1917), 432; H. W. Boynton, "A Stroll Through the Fair of Fiction," The Bookman, 46 (Nov. 1917), 337-342; H. W. Boynton, "Outstanding Novels of the Year," The Nation, 105 (29 Nov. 1917), 600-601; John Macy, "The Story of a Failure," The Dial, 63 (22 Nov. 1917), 522. Kate Holladay Claghorn in her review of the novel for Survey, 39 (1 Dec. 1917), 260, 262, agreed with most of the critics in seeing it simply as the story of a greedy, predatory immigrant. She contrasted Levinsky to Montague Glass's Potash and Perlmutter, our "loveable, amiable, and human friends."

SELECTED BIBLIOGRAPHY

The list of primary works includes the fiction cited in the text with the exceptions of British titles, those which do not fall in the 1880-1920 period, and a few works mentioned in passing but not directly related to aspects of the subject. It is not intended as a complete list of slum or ghetto fiction, and readers who wish to go beyond this list should consult the published bibliographies listed among the secondary works below, including my own annotated bibliography of ghetto fiction.

As to the secondary list, I have excluded some works cited in the text or notes which are not central to the study, and I have included a number of titles not acknowledged in the notes because they are not directly cited but which added to my understanding of the subject. A sampling of book reviews is included. Reviews were chosen either for the typicality of the opinion expressed, the prestige of the reviewer, or the unusual perceptiveness revealed. I have briefly annotated the reviews to indicate their content.

PRIMARY--NOVELS

Beckley, Zoe. A Chance to Live. New York: Macmillan, 1918.

Berman, Henry. Worshippers. New York: Grafton, 1906.

Bernstein, Herman. Contrite Hearts. New York: A. Wessels, 1905.

Brudno, Ezra. The Fugitive. New York: Doubleday, Page, 1904.

_____. The Tether. New York: Lippincott, 1908.

Cahan, Abraham. The Rise of David Levinsky. New York: Harper and Bros., 1917.

_____. Yekl: A Tale of the New York Ghetto. New York: Appleton, 1896.

Campbell, Helen. Miss Melinda's Opportunity. Boston: Roberts Bros., 1886.

_____ . Mrs. Herndon's Income. Boston: Roberts Bros. , 1886.

Converse, Florence. The Children of Light. Boston: Houghton, Mifflin, 1912.

Crane, Stephen. Maggie: A Girl of the Streets. New York, n. p. , 1893.

Donnelly, Ignatius. Caesar's Column: A Story of the Twentieth Century, ed. by W. Rideout. Cambridge, Mass. : Harvard University Press, 1960.

Edwards, Albert [i. e. , Arthur Bullard]. Comrade Yetta. New York: Macmillan, 1913.

Fawcett, Edgar. The Evil That Men Do. New York: Belford, 1889.

Ford, Peter Leicester. The Honorable Peter Stirling. New York: Henry Holt, 1900. [1894]

Frankel, A. H. In Gold We Trust. Philadelphia: Wm. Piles' Sons, 1898.

Friedman, Isaac Kahn. By Bread Alone. New York: McClure, Phillips, 1901.

_____ . Poor People. Boston: Houghton, Mifflin, 1900.

Fuller, Edward. The Complaining Millions of Men. New York: Harper and Bros. , 1893.

Harris, Frank. The Bomb. London: John Long, 1908.

Howells, William Dean. A Hazard of New Fortunes. New York: Harper and Bros. , 1890.

King, Edward Smith. Joseph Zalmonah. New York: Lee and Shepard, 1893.

Kussy, Nathan. The Abyss. New York: Macmillan, 1916.

London, Jack. Mutiny on the Elsinore. New York: Macmillan, 1914.

_____ . The Valley of the Moon. New York: Macmillan, 1913.

Luska, Sidney [i. e. , Henry Harland]. As It Was Written: A Jewish Musician's Story. New York: Cassell, 1885.

_____ . Mrs. Peixada. New York: Cassell, 1886.

_____ . The Yoke of the Thorah. New York: Cassell, 1887.

McCardell, Roy. Wage Slaves of New York. New York: Dilling-
      ham, 1899.

Mead, Lucia True [i. e., Lucia True Ames]. Memoirs of a Million-
      aire. Boston: Houghton, Mifflin, 1889.

Nyburg, Sidney. The Chosen People. Philadelphia: J. B. Lippin-
      cott, 1917.

Oppenheim, James. The Nine-Tenths. New York: Harper Bros.,
      1911.

Rollins, Alice. Uncle Tom's Tenement. New York: Smythe, 1886.

Roof, Katherine Metcalf. The Stranger at the Hearth. Boston:
      Small, Maynard, 1916.

Scudder, Vida. A Listener in Babel: Being a Series of Imaginary
      Conversations Held at the Close of the Last Century and Re-
      ported. Boston: Houghton, Mifflin, 1903.

Sinclair, Upton. The Jungle. New York: Doubleday, Page, 1906.

Steiner, Edward. The Mediator. New York: Fleming H. Revell,
      1907.

Sterner, Lawrence. The UnChristian Jew. New York: Neale, 1917.

Teller, Charlotte. The Cage. New York: Appleton, 1907.

Tobenkin, Elias. The House of Conrad. New York: F. Stokes,
      1918.

_____. Witte Arrives. New York: F. Stokes, 1916.

Townsend, Edward. A Daughter of the Tenements. New York:
      Lovell, Coryell, 1895.

                    PRIMARY--STORY COLLECTIONS

Bernstein, Herman. In the Gates of Israel: Stories of the Jews.
      New York: J. F. Taylor, 1902.

Bunner, Henry Cuyle. Jersey Street and Jersey Lane: Urban and
      Suburban Sketches. New York: Scribner's, 1896. (The
      sketch "Jersey and Mulberry" is relevant.)

Cahan, Abraham. The Imported Bridegroom and Other Stories of
      the New York Ghetto. Boston: Houghton, Mifflin, 1898.

Dunne, Finley Peter. Observations by Mr. Dooley. New York:
      R. H. Russell, 1906.

Friedman, Isaac Kahn. The Lucky Number. Chicago: Way and
    Williams, 1896.

Glass, Montague. Abe and Mawruss: Being Further Adventures of
    Potash and Perlmutter. Garden City, N. Y. : Doubleday,
    Page, 1911.

_____. Potash and Perlmutter. Philadelphia: Henry Altemus,
    1909.

Hapgood, Hutchins. Types from City Streets. New York: Funk
    and Wagnalls, 1910.

Kelly, Myra. Little Aliens. New York: Scribner's, 1910.

_____. Little Citizens. New York: McClure, Phillips, 1904.

_____. Wards of Liberty. New York: McClure, 1907.

Lessing, Bruno [i. e. , Rudolph Block]. Children of Men. New
    York: McClure, Phillips, 1903.

_____. "Lapidowitz the Schnorrer": With the Best Intention.
    New York: Hearst's International Library, 1914.

Matthews, Brander. Vignettes of Manhattan. New York: Harper
    and Bros. , 1894.

Oppenheim, James. Dr. Rast. New York: Sturgis and Walton,
    1909.

_____. Pay Envelopes. New York: B. W. Huebsch, 1911.

Ralph, Julian. People We Pass: Stories of Life Among the Masses
    of New York City. New York: Harper and Bros. , 1896.

Riis, Jacob. Neighbors: Life Stories of the Other Half. New York:
    Macmillan, 1914.

_____. Out of Mulberry Street: Stories of Tenement Life in
    New York City. New York: Century, 1898. (Reprinted by
    Macmillan as Children of the Tenement, 1903.)

Sanborn, Alvan Francis. Moody's Lodging House and Other Tene-
    ment Sketches. Boston: Copeland and Day, 1895.

_____. Meg McIntyre's Raffle and Other Stories. Boston: Cope-
    land and Day, 1896.

Sullivan, James. Tenement Tales of New York. New York: Henry
    Holt, 1895.

Townsend, Edward. Chimmie Fadden; Major Max; and Other Stories.
    New York: Lovell, Coryell, 1895.

Warfield, David, and Margherita Hamm. Ghetto Silhouettes. New
    York: James Pott, 1907.

PRIMARY--UNCOLLECTED STORIES

Cahan, Abraham. "The Daughter of Reb Avrom Leib," Cosmopoli-
    tan, 29 (May 1900), 53-64.

_____. "Dumitru and Sigrid," Cosmopolitan, 30 (March 1901),
    493-501.

_____. "Imaginary America: How a Young Man Pictured It,"
    New York Commercial Advertiser, Saturday Supplement, 6
    Aug. 1898. Reprinted in Rischin, "Abraham Cahan and the
    New York Commercial Advertiser, 1897-1900: A Study in
    Acculturation," Publication of the American Jewish Historical
    Society, 43 (Sept. 1953), 15-17.

_____. "A Marriage by Proxy: A Story of the City," Everybody's
    Magazine, 3 (Dec. 1900), 569-575.

_____. "Rabbi Eliezer's Christmas," Scribner's, 26 (Dec. 1899),
    661-668.

_____. "Tzinchadzi of the Catskills," Atlantic Monthly, 88 (Aug.
    1901), 221-226.

Willisie, Honoré. "What Is an American?" Collier's, 50 (9 Nov.
    1912), 14.

SECONDARY--BOOKS AND ARTICLES

Addams, Jane. Democracy and Social Ethics. New York: Mac-
    millan, 1902.

_____. Philanthropy and Social Progress: Seven Essays. New
    York: T. Crowell, 1893.

_____. Twenty Years at Hull House. New York: Macmillan,
    1910.

Antin, Mary. The Promised Land. Boston: Houghton, Mifflin,
    1912.

Bassan, Maurice, ed. Stephen Crane's Maggie: Text and Context.
    Belmont, Calif.: Wadsworth, 1966.

Bernheimer, Charles, ed. The Russian Jew in the United States.
    Philadelphia: J. Winston, 1905.

Bourne, Randolph. "Trans-National America," Atlantic Monthly,
      118 (July 1916), 86-97.

Bremner, Robert. From the Depths: The Discovery of Poverty in
      the United States. New York: New York University Press,
      1956.

Brooks, Van Wyck. The Confident Years, 1885-1915. New York:
      E. P. Dutton, 1952.

Cady, Edwin. "Stephen Crane: Maggie, A Girl of the Streets,"
      in Hennig Cohen, ed. , Landmarks of American Writing. New
      York: Basic Books, 1961.

Cahan, Abraham. The Education of Abraham Cahan, trans. by Leon
      Stein, Abraham P. Conan, and Lynn Davison. Philadelphia:
      Jewish Publication Society of America, 1969. (Translation of
      the first part (vols. 1 & 2) of Cahan's five-vol. autobiography,
      Bleter fun mein Leben).

_____. "The Russian Jew in America," Atlantic Monthly, 82
      (July 1898), 128-139.

Colvert, James. Introduction to Stephen Crane: The Bowery Tales,
      ed. by Fredson Bowers. Charlottesville, Va. : University
      Press of Virginia, 1969.

Cunliffe, Marcus. "Stephen Crane and the American Background of
      Maggie," American Quarterly, 7 (spring 1955), 31-34.

David, Henry. The History of the Haymarket Affair. New York:
      Russell and Russell, 1958.

Fiedler, Leslie. "Genesis: The American Jewish Novel Through
      the Twenties," Midstream, 4 (summer 1958), 21-33.

Fine, David. "Abraham Cahan, Stephen Crane and the Romantic
      Tenement Tale of the Nineties," American Studies, 14 (spring
      1973), 95-108.

_____. "Attitudes Toward Acculturation in the English Fiction of
      the Jewish Immigrant, 1900-1917," American Jewish Histori-
      cal Quarterly, 63 (Sept. 1973), 45-56.

_____. "Immigrant Ghetto Fiction, 1885-1918: An Annotated Bib-
      liography," American Literary Realism 1870-1910, 6 (summer
      1973), 169-196.

Flower, Benjamin Orange. Progressive Men, Women, and Move-
      ments of the Past Twenty-five Years. Boston: New Arena,
      1914.

Gartner, Carol Blicker. "A New Mirror for America: The Fiction

of the Immigrant of the Ghetto, 1890-1930. " Unpubl. diss. ,
New York University, 1970.

Gleason, Philip. "The Melting Pot: Symbol of Fusion or Confusion?" American Quarterly, 16 (spring 1964), 20-46.

Goodchild, A. F. "The Sweating System in Philadelphia," The
Arena, 11 (1895), 261-265.

Gordon, Milton. Assimilation in America: The Role of Race, Religion, and National Origins. New York: Oxford University
Press, 1964.

Gordon, Nicholas. "Jewish and American: A Critical Study of the
Fiction of Abraham Cahan, Anzia Yezierska, Waldo Frank,
and Ludwig Lewisohn. " Unpubl. diss. , Stanford University,
1967.

Gossett, Thomas. Race: The History of an Idea in America. Dallas: Southern Methodist University Press, 1963.

Grant, Madison. The Passing of the Great Race, 3rd ed. New
York: DeForest Grant, 1944.

Grant, Percy Stickney. "American Ideals and the Race Mixture,"
North American Review, 195 (1912), 513-535.

Green, Rose Basile. The Italian American Novel: A Document of
the Interaction of Two Cultures. Teaneck, N. J. : Fairleigh
Dickinson University Press, 1974.

Gulbenkian, Vahe. "The Slum Movement in English and American
Fiction, 1880-1920: A Chapter in the History of the American Novel. " Unpubl. diss. , Case Western Reserve University, 1951.

Guttman, Allen. The Jewish Writer in America: Assimilation and
the Crisis of Identity. New York: Oxford University Press,
1971.

Hall, Prescott. Immigration and Its Effects on the United States.
New York: Holt, 1906.

Halper, Albert. "Notes on Jewish-American Fiction," Menorah
Journal, 20 (spring 1932), 61-69.

Handlin, Oscar. Race and Nationality in American Life. Garden
City, N. Y. : Doubleday Anchor, 1957.

_____ . The Uprooted: The Epic Story of the Great Migrations
That Made the American People. New York: Grosset and
Dunlap, 1951.

_____, ed. Immigration As a Factor in American History.
Englewood Cliffs, N. J. : Prentice-Hall, 1959.

Hanson, Marcus Lee. The Immigrant in American History. Cambridge, Mass. : Harvard University Press, 1940.

Hapgood, Hutchins. The Spirit of the Ghetto: Studies of the Jewish
Quarter of New York. New York: Funk & Wagnalls, 1902.

Hapgood, Norman. "The Jews and American Democracy," Menorah
Journal, 2 (1916), 201.

Harap, Louis. The Image of the Jew in American Literature.
Philadelphia: Jewish Publication Society of America, 1974.

Higham, John. Introduction to The Rise of David Levinsky by Abraham Cahan. New York: Harper, 1960, pp. v-xii.

_____. Strangers in the Land: Patterns of American Nativism
1860-1920. New Brunswick, N. J. : Rutgers University Press,
1955.

Hindus, Milton. "Edward Smith King and the Old East Side," American Jewish Historical Quarterly, 64 (June 1975), 321-330.

_____, ed. The Old East Side: An Anthology. Philadelphia:
Jewish Publication Society of America, 1969.

Holton, Milne. "The Sparrow's Fall and the Sparrow's Eyes:
Crane's Maggie," Studia Neophilologica, 41 (1969), 115-129.

Howells, William Dean. "An East Side Ramble," in Impressions
and Experiences. New York: Harper and Bros. , 1896, 127-
149.

Hull, William. "The Children of the Other Half," The Arena, 17
(June 1897), 1039-1050.

James, Henry. The American Scene, ed. by Leon Edel. Bloomington: University of Indiana Press, 1968.

Janeway, William Ralph. Bibliography of Immigration in the United
States, 1900-1930. Columbus, Ohio: A. L. Hedrick, 1934.

Jeshurin, Ephim, ed. "Der Vilner: Dedicated to Abraham Cahan's
80th Birthday. " Issued by the United Vilner Relief Committee,
22 Feb. 1941. (Listings of Cahan's works and articles about
him in English, Yiddish, and Russian, to 1941.)

Jones, Howard Mumford. "American Literature and the Melting
Pot, " in Ideas in America. Cambridge, Mass. : Harvard
University Press, 1944; pp. 185-205.

Jones, Maldwyn Allen. American Immigration. Chicago: University
of Chicago Press, 1960.

Kallen, Horace. "Democracy versus the Melting Pot," The Nation,
100 (18 Feb. 1915), 190-194; (25 Feb. 1915), 217-220.

Kelley, Florence. "The Sweating System," in Hull House Maps
and Papers. Chicago: Thomas Crowell, 1895; pp. 27-44.

Kirk, Rudolph and Clara Kirk. "Abraham Cahan and W. D. Howells:
The Story of a Friendship," American Jewish Historical Quarterly, 52 (Sept. 1962), 27-57.

Lawrence, Elwood. "The Immigrant in American Fiction: 1890-
1920." Unpubl. diss., Case Western Reserve University,
1944.

Liptzen, Solomon. The Jew in American Literature. New York:
Bloch, 1966.

Lodge, Henry Cabot. "The Restriction of Immigration," North American Review, 152 (1891), 27-36.

Lubove, Roy. The Progressives and the Slums: Tenement House
Reform in New York City, 1890-1917. Pittsburgh: University of Pittsburgh Press, 1962.

Marovitz, Sanford. "Howells and the Ghetto: The Mystery of
Misery," Modern Fiction Studies, 16 (1970), 345-362.

_____. "The Lonely New Americans of Abraham Cahan," Ameri-
can Quarterly, 20 (summer 1968), 196-210.

_____. "Yekl: The Ghetto Realism of Abraham Cahan," Ameri-
can Literary Realism 1870-1910, 2 (fall 1969), 271-273.

_____, and Lewis Freed. "Abraham Cahan: An Annotated Bib-
liography," American Literary Realism 1870-1910, 3 (summer
1970), 197-243.

Matthews, Brander. "A Study of Nativities," The Forum, 26 (Jan.
1899), 621-627.

May, Henry F. The End of Innocence: A Study of the First Years
of Our Own Time, 1912-1917. New York: Knopf, 1959.

Park, Robert, and Herbert A. Miller. Old World Traits Trans-
planted. New York: Harper and Bros., 1921.

Peragallo, Olga. Italian American Authors and Their Contribution
to American Literature. New York: S. F. Vanni, 1949.

Pollock, Theodore. "The Solitary Clarinetist: A Critical Biography

of Abraham Cahan, 1860-1917." Unpubl. diss., Columbia
University, 1959.

Poole, Ernest. "Abraham Cahan: Socialist, Journalist, Friend of
the Ghetto," The Outlook, 99 (28 Oct. 1911), 467-478. (See
note number 1, Chapter III, p. 153.)

Powderly, Terence. "A Menacing Irruption," North American Review, 147 (1888), 165-174.

Rideout, Walter. The Radical Novel in the United States. New
York: Hill and Wang, 1956.

Riis, Jacob. How the Other Half Lives. New York: Scribner's, 1890.

Rischin, Moses. "Abraham Cahan and the New York Commercial
Advertiser, 1897-1900: A Study in Acculturation," American
Jewish Historical Quarterly, 43 (Sept. 1953), 10-36.

_____. The Promised City: New York's Jews, 1870-1914. Cam-
bridge, Mass.: Harvard University Press, 1962. (Reprint,
New York: Corinth, 1964.)

Rosenfeld, Isaac. "America, the Land of the Sad Millionaire," Commentary, 14 (Aug. 1952), 131-135.

Ross, Edward A. "The Causes of Racial Superiority," Annals of the
American Academy of Political and Social Sciences, 18 (1901),
67-89.

_____. The Old World and the New. New York: Century, 1914.

Roucek, Joseph, Alice Hero, and Jean Downey. The Immigrant in
Fiction and Biography. New York: Bureau for International
Education, 1945. (An annotated bibliography.)

Round, W. M. F. "Immigration and Crime," The Forum, 8 (1890),
428-440.

Sanders, Ronald. The Downtown Jews: Portraits of an Immigrant
Generation. New York: Harper and Row, 1969.

Schoener, Allon, ed. Portal to America: The Lower East Side,
1870-1925. New York: Jewish Theological Seminary of America, 1966.

Shumsky, Neil. "Zangwill's The Melting Pot: Ethnic Tensions on
Stage," American Quarterly, 27 (spring 1975), 29-41.

Singer, David. "David Levinsky's Fall: A Note on the Liebman
Thesis," American Quarterly, 19 (winter 1967), 696-706.

Solomon, Barbara. "The Intellectual Background of the Immigrant
Restriction Movement in New England," New England Quarterly, 25 (1952), 47-59.

Steffens, Lincoln. The Autobiography of Lincoln Steffens. New York: Harcourt, Brace, 1931.

_____. "Jacob Riis, Reporter, Reformer and American Citizen," McClure's, 21 (1903), 419-425.

Strong, Josiah. Our Country: Its Possible Future and Its Present Decay. New York: American Home Missionary Society, 1885.

United States. Library of Congress. A List of Books (with Reference to Periodicals) on Immigration, comp. under direction of Appleton Prentiss Clark Griffin. Washington, D. C. : U. S. Gov. Printing Office, 1907.

Van Etten, Ida. "Russian Jews As Desirable Immigrants," The Forum, 15 (1893), 172-182.

Velikonja, Joseph, ed. Italians in the United States. Carbondale: Southern Illinois University Press, 1963.

Walker, Francis. "Immigration and Degradation," The Forum, 11 (1891), 634-644.

_____. "Restriction of Immigration," Atlantic Monthly, 77 (1896), 822-829.

Ward, David. Cities and Immigrants: A Geography of Change in Nineteenth Century America. New York: Oxford University Press, 1971.

Ward, Robert deCourcy. "National Eugenics in Relation to Immigration," North American Review, 192 (1910), 56-67.

_____. "Our Immigration Laws from the Standpoint of National Eugenics," National Geographic Magazine, 23 (Jan. 1912), 38-41.

Warner, John DeWitt. "The Sweating System in New York City," Harper's Weekly, 29 (2 Feb. 1895), 135-136.

Weinstein, Gregory. The Ardent Eighties. New York: International Press, 1928.

Wirth, Louis. The Ghetto. Chicago: University of Chicago Press, 1928.

Wish, Harvey. Society and Thought in Modern America: A Social and Intellectual History of the American People from 1865. New York: McKay, 1962.

Wister, Owen. "The Evolution of the Cowpuncher," in The Writings of Owen Wister, vol. 6. New York: Macmillan, 1928; pp. vii-xxiv.

Wittke, Carl. "Melting Pot Literature," College English, 7 (Jan. 1946), 189-197.

Ziff, Larzer. The American 1890's: Life and Times of a Lost Generation. New York: Viking, 1966.

SECONDARY--REVIEWS

Atherton, Gertrude. "The Alpine School of Fiction," The Bookman, 55 (1922), 26-33. (Caustic Anglo-Saxon nativist attack on recent American fiction.)

Banks, Nancy Houston. "The New York Ghetto," The Bookman, 4 (Oct. 1896), 157-158. (Attacks the sordidness of Cahan's Yekl.)

Bourne, Randolph. "Clipped Wings," The Dial, 64 (11 April 1918), 358-359. (Sarcastic denunciation of the Americanization message of Tobenkin's House of Conrad.)

Boynton, H. W. "Outstanding Novels of the Year," The Nation, 105 (29 Nov. 1917), 599-601. (Contrasts David Levinsky unfavorably to The Chosen People.)

_____. "A Stroll Through the Fair of Fiction," The Bookman, 46 (Nov. 1917), 337-342. (Refers to The Rise of David Levinsky as "an unsparing interpretation of the predatory immigrant.")

_____. "Witte Arrives," The Bookman, 44 (Oct. 1916), 183. (Praises Tobenkin's novel for its assimilation message.)

Cahan, Abraham. "The New Writers of the Ghetto," The Bookman, 39 (Aug. 1914), 631-637. (A review of Yiddish writers of the New York ghetto.)

"Chronicle and Comment: Portrayal of Jewish Life by Cahan," The Bookman, 10 (Jan. 1900), 428-430. (A defense of Cahan against the attacks on his "sordidness.")

Claghorn, Kate Holladay. "The Rise of David Levinsky," Survey, 39 (1 Dec. 1917), 260-262. (Another misinterpretation of Levinsky seeing it as simply the story of a greedy and predatory Jew.)

"Dreams and the Main Change," The Nation, 106 (14 March 1918), 295-296. (Favorable review of Tobenkin's The House of Conrad.)

"Glimpses of Reality," The Nation, 105 (18 Oct. 1917), 430-433. (Still another attack on The Rise of David Levinsky and the character of its protagonist, whom the reviewer sees as a "sneaking, malodorous animal.")

Hale, Edward. "Recent Fiction," The Dial, 61 (21 Sept. 1916), 193-
    196. (Favorable response to Tobenkin's "melting pot" novels.)

"The House of Conrad," New York Times, 10 March 1918, p. 94.
    (In typical fashion praises Tobenkin's novel for "its very
    great value as a picture of the unconscious processes of
    Americanization at work on the minds and souls of immi-
    grants.")

Howells, William Dean. "American Letter: Some Books of Short
    Stories," Literature, 3 (31 Dec. 1898), 628-629. (His favor-
    able reaction to Cahan's The Imported Bridegroom....)

_____. "Editor's Easy Chair," Harper's Monthly, 130 (May 1915),
    958-961. (A review of recent urban fiction praising Abraham
    Cahan, Fannie Hurst, and Montague Glass.)

_____. "Life and Letters," Harper's Weekly 39 (1 June 1895), 508.
    (On Townsend's "Chimmie Fadden" and idealizing slum life in
    fiction.)

_____. "New York Low Life in Fiction," New York World, 26
    July 1896, II, p. 18. (Reviews Maggie, George's Mother,
    and Cahan's Yekl, praising all three for their realistic treat-
    ment of characters "struggling vainly with an inexorable fate.")

Macy, John. "The Story of a Failure," The Dial, 63 (22 Nov. 1917),
    521-523. (A perceptive discussion of The Rise of David Le-
    vinsky and one of the few early reviews to recognize the irony
    of Levinsky's "rise.")

Marcosson, J. F. "Love in the Ghetto," The Bookman, 7 (Aug.
    1898), 513-514. (Very sympathetic review of The Imported
    Bridegroom....)

Mayer, Annie Nathan, and Martin B. Ellis. "The Ghetto in Fiction,"
    The Bookman, 10 (Feb. 1900), 532-534. (Two responses to
    the negative German-Jewish criticism of Zangwill's and Ca-
    han's ghetto fiction reported in The Bookman previously.)

"The Mediator," The Outlook, 87 (23 Nov. 1907), 623. (Favorable
    review of Steiner's novel, stressing its optimistic reconcilia-
    tion theme.)

"Mr. Zangwill's New Dramatic Gospel," Current Literature, 45 (Dec.
    1908), 667-673. (Reviews various opinions of The Melting Pot.)

Oppenheim, James. "Potash and Perlmutter," The Bookman, 31
    (Aug. 1910), 630-631. (Lavish praise for Glass's humanity.)

Rascoe, Burton. "A. Cahan's Novel of an Immigrant," Chicago
    Daily Tribune, 3 Nov. 1917, p. 11. (A lengthy and incisive
    discussion of the novel, focusing on Levinsky's intensity both

as a Talmudist and industrialist, a man tortured by conscience and hypocrisy.)

Trail, H. D. "The New Realism," Fortnightly Review, 68 (Jan.
1897), 63-67.   (Hostile British reaction to Crane and other
explorers of slums; compare with Banks above.)

"Witte Arrives," New York Times Book Review, 27 Aug. 1916, p.
334.   (Favorable but confusing review which suggests some
of the confusion surrounding the melting pot concept in the
war years.)

INDEX

"Uprising of the Twenty Thou-
sand" 78, 95 see also
Great Revolt
"Uses of Adversity, The" (Myra
Kelly) 70

Wage Slaves of New York (Roy
McCardell) 44
Wald, Lillian 28
Walker, Francis A. 6, 78
Ward, Robert DeCourcy 6-7
Wards of Liberty (Myra Kelly)
69
Warfield, David 62-63
Warren, Fred D. 81-82
Weinstein, Gregory 157n.
Wendell, Barrett 105
"What Is an American?" (Honore
Willisie) 13
"Wilder: Prophet of the Genteel
Christ" (Mike Gold) v
Williamsburg Trilogy (Daniel
Fuchs) v, 142
Willisie, Honore 13
Wirth, Louis 23
Wister, Owen 12
Witte Arrives (Elias Tobenkin)
105-108, 116
Women's Trade Union League
95
Worshippers (Henry Berman) 67
Wright, Henry J. 123
Wright, Richard 142

Yekl, A Tale of the New York
Ghetto (Abraham Cahan) 22,
38-40, 51-55, 67, 122
"Yellow Kid, The" (Richard Out-
cault and George Luks) 48
Yezierska, Anzia vi, 139-140,
141, 145, 146, 147
Yoke of the Thorah, The (Henry
Harland) 24-25

Zangwill, Israel 22, 34, 109-
111, 116
Ziff, Larzer 53, 57
Zola, Emile 40